Politics and Film

Politics and Film

The Political Culture of Television and Movies

Second Edition

Daniel P. Franklin

ROWMAN & LITTLEFIELD
Lanham • Boulder • New York • London

Published by Rowman & Littlefield
A wholly owned subsidiary of The Rowman & Littlefield Publishing Group, Inc.
4501 Forbes Boulevard, Suite 200, Lanham, Maryland 20706
www.rowman.com

Unit A, Whitacre Mews, 26–34 Stannary Street, London SE11 4AB

British Library Cataloguing in Publication Information Available

Library of Congress Cataloging-in-Publication Data

Names: Franklin, Daniel P. author.
Title: Politics and film : the political culture of television and movies / Daniel P. Franklin.
Description: Second edition. | Lanham : Rowman & Littlefield, 2016. | Includes bibliographical references and index. | Includes filmography.
Identifiers: LCCN 2016018529 (print) | LCCN 2016024155 (ebook) | ISBN 9781442262409 (cloth : alk. paper) | ISBN 9781442262324 (pbk. : alk. paper) | ISBN 9781442262331 (electronic)
Subjects: LCSH: Motion pictures—Political aspects—United States. | Culture in motion pictures.
Classification: LCC PN1995.9.P6 F73 2016 (print) | LCC PN1995.9.P6 (ebook) | DDC 791.43/6581—dc23
LC record available at https://lccn.loc.gov/2016018529

Printed in the United States of America

Contents

Foreword to the Second Edition

The theme of this edition is the same as the first and still quite simple: *the audience for film determines the content of film.* This thesis cuts through the haze of polemical criticisms of the film industry that feature, on the Right, arguments that Hollywood liberals are out to corrupt the morals of our youth and, on the Left, insinuations that the military-industrial complex manipulates the content of entertainment for its benefit. I am as unmoved by these arguments today as I was a decade ago when I published the first edition of *Politics and Film*.

But that is not to say that much hasn't changed since then. I ended the last edition on an optimistic note, suggesting that we had now entered the real Golden Age of Hollywood. The advent of technological advances such as improved digital photography and storage had made filmmaking accessible to even the most independent of independent filmmakers. What I did not anticipate, and what will now be a new theme for this book, is the advent of digital transmission of entertainment, on demand. In retrospect, in 2006 we already saw signs of that coming. But even back then we were still locked in a world that required physical media to transport films. Many of us still own DVD players that will soon begin to gather dust along with VHS players, floppy discs, and turntables.

As I note in the text of this book, technology is one of the main engines of change in the entertainment media industry. This is no more so the case in the last ten years. It is now the case that very little filmmaking is on film. In January 2014, Paramount announced that *Anchorman 2* would be the last film it would release in 35mm prints. After all, at that point less than 10 percent of film theaters in American projected movies on film. Nowadays, movies are delivered electronically to theaters much as if they were video streamed.

That shift brings to mind the second major technological change relevant to the entertainment industry in the last ten years: the advent of video streaming on demand. This innovation was made possible by the conversion in the late 2010s from analog to digital transmission. Because digital transmission allows more capacity on the same bandwidth of higher quality, it is now possible to stream high-resolution images to the home. This has made it possible for families to watch content at home, on demand, at a total price lower than going to the movies.

This has fundamentally changed the moviegoing experience. But more important, for the purposes of this book, these changes in technology have fundamentally changed the audience for film. Not only for demographic reasons, as filmgoers are growing older, the availability and affordability of film has also broadened the audience to stay-at-home moms and dads, to the elderly and disabled, and even to the religiously inclined. That, in turn, has altered the content and the political message of film.

So even while the central argument of this book remains very much the same (and I expect the same to be true for the next edition and the one after that), the environment for film is very different. Thus, the conclusions we draw based on the content of film must reflect the tastes and predilections of an entirely different audience. Or, more to the point, in the last ten years, films got older.

Therefore, among the other topics discussed in this edition of *Politics and Film* will be the effects of a different audience on the content of film. In response to reviewers, and out of a desire to keep things fresh, I will reorder the chapters and feature many different films, films that the readers of this book will likely have seen, and include the results of updated surveys that point to a new audience for film.

But one thing that won't change will be the central argument of the book, now simply reinforced with new data. Along with updated survey analysis, I will revise the discussion of the legal definition of pornography and update the scientific literature on the connection between filmed and actual violence. Finally, I will reorder the chapters to bring the discussion of film criticism to the fore. For students of film criticism, I will discuss briefly the process of deconstruction and how the analysis of film can be similar to the analysis of literature or the arts.

And now a note on the title: In some sense, even the title of this book has grown obsolete. Movies are no longer shot on film.[1] However, in the same way that we say that we are "dialing" a phone or "turning" something on or "rolling up" a window, describing a movie as a film evokes an earlier era. Maybe, at some point, nobody will know what I am talking about when I call a movie a film. But until then, calling a film a digital stream or a pay per view just doesn't alliterate.

Note

1. This is with the exception of the recently released *Hateful Eight* (2016). That film is not doing well, and with the added cost of shooting on film—film stock is expensive, the equipment is becoming harder to find, and the product cycle is extended—I don't think there is going to be much more of this. Who would be willing to finance it?

Introduction

Seth Rogen and James Franco have developed a niche market for small-scale, profitable comedy films. With the production of *The Interview*, they were on track to produce a moderately successful ensemble comedy every eighteen months or so. Their previous collaboration, *This Is the End* (2013), had grossed $136 million on a $32 million budget—successful by Hollywood standards but not a blockbuster. Their collaboration before that, *Pineapple Express* (2008), had grossed $100 million on a budget of $27 million. Rogen and Franco were on the road to a franchise. And each film was better than the one before. They were really beginning to perfect their craft—until, that is, North Korean dictator Kim Jong-un took umbrage to the plotline of their latest film.

The Interview is the story of a dense, preening talk show host and his frustrated producer who wants to be a journalist but has to settle for celebrity interviews and the phony news of *Entertainment Tonight*. Then the producer has an idea. When he finds out that his show is a favorite of North Korean dictator Kim Jong-un, he offers an interview to the reclusive Kim. Of course, the talk show host barely knows who his producer is talking about, but he is game as long as it's good for the ratings. The producer, being just the slightest bit smarter, has some qualms about providing the murderous dictator a platform, but, wow, what ratings potential this interview has! In any event, through a series twists and turns the duo gets the interview and heads off to North Korea.

In the meantime, they are recruited by the CIA to assassinate Kim. It's not entirely clear why they are willing to go along and risk their lives. Was it to be in service to their country, or was it because they were competing for the attention of the pretty CIA recruiter? Most probably the latter. That's the kind of guys they are. I won't spoil the plot by revealing the outcome, but let's just say that in real life, the North Koreans weren't amused. In June 2014, the North Korean government denounced the film as "an act of terrorism," promising "merciless retaliation" if the film was released.[1]

The film was slated for release on Christmas Day 2014.

On November 22, employees at Sony USA began seeing strange messages, including the images of skulls, on their computer screens at work. Then many of their computer workstations broke down. Sony employees began communicating by paper and pen, and employees broke out their old fax machines. Sony's computers had been hacked, compromising employment records, payroll information, and the emails of executives discussing proprietary business. A copy of Sony's not-yet-released *Annie* was stolen and began to show up on illegal data-sharing sites. The location of the hackers was traced back to Bangkok, Thailand. The electronic fingerprint of the hack bore some resemblance to the previous activities of the North Korean government.

Sony Corporation was in a particularly delicate position with regard to North Korea. Sony in its origins is a Japanese company, and there is still plenty of bad blood between the Japanese and the Koreans over the Japanese occupation of Korea prior to and during World War II. Americans are far away and can posture or laugh off the provocations of the North Koreans. But Pyongyang is only about seven hundred miles from Tokyo, and the North Koreans do have nuclear weapons. In response to North Korean posturing combined with its unpredictability, the Japanese had to be getting nervous.

Among the other things that the hackers did when they compromised Sony's computers was to make threats to the screenings of *The Interview*. Theater chains and movie studios were particularly sensitive to this sort of thing after a gunman shot up a movie theater in Aurora, Colorado, in 2012 during a screening of *The Dark Knight Rises*, killing a dozen people and wounding another seventy.

On December 17, Sony offered to allow movie theater chains to cancel their screenings of *The Interview*. Carmike Cinemas, with 247 theaters, was the first to cancel. The other major chains followed soon thereafter. Sony then cancelled the release.

Then the other side weighed in. Sony was criticized from both the Left and the Right for caving in to North Korean threats. President Obama termed Sony's decision a "mistake." The business community was concerned as well. How was Sony going to recoup the reported $100 million budget of the film? A small group of independent theater operators, sensing an opportunity to flank the corporate movie chains, wrote a letter to Sony asking to screen the film. Sony relented, and *The Interview* opened as scheduled on Christmas Day in 331 theaters.[2] Because of its limited opening and the negative "buzz" associated with the film, *The Interview* grossed just over $6 million. As Joe Pesci's character in *Casino* once said, "You just knew that somebody was going to get whacked." Sony Pictures Digital president Bob Osher was fired six weeks later.

The United States, accusing the North Koreans of being responsible for the Sony hack, moved to impose enhanced sanctions on North Korea.

However, as there are virtually no commercial or diplomatic relations between North Korea and the United States, it was not clear what more could be done.

Coincidentally, a week after the scheduled release of the film, North Korean access to the Internet began to fail, and for a week thereafter, Internet service in North Korea ranged from slow to nonexistent. No one claimed responsibility, and no cause has ever been established. However, it is widely believed that the US government was involved.[3]

On display in this incident are all of the modern elements of political film. Inasmuch as 70 percent of the revenue of American film is derived from foreign sources, the content of American film is constantly under scrutiny for cultural disconnects. American producers have to be sensitive to foreign sensibilities, even more so today when so much revenue is derived from abroad.

However, American films don't screen in North Korea, so for the North Koreans an economic boycott was not an option. Besides, the North Korean market is too small. Nevertheless, the Korean communists did manage to push the right buttons and ruin the premiere of *The Interview*. And while Americans didn't appreciate being pushed around by Kim and his thugs, Hollywood could see the writing on the wall, and it is unlikely that any new films will be made that make fun of Kim Jong-un, at least until he is gone.[4]

The story of *The Interview* is a modern cautionary tale of the politics of film. Movies are not produced in a vacuum, and they are closely scrutinized both at home and abroad for their content. For example, it has for some time been in vogue for politicians, film critics, and academics to decry the degeneracy of American film. In general, the argument goes something like this: Hollywood movie moguls, out of touch with the mainstream of American society, are producing films that appeal to our basest instincts. Furthermore, many a film contains a hidden agenda, an attempt to corrupt the morals of our youth and push a particular moral and political point of view.[5]

That is where criticisms of American film divide into two variations. From the Right, the argument is that because the Hollywood movie community is generally leftist in its political orientation, American feature films have become a medium for promoting all sorts of radical left-wing political and social agendas. The more society sees of this degeneracy on screen, the more likely that the members of the viewing public will become inured to the fictional violence and sexual promiscuity on screen and vote Democratic.

From the Left, the argument is somewhat different, and yet somewhat the same. Because the Hollywood community is a propaganda arm of the military-industrial complex, the messages of film never challenge the dominance of the ruling class. Serious films ignore the reality of the exploitation of the working class. And films intended to simply entertain are the modern-day equivalent of bread and circuses and the games in the Roman Coliseum.

In this book, I will argue that both arguments are wrong. But that is not to say that there aren't politics in film. Rather, we need to use a more sophisticated analysis. We need to deconstruct the content of film. To deconstruct a film, we need to be aware of not only the plot of the film but also the choices the director makes in technique, pacing, editing, and even music and design. All of the decisions made to construct a film are editorial in the sense that they are intended to make a point. In addition, a film cannot be made that is not in some ways intentionally and some ways unintentionally a product of circumstance. The film's producers must be aware of and are themselves a product of the culture in which the film—or any work of art, for that matter—is made.

Deconstruction is a technique for analyzing the underlying meaning of literature and the arts. Based on the works of philosophers Martin Heidegger and Jacques Derrida, deconstructionists suggest that only in the deconstruction of a piece of art we can derive the meaning of that art within the context of history. Therefore, we are cautioned to avoid looking at a piece of art through a modern lens at the risk of misinterpreting the true meaning of what the artist at the time was trying to say. Thus, art and literature become artifacts for understanding the characteristics of the society in which they were produced (and, in their modern, nondeconstructionist interpretation, become a product of their own time).[6]

Examine the two paintings shown on the following pages. Both pictures are in their own ways products of the French Revolution. The first is a painting titled *The Swing* by Jean-Honoré Fragonard. Let's start with the obvious: *The Swing* depicts a young girl on a swing. As her dress flies up, a young man hidden in the bushes looks up her skirt. The structure of the painting is traditional, with the ropes of the swing directing our attention to the girl, who, in a pink dress, stands out in distinct contrast to the dark green foliage in the background. The colors of the painting are generally soft in the range of pastels. The well-defined brushstrokes are round rather than angular and soft and gauzy rather than sharp, creating an impression of an atmosphere of luxuriance and pleasure.

Now, let's get to the context. Fragonard was a decorative artist of French aristocracy. *The Swing* was intended to be hung in the drawing room of a French villa or apartment. It was meant to supplement the décor of a space modeled in what was known as a Rococo design. (*Rococo* is the term used to describe the opulence of the French court in the late eighteenth century.)

The Swing is also a symbol of the disconnect between the French aristocracy and the lives of most of the ordinary citizens of France. It is that dis-

The Swing, Jean-Honoré Fragonard, 1767
Wikipedia Commons

tance and the obliviousness of the French aristocracy to that distance that eventually blew up into the French Revolution. Only a few years later, the king himself was executed in the public square. What was to follow was a revolutionary government symbolized in the next painting.

The Death of Marat was painted by Jacques-Louis David. Jean-Paul Marat, subject of the painting, was a journalist and a radical supporter of the French Revolution. He was assassinated by Charlotte Corday, a daughter of the aristocracy who held Marat responsible for the wave of executions associated with Robespierre's "reign of terror," including the execution of King Louis XVI. Corday gained entry to Marat by claiming that she had a list of people who were traitors to the revolution.[7]

The Death of Marat, Jacques-Louis David, 1793
Wikipedia Commons

Again, let's start with the obvious. Marat lies dead, stabbed to death, in his bathtub. The bathroom seems an unusual setting, but because he had a serious skin affliction, Marat spent much of his day submerged in water. The form of the painting is conventional, with Marat's outstretched arm drawing us to the center of the painting. But that is where the similarity in style to *The Swing* ends.

The Death of Marat is in what is called the neoclassical style. Painters of the French Revolution were often inspired by the exploits of the pre-Christian classics of Greco-Roman mythology as French revolutionaries were urged to renounce Christianity in favor of a civic religion, one that favored heroism and sacrifice to the community. Classical allegories were common in the substance and form of neoclassical painting. In *The Death of Marat*, Marat's body is not so much human as it is a statue. The skin has the look and "feel" of stone. The colors are basic as opposed to the pastels of *The Swing*, and the lines of the painting are sharp, angular, and well defined. In his hand, Marat is holding the note from the assassin.

In death, Marat becomes a martyr to the revolution. The artist, David, was as much a painter to the revolution as Fragonard was a painter to the aristocracy. David also happened to be a member of the Revolutionary Council, which quite frequently sentenced people to death. David paints not so much a picture as a poster. The painting is not intended to be hung in a parlor but in a public building. It is meant to inspire and certainly not to amuse.

That is an example of the use of deconstruction. The same technique can and should be applied to literature, music, and other forms of expression, if for no other reason than to put these activities into context. In the pages to follow, I am going to deconstruct American film. That means that while I will discuss some films that are expressly political in their content, I will be just as focused on films that are not. Indeed, some of the most profound insights into political film will be gleaned from films that are not self-consciously political in content. That is because the politics in an ostensibly apolitical film are unencumbered by conscious decisions about how to construct an ideological position. In apolitical film, the content is just there without the self-conscious filter of a political agenda.

This book is an examination of the role of film in American political culture. It is important to state at the outset that the influence of the entertainment industry is only a part of the formation of American political culture, and the influence of feature film is a smaller part even still. In this book, I want to make it clear that I am not evaluating media as a whole. If media can be defined as "organizations of communication that take different forms, such as broadcasting and print and create and transmit a vast array of content,"[8] then feature films are a particular type of entertainment media distinguishable from music, theater, and the arts.

Furthermore, the media can more accurately be divided into two parts: the entertainment and journalistic media. This book is not about journalism, and what I may say about the entertainment media will not pertain to journalists. For example, I will argue that marketization of the entertainment industry is generally to the good. The marketization of journalism, however, may not have the same beneficial effects. But that is a topic for another book. This book is about entertainment, and a limited portion of the entertainment medium at that.

Feature motion pictures are those films made for commercial exhibition by for-profit enterprises. I am not studying television here, except to the extent that movies are screened on television in a digital format such as streaming video and pay per view. Since I wrote the last edition of this book, there has emerged a revolution of television content featuring serialized dramas, such as *House of Cards* and *Orange Is the New Black*, which can only exist in an on-demand environment. Prior to the advent of streaming video, each episode of a television show had to be self-explanatory and self-contained, so that the viewer could watch and understand the show without having seen previous episodes in the series. Now, viewers can watch a television series, on demand, in sequence. This allows for character and plotline development that would have been impossible in the days of the sitcom and will always be impossible in the traditional feature film. Those serialized television shows will also be considered here as they are in some sense the new movies. To what extent do films guide or reflect American political culture?

THE CONCEPT OF POLITICAL CULTURE

Political culture, or the societal context in which distributive decisions are made, is influenced by a number of historical, geographical, and cultural factors. While there is quite a bit of disagreement over the definition of the term and even its relation to politics, the classic formulation of the concept is contained in the groundbreaking work of political scientists Gabriel Almond and Sidney Verba. In their 1963 cross-cultural opinion survey of five countries, *The Civic Culture*, Almond and Verba sought to identify differences between the political cultures of nations and thereby explain, among other things, differences between states in public policy and planning.[9]

Almond and Verba defined *political culture* as "the specifically political orientations-attitudes towards the political system and its various parts, and attitudes towards self in the system."[10] As such, Almond and Verba identified political culture as the "connecting link" between micro politics (the attitudes of the individual) and macro politics (the structure of the political system). What makes political culture political is that attitudes, particularly in a democracy, are translated into public policy through political participation. To the extent that the media form and reinforce this political culture, they become part of the process that guides the formation of public policy. For example, if the public perceives that the level of crime has increased, a perception that can be created by the media, there is likely to be pressure on the government to adopt more extensive public policy measures against crime.

American political culture is shaped by a unique national heritage. As an isolated continent—separated for most of its early history from the rest of the world by thousands of miles of ocean, with a relatively wide-open frontier—the United States has developed a culture that is unlike any other. Furthermore, because the United States was populated *de novo* by political and economic refugees of one kind or another, the political context of this country is heavily influenced by this shared experience of flight from governmental oppression and class-oriented societies abroad. Finally, because most of the original settlers (at least those who had any say in matters of politics) were from Western Europe, American politics reflects the overwhelming influence of European politics of the eighteenth century, when our constitution was written. The result is a culture that is a product of both the Wild West, where anything goes, and the Puritans, Pilgrims, and Plymouth Rock. These two strains of thought—liberal freedom and Protestant asceticism—come to clash in matters of freedom of thought and expression.[11]

There are any number of reasons that make the politics of film a difficult topic to discuss in any systematic way. The main problem with evaluating the psychological and political effects of film is that, at a superficial level, films are so easy to understand. Who am I to say what a film means or doesn't mean? Films are so intentionally accessible that even the most unschooled viewer can have a legitimate opinion about whether *Citizen Kane* (1941; considered one of the greatest films of all time) is a good film. But the popularity of and praise for *Citizen Kane* may have subtle meaning beyond the film's artistic merit. To explore the subtle meaning of an art form so purposely designed for popular consumption is a very difficult task, requiring the observer to go beyond the superficial level and put the film in societal context.

In the main, the problems of discussing film and society are associated with making connections. What is the influence of film, if any, on the individual and thus on society? What is the *direction* of causality, and, even if there were an established link between movie viewing and behavior, is that behavior necessarily a problem at all? The evidence is not altogether clear that, for most of us, there is any relationship between what we view on the screen and how we behave. Furthermore, even if it is true that viewing a motion picture influences behavior, it is not clear whether the "good" balances or even compensates for the "bad" in motion pictures.

Finally, what if it is the case that films "influence" the behavior of particularly susceptible individuals? Even if that is true, what, then, do we do? We can forbid children from viewing objectionable material, but can we selectively ban certain individuals from the theater or restrict what the rest of society sees because a film negatively affects just a few?

CAUSALITY AND THE INFLUENCE OF FILM

It is difficult to even establish a direction of causality. Is film an influence on or a mirror of society? The answer is that it is probably both. Filmmakers decide what we are going to see on screen. However, we decide what we are going to pay to see. Thus, commercial filmmakers are constrained by financing at both the front end and the back end of production. Backers will not come up with the money to produce a script without at least some assurance that the film will make a profit. However, that sort of judgment is by no means a science. Audiences are notoriously fickle. What looks profitable on paper may not be so in the suburban multiplex cinema. Thus, if anything, we would expect filmmakers to be rather conservative in making decisions about what type of films to produce, at least for the consumer market. This is not to say that filmmaking is politically conservative but that the choices made in producing a film are driven by market demands that emphasize reliance on proven formulas.

Common sense tells us that, from a business perspective, filmmakers—if they want to make a profit—have to be responsive to the market. This doesn't just mean that they have to produce a product that delights the eyes, nor does it mean that special effects alone are enough. Anyone who doubts this should see the abysmal 2001 remake of the classic science fiction film *Planet of the Apes* (1968). Films also must be made to please the mind, not just in terms of satisfying our desire to be entertained (although that alone is sometimes enough) but also in terms of satisfying our curiosity about people, ideas, and problems that we may confront in everyday life. In that respect, even commercial films are political. They reflect the values with which we are comfortable or interested, or else we wouldn't go to see these films at all. This is not to say that there isn't lots of brain-dead filmmaking. But when it comes to successful films, in those expansive box office receipts is a message about American political culture. In the tradition of those who have said, "You are what you eat," I would further assert, "You are what you pay to see." Consequently, I argue in this book that to a certain extent American film reflects the culture of American society.

Thus, there are three central questions that need to be considered in discussing the relationship of film and politics in the United States. At the individual level, is film a behavioral influence, and, if so, in what direction does the influence flow? Second, at the societal level, is commercial film "art" or simply another "product" with all the attendant legal and constitutional implications thereof? Finally, at the systemic level, which beliefs, values, and notions of justice special to the American political context and culture are promoted by and reflected in American film? The answers are, respectively, yes (but in both directions), product, and American liberalism. Allow me to elaborate.

There is extensive evidence to suggest that at least some individuals are influenced by what they see in the movie theater. But this doesn't necessarily mean that films "cause" certain types of behaviors. To make that connection requires establishing a linkage that connects behavior on a screen with an actual act. Establishing this connection requires some sort of actual evidence, and just because a theory seems to make sense doesn't make it so. In the chapters to follow, I examine the strength of the evidence in this regard. For instance, is it in fact true that film violence causes similar behavior? And if so, how widespread is the effect, and does the effect of influence extend to other areas of thought and behavior?

There seems to be quite a bit of evidence to suggest that the media does influence our behavior. This behavior is affected by what I call first-, second-, and third-order effects. First-order effects are the direct connections between what we see on the screen and what we do. Violence in films, racism in film, or simple incivility can influence our behavior by increasing our tolerance for such behavior and, at times and for some people, suggest a mode of seemingly acceptable behavior. Thus, children who see people punch one another in cartoons may be tempted to do the same with their peers. That is an example of a first-order behavioral effect. At another level, the media and film create a worldview that influences our behavior. If young black men are seen in handcuffs at the beginning of every evening television newscast, then the perception is created that, in general, young black men are dangerous. People will respond to this perception, and the second-order behavioral effect will become manifest. Finally, when someone watches a film, they cannot be doing something else; thus, this form of entertainment has a "crowding out" effect. What is lost when someone is in a theater or at home watching a movie, a third-order effect? For example, it has been suggested that the effect of television is to atomize a society in such a way that people are increasingly less likely to interact in social settings.

To the extent that it can be established that the viewing of film violence causes actual violence, we are obligated to act. Already as a society we have adopted a number of strategies to mitigate what we perceive as the negative effects of film content on behavior. These strategies range from outright government censorship, to an industry-imposed ratings system, to reliance on the controls of the market better known as laissez-faire. But the suppression of undesirable film content does not come without a cost. At risk are other societal values just as important, such as the freedom of speech and artistic expression. A clear and sober analysis of exactly what negative effects films have on societal behavior is the first step in deciding in what ways and how far we should go in controlling film content. I would add that it's not just film violence that should be of concern. There are those who find equally dangerous in films explicit sexual relations and just plain, old-fashioned immorality. If film content causes those behaviors, just what trade-offs should we make to control film content in that regard? More to the point, what is a "bad" movie, and what should we do about it?

CONTROLLING THE CONTENT OF FILM

The whole question of whether we can or should "do" something about the content of film is strongly related to whether film is product or art. Our laws and customs make it easier, in both the legal and the philosophical sense, to regulate a dangerous product through product-liability laws. An objectionable work of art, however, is presumably protected under the First Amendment. Part of the controversy concerning the content of film can be traced at its source to disagreements over whether films should be considered product or art. A commercially produced film is not strictly a work of art. In the consumer market, art may not sell, which is the case more often than not. Therefore, commercial motion pictures can best be described as a product, shaped by a craftsman's or craftswoman's touch and with perhaps an artistic influence. Primarily, however, motion pictures are commercial goods. As noted, this question of art versus industry is not as esoteric as it seems. Depending on what we judge feature motion pictures to be—art or commercial good—may determine their legal status, including the banning of a commercial film.

This brings us to the legal-constitutional component of the politics of film—the problem of regulating the motion picture industry. If motion pictures are simply another industrial product, there is no reason that the government cannot intervene to protect the public interest. However, motion pictures exist on the cusp of expression and industry. Filmmakers are fond of asserting their right of protection pursuant to the First Amendment admonition against restrictions of free expression. Is this a phony claim? Does the commerce clause of the Constitution or the right of the federal government to regulate interstate commerce trump the First Amendment in this case? All of this exists in the gray area of the law because of the hybrid status of motion pictures. Furthermore, do local communities have the right to restrict the screening of films that they find objectionable?

Not only is this a First Amendment issue, but it is also an issue of states' rights. With the "new federalism" that is now so much in vogue, can we expect local governments to be more active in the censorship of film, and will the federal government let them get away with it?

THE SUBLIMINAL MESSAGES OF FILM

What are the subtle and not-so-subtle messages sent to the public through the medium of film? What do we learn, and what do we allow? I assume that there are messages so repulsive to the public that they would not be acceptable when translated into films. Those films would at least fail in the box office (if not effectively end the careers of those people associated with their production). Public beliefs probably form a sort of philosophical and moral range within which film content is acceptable. A film that attacks a widely held understanding of American history—the treatment, for example, in the recent film *Selma* (2014) of Lyndon Johnson's role in the civil rights movement comes to mind—violates the sensibilities of a large portion of the American public and is therefore rejected regardless of whether it is true.

What are the limits to the range of the acceptable? That is certainly one of the most important questions to ask. The answer gets to the bedrock foundations of American beliefs. Why is it more tolerable to an American audience to watch two men kill each other, something we see all the time on screen, than it is to see them make love to one another? Furthermore, the fact that attitudes regarding the homosexual act are changing gives us insights into how the thinking of American audiences evolves.

On the other hand, is the heightened level of societal permissiveness in regard to homosexuality (and violence and liberal/conservative politics) a function of the subliminal messages of film? Presumably, filmmakers have room to maneuver within a certain range. Therefore, within that range there also lays considerable leeway to suggest, connote, and imply certain points of view, both moral and political. Can that also be true?

What is the nature of the interaction between audience beliefs and the apparent increasing violence and explicit sexuality in American films? Are we more tolerant of that sort of thing because of the influence of the rest of the media, including film, or is it the other way around? The answer to this question is probably so complex and nuanced as to not be completely knowable. Nevertheless, it is almost certainly the case that some of what we learn about how to dress, how to act, and how to think comes from the entertainment media.

WHO GOES TO THE MOVIES?

It is often the case that the audience for movies is analogous to the American public, but this brings to mind yet another consideration. Who goes to the movies? I assume that the filmgoing audience is not necessarily representative of a cross section of American society—that is, films are geared toward a special, moviegoing public and not the American public at large. Thus, the objections so commonly heard about the nature of film content may be largely the complaints of a group of people who don't go to movies in general or to a film not made with them in mind. If I go to an X-rated movie (now NC-17), I will certainly see a lot of nudity and explicit sexuality. I really can't complain about that. No one forced me into the theater. If there is a market for those types of films, then my public complaints about nudity and sex in X-rated films are a thinly veiled attempt to control the viewing habits of others—presumably a violation of rights of individuals in a free society. I might assume, then, that those who complain about film content and seek government controls have a hidden antidemocratic agenda. I can only assume that to be the case because, if those films (with excessive sexuality or violence) were really objectionable to the moviegoing public, nobody would go to see them. Those films would wither on the economic vine (and, indeed, many do). Thus, the ongoing controversy about film content and our degenerate moral culture is almost certainly part of a much larger political debate.

Ultimately, I argue that commercial film is a reflection of a large part of American political culture, warts and all. While sexism, racism, and social Darwinism are generally not, and increasingly less so, a strain of American political ideology, they are a part of our history. As such, and being that films reflect and guide our culture, American motion pictures are sometimes racist, sexist, and excessively violent even still.

By the same token, film can also reflect the good in society, the power and scope of democratization, or the positive effects of capitalism. Thus, the effect and reflections of American film can be a mixed bag. At their best, films inspire and motivate us in the best of American tradition. At their worst, film taps the darker side of our nature and of our society. In that way, films are a twentieth-century and now twenty-first-century historical record of American popular culture—modern hieroglyphics, if you will. For instance, films of the 1950s reflect a concern about the Soviet communist menace, films of the 1930s reflect the burden of the Great Depression, and so on. I also argue that, whatever the decade or the studio or the stars or the screenplay, American films reflect enduring notions of justice in American political culture.

OUTLINE OF THE BOOK

In the first chapter of this book, I examine American political culture and how that culture influences the stories that are told in the movies about American life. Thus, commercial films become a marker of the evolution of American ideologies, but only a partial marker. Commercial films have been produced since only the beginning of the twentieth century. I want to distinguish between political culture, which is an enduring iconography of American society, and popular culture, which is reflective of a more transient form of expression. Furthermore, as we shall see, film content tends to interact with the political economy of the modern film industry.

Chapter 2 puts the development of American film into context. This chapter is a short history of the political economy of American film—a transformation from the studio-driven monopoly of the "golden era" of American cinema to the relatively unfettered market for and production of American films today. What are the consequences for the content of American film of such a transformation?

Chapter 3 is an examination of who makes the movies and who watches them. What are the connections between the producers/consumers of the product and the product itself? This chapter will include an examination of both the demographic profile of Hollywood and the audience for film. It can be argued that in service to its most lucrative market, Hollywood makes films that may be objectionable to the religious community—who don't go to the movies anyway.

Chapter 4 gets to the heart of the matter of causality. What evidence is there to suggest that feature films stimulate or discourage some types of behavior? Ultimately, I argue in this section that because the financing of feature films is so expensive, investments made in movie projects generally follow rather than lead the market. Financiers take enough of a risk when they sponsor an expensive film venture without having to anticipate the market. Thus, feature films are more a reflection of perceived demand than they are a stimulant to any particular interest or behavior. Nevertheless, there may be an interactive influence at work in the sense that films reinforce existing perceptions and behaviors.

In chapter 5, I discuss the evaluation of films. In order to criticize the content of films, we must attempt to develop some standards. More simply put, we must answer the question: What is a "bad" movie? It is my contention that because moviegoing is a very personal experience, a bad movie is one that offends the person but not the society. Films that offend the broad expanse of the viewing public will not get made and, if they do, will not get seen (or, in other words, will not make a profit). This argument, however, comes with a qualifier. Given the marketization of the industry, it is now possible to make and profit from niche films that may offend many to appeal to the few. Thus, there is more of a chance than ever that someone may wander into a film that is made with another audience in mind and may be offended.

In chapter 6, I address the issue of why films "aren't what they used to be." The fact of the matter is that times and taste change. What was acceptable in the past may be unthinkable today and the other way around. I have some fun with this idea by rewriting the story line of a classic film so that it conforms to modern sensibilities. By doing so, I hope to illustrate the transient nature of American tastes and beliefs. Nevertheless, there are, as I argue in chapter 1, certain ideas and standards that endure.

In chapter 7, I turn to the constitutional debate. Can movies be censored, and can communities act to forbid the screening of a film? At first this seems to be a simple open-and-shut case, governed by the dictates of the First Amendment. However, feature films are not "speech" in the strictest sense. They are also commercial products manufactured for the market. As such, they may also be subject to the commerce clause of the Constitution. In this chapter, I examine the constitutional case for both restricting and not restricting the exhibition of feature films. Does the First Amendment trump the commerce clause?

At the end of each chapter, I review a feature film. This film is examined from the perspective presented in the chapter. Each of these minireviews illustrates *how* the issues presented here can be translated into a perspective from which a film can be viewed. Readers are then invited to review a film of their own choosing from that particular historical, philosophical, economic, or legal perspective.

Ultimately, I argue that feature films are the hieroglyphics of our time. Future generations may be able to tell more about our culture from viewing our films than from any other single source. That is why this subject is so important. While the answers to the questions of cause and effect and of societal limits may be difficult to answer, there lies at the end of that pursuit an essential and fruitful examination of American society in the twenty-first century.

On a final note, this book is about film and politics in the United States. This limitation should not be taken to mean that other nations do not have a tradition of filmmaking worthy of mention.[12] In fact, I believe that choosing to examine the films of France, Italy, Germany, or Japan can tell us much about the politics and sensibilities of those countries, giving us the types of insights that would take years to collect in any other way. I hope that with this book I can establish a model that other scholars can follow in examining and explaining the countries that they choose to study.

Feature Film: *Fifty Shades of Grey*

First of all, this is an appallingly bad movie. The production values are fine and the acting is as good as it can be given the unfortunate script and the preposterous story. The movie is adapted from a book of the same name about which Salman Rushdie said, "I've never read anything so badly written that got published." The film has also grossed to this point $569 million on a $40 million budget. That means that we are going to have to endure two other installments to finish the trilogy.

Nevertheless, the producers had an interesting problem on their hands. As is the case with most feature films, *Fifty Shades* made much of its money in the first two weeks of release, an exceptional amount of money, but after that, the word got out that the film was so bad that people quit going. I saw the film on a Saturday night, about a month after

Fifty Shades of Grey, **Focus Features, 2015**

the release, and there were no more than ten people in the theater. There were times during the film when the audience literally laughed at the film—during the parts that weren't supposed to be funny. *Box Office Mojo,* a website that measures this sort of thing, has a metric, weekly gross that tracks the "word of mouth" on a film. *Fifty Shades* was released on February 13, the day before Valentine's Day in 2014. It made $106 million in its first week and then dropped off 72 percent in the week after that (the lion's share of the rest of the gross is from overseas). That is an exceptional decline for any film and reflects a negative word of mouth.

What turned people off? I would argue that it turns out to be awfully hard to do good pornography. Anybody can shoot the mechanics of sex, but constructing a sensual environment, especially around whips and chains, is possible, I suppose, but it isn't done well here. Dakota Johnson, daughter of Melanie Griffith and Don Johnson, has entered the family business, and I get a sense of nostalgic continuity, as I probably saw her mother's bosom before she did. I expect that Jamie Dornan, the actor who plays Grey, will probably survive this movie, if only to be embarrassed by it for the rest of his life.

Fifty Shades is one in a line of movies, like *Pretty Woman* and *Working Girl*, stretching all the way back to the works of Jane Austen and William Makepeace Thackeray (*Vanity Fair*), where a young girl sleeps her way to the top. Except in the modern world of women's rights, this sort of thing is supposed to be no longer in vogue or necessary.

Basically, the plot of this film is that a young college girl, Anastasia "Ana" Steele, is sent off to interview a dotcom billionaire by her friend, who is a reporter for the campus newspaper. For some reason the billionaire, Christian Grey, takes to Ana, and they start an affair. The "gimmick" in this story is that Grey is a bondage enthusiast. We get some shadowy hints about some kind of relationship he had with an older woman when he was a boy. I suppose we'll find out more about that later.

I'm no expert on these things, but it is my understanding that guys like Grey, men of power, are less likely to want to give than receive punishment, but that would seriously cramp the plot of the movie because Ana doesn't really seem to be into bondage. She spends most of her time between spankings complaining about a lack of intimacy, which seems a rather conventional complaint when matched up against Grey's peccadillos.

So here's the problem with this movie: If you want to see porno, this movie is not for you. The sex scenes, even the ones with whips and chains, are really pretty flat and, to be frank, for the bondage enthusiast, they aren't graphic enough. The plotline is archaic and not just a little insulting to women. So, the movie is a kind of "tweener." It not dirty enough to satisfy the audience for pornography and not modern enough to be anything but insulting.

So why did it succeed? Because it had a brilliant rollout. Who doesn't want to find a shortcut to get your girl/guy in the mood on Valentine's Day?

Don't agree? What do you think?

EXERCISE

Select the film that is currently leading in box office receipts. Write a review of that film from the perspective of a social scientist. What does the popularity of that film tell us about the politics of the audience that watches it and the filmmakers who produced it?

SUGGESTED READINGS

Brownell, Kathryn Cramer. *Showbiz Politics: Hollywood in American Political Life*. Chapel Hill: University of North Carolina Press, 2014.

Danesi, Marcel. *Popular Culture: Introductory Perspectives*. Lanham, MD: Rowman & Littlefield, 2015.

Decherney, Peter. *Hollywood: A Very Short Introduction*. Oxford: Oxford University Press, 2015.

Haas, Peter J., and Terry Christensen. *Projecting Politics: Political Messages in American Films*. New York: Routledge, 2015.

Kelley, Beverly Merrill. *Reelpolitik Ideologies in American Political Film*. Lanham, MD: Rowman & Littlefield, 2012.

McVeigh, Stephen. *The American Western*. Oxford: Oxford University Press, 2007.

Wiatrowski, Myc, and Cory Barker, eds. *Popular Culture in the Twenty-First Century*. Newcastle upon Tyne: Cambridge Scholars, 2014.

NOTES

1. Sam Frizell, "Kim Jong Un Swears 'Merciless' Retaliation If New Seth Rogen Film Released," *Time Online*, June 25, 2014, http://time.com/2921071/kim-jong-un-seth-rogen-the-interview-james-franco/ (accessed January 13, 2016).

2. *The Hobbit*, by contrast, opened in over 3,800 theaters on the same day.

3. Nicole Perlroth and David E. Sanger, "North Korea Loses Its Link to the Internet," *New York Times*, December 22, 2014, http://www.nytimes.com/2014/12/23/world/asia/attack-is-suspected-as-north-korean-internet-collapses.html?_r=0 (accessed January 13, 2016).

4. Perhaps Franco and Rogen were trying to walk in the footsteps of Charlie Chaplin, who made a parody of Adolf Hitler titled *The Great Dictator*, released in 1940. It was Chaplin's first "talkie" and his most successful commercial film. The genesis of the film was Chaplin's attendance at a screening of *The Triumph of the Will*, Leni Riefenstahl's paean to the Nazi movement and Adolf Hitler. Chaplin thought the film was very funny and believed that Hitler would make a great subject for parody.

In some sense, *The Great Dictator* could have suffered the same fate as *The Interview*. While the film was being shot in 1938, the British in their effort to appease Hitler and a number of other countries with influential fascist movements let it be known that they would not screen the film. Chaplin was labeled in Germany a degenerate Jew (he wasn't Jewish). But by the time the film was released, Hitler had invaded Poland and most of the world was at war. Hitler would no longer be appeased, and *The Great Dictator* opened to enthusiastic audiences in Great Britain and the United States.

5. Ronald Radosh and Allis Radosh, *Red Star over Hollywood: The Film Colony's Long Romance with the Left* (San Francisco: Encounter Books, 2005); Allan H. Ryskind, *Hollywood Traitors: Blacklisted Screenwriters—Agents of Stalin, Allies of Hitler* (Washington, DC: Regnery History, 2015); or, from the Left, Eric Foner, *Who Owns History? Rethinking the Past in a Changing World* (New York: Hill and Wang, 2002).

6. There is massive literature on the theory of deconstruction; see Jacques Derrida and John D. Caputo, *Deconstruction in a Nutshell: A Conversation with Jacques Derrida* (New York: Fordham University Press, 1997); Susanne Lüdemann and Erik Butler, *Politics of Deconstruction: A New Introduction to Jacques Derrida* (Stanford, CA: Stanford University Press, 2014).

7. She was later executed on the guillotine.

8. David L. Paletz, *The Media in American Politics: Contents and Consequences* (New York: Longman, 1998).

9. Gabriel A. Almond and Sidney Verba, *The Civic Culture: Political Attitudes and Democracy in Five Nations* (Newbury Park, CA: Sage, 1989). Also, for a good discussion of the concept of political culture, see Ronald P. Formisano, "The Concept of Political Culture," *Journal of Interdisciplinary History* 31, no. 3 (2001): 393–426.

10. Almond and Verba, *The Civic Culture*, 12.

11. For discussions of American exceptionalism, see John D. Wilsey, *American Exceptionalism and Civil Religion: Reassessing the History of an Idea* (Westmont, IL: InterVarsity Press, 2015); Seymour Martin Lipset, *American Exceptionalism: A Double-Edged Sword* (New York: W. W. Norton, 1997); and the classic Louis Hartz, *The Liberal Tradition in America: An Interpretation of American Political Thought since the Revolution* (San Diego: Harcourt Brace Jovanovich, 1991).

12. An added complication is that it is increasingly the case with the globalization of industry that many films are the result of a multinational effort. I will consider films "American" if they are made and distributed by one of the major American studios.

1

Movies, the Media, and American Tales

In his classic examination of political systems, David Easton suggests that the media play an important role in what he calls the "feedback loop" of politics.[1] Feedback in political systems is the information transmitted to the public, mainly by the media that inform the public as to the actions of government and guides the public to their responses, which in turn gives direction to the government for further action. In most political systems, even authoritarian ones but particularly in democracies, the government is constantly tweaking policy to conform to public opinion. The media play a crucial role in this feedback process. Particularly for those not directly affected by a particular policy, the media play a crucial role in providing information and interpreting the effects of public policy. Thus, the conversation of politics is carried on through this feedback loop. While we generally think about media primarily as a journalistic enterprise (the journalistic media can include anything from television and radio journalism to the newspapers), as a subset of the media there is also the entertainment industry, of which feature films are a part. While the role of the entertainment media in this feedback loop is much more subtle, what we view as entertainment informs, forms, and transmits our concerns. How the entertainment industry addresses social problems should be of interest to decision makers. After all, in viewing and thus financing films, the public "votes" with its dollars in expressing its interests, concerns, and beliefs.

In fact, decision makers do seem to monitor our moviegoing. The language of movies often slips into the political debate. "Read my lips" (no new taxes), "make my day" (in reference to a presidential veto threat), "you had me at hello," "show me the money," and "you can't handle the truth" are just a few examples of movie lines that have become modern jargon.[2]

Politicians assume, and rightly so, that most people will know what complex ideas a phrase like "make my day" connotes. That phrase captures exactly the point that political candidates are trying to make, and, in being test marketed at the theater, the language of the movies becomes a surefire appeal to a specific audience. In fact, after sports analogies (the sports industry is another component of the entertainment media), references from the movies are some of the most commonly used metaphors in the language of American politics.

Feedback through the media is not strictly in one direction or the other, to the bottom up or from the top down. Not only does the public register its concerns and interests in its choice of entertainment and news, but there is also clearly an influence going in the other direction. News editors are constantly making decisions about what stories to cover, what points in a news story to emphasize, and how to place a news story into a broader context. So it is too with the movies. Movies (and literature in general) place a spin on the events of the world. The choices that film producers make in editing, marketing, financing, casting, and scripting all represent editorial decisions of a kind. Who decides what we see in the theater and how that product is presented is the result of a multitude of editorial decisions. Whether those decisions are a function of the personal bias of the people who make those decisions is a matter for debate. One thing seems to be certain, however—the journalistic and entertainment media are not clear, unfiltered reflections of public interests and concerns.[3]

Thus, we need to think of films as being influenced by and influencing public opinion. A most obvious example of this sort of phenomenon is that of *The China Syndrome* (1979), a film that evoked the concern shared by many about the dangers of nuclear power. That film is an obvious example of popular culture reflecting contemporary problems. Cable and network television produce shows that are almost contemporaneous with current events and our modern lives. Given the longer lead time for their production and the broader market for their product, filmmakers are somewhat less current but are nevertheless cognizant of current events and political trends. *The Contender* (2000), a story about a politician, in this case a woman, accused of sexual indiscretions, along with *Primary Colors* (1998), are clearly comments on the politics of the Clinton era. But the contemporary political and social commentary of film can be even subtler than that. In the era of the Great Depression, *Mr. Smith Goes to Washington* (1939), *Gabriel over the White House* (1933), and *Meet John Doe* (1941) all evinced a growing concern about the viability of democracy in the face of fascism, political corruption, and economic decline. In the 1940s, during World War II, films taught us about how to act as patriots and why we should fight our enemies. And after the war came the doubts about American life in peacetime, evoked in an entire genre of films collectively known as film noir (one of the best examples of which is *The Big Sleep* [1946]). In the 1950s, both directly and metaphorically, the red menace was on display, and so on throughout the twentieth century.

To what extent and in what ways the entertainment media reflect and drive the concerns of the public who consume its product is hard to say. It is not necessarily true that the financial success of *Silence of the Lambs* (1991) or *The Godfather* (1972) expresses an overwhelming public fascination with serial killers and the Mafia, but it is not too difficult to suggest that the focus on crime in film in general both reflects and transmits some degree of societal enthrallment with the Mafia and a concern with violence and crime. Certainly, the increasing acceptance of graphic violence on screen indicates, if nothing else, a higher degree of tolerance for that sort of depiction.

Whether this tolerance then translates into greater tolerance for real-life violence in the form of, say, the death penalty or war is an open question. Establishing that sort of connection would require exploring one more link on the causal chain. Does film violence beget actual violence?

But even if that were true, film violence could work in the opposite way. Depictions of violence can lead to a certain type of revulsion and outrage. Steven Spielberg, it is said, made the battle scenes in *Saving Private Ryan* (1998) as graphic as they were in order to accurately depict the horrors of war. Anyone watching those scenes would probably think twice about favoring war as a policy option. News footage of civil rights demonstrators being clubbed by local police in Selma, Alabama, in 1964 had the effect of nudging a large segment of the American public to support civil rights legislation. By the same token, it makes sense that films extolling the glory of war or the repulsiveness of crime would drive public sensibilities in another direction.

As part of the feedback loop, the entertainment media play a subtle but important role in American politics. To the extent that public opinion in a democracy influences politics and to the extent that politics determines "who gets what, when and how," the media and even the entertainment media become an important influence on how we prosper and how we lead our lives.[4] In the chapters to follow, I discuss in detail some of the issues introduced here. I am particularly interested in the issue of films as cause and effect—at both the market and the individual level. How much influence does the market have on the content of film as opposed to the beliefs and prejudices of filmmakers themselves? Furthermore, at the individual level, how do film messages translate into actual behavior? In other words, where does film exist on the feedback loop?

There are three general ways that the information transmitted through the feedback loop can be altered. At one level, the message of the media can be affected by the biases of the industry itself. This issue encompasses the debate concerning the liberal or conservative bias of the media. I examine those biases in chapter 3. At another level, the media can be influenced by their structures. The fact that in the former Soviet Union *Pravda* was published in a totalitarian state and that the *New York Times* is published in a capitalistic democratic state certainly affects the journalistic tone and content of those newspapers. I examine this political economy of the film industry in chapter 2. Finally, media can be influenced in their relationships to a state's political culture. In this chapter, I examine the effects on the media feedback loop of American political culture.

MOVIES AS PART OF POLITICAL CULTURE

Easton also writes of the environmental context in which a political system operates. By environmental context, I mean the deep-seated beliefs of our society that affect public policy. More specifically, political culture has been described as "a 'mind set' that has the effect of limiting attention to less than the full range of alternate behaviors."[5]

For example, the selection or tolerance by the public of an overtly authoritarian government may be possible in Algeria or Russia or even Italy (in the 1920s), but it would be unlikely in largely liberal political systems such as the United States. After all, classical liberals believe, as do most Americans, that the government that governs best governs least.

While there is some intramural disagreement over the size and scope of government, the communitarian perspective—or the belief in the importance of a collective identity and response—never gained much traction in the United States. By the same token, the heroic sacrifice of the individual to the needs of the all-encompassing state, a perspective central to fascist ideology, never gained much leverage in the United States, either. Americans are just too independent for that sort of political involvement. Thus, the spectrum of American political debate and the range of the acceptable political messages are delimited by a rejection of the communal approach to politics. Even rather limited proposals that require Americans to act as a community, such as affirmative action (or national health care or Social Security, for that matter), are highly controversial because they regard certain persons as part of a protected class rather than as persons deserving rewards on the basis of individual merit.[6]

These parameters of the American political debate influence the media. As noted film critic Andrew Sarris has written,

> Simply by looking at movies again and again I began to see them in terms of recurring myths and fables deep within our psyches rather than as transient impressions of the surface of our society. Also, I began to realize that the cin-

ema did not faithfully record all the realities of politics. . . . The enormous expense of production, and the publicity attendant on exhibition make it mandatory for films to be in tune either with their society or with at least a sympathetic subculture within that society.[7]

Thus, a serious (not mocking) depiction of socialism is rarely seen on American television or at the movies. With the exception of the film *Reds* (1981), a reasonably successful film about the life of socialist writer Jack Reed, most American films ignore the socialist revolution in Russia (*Enemy at the Gates*, 2001), mock its results (*Dr. Zhivago*, 1965), or remember nostalgically the rule of the czar (*Nicholas and Alexandra*, 1971). Without getting into a discussion of which of these depictions are most accurate, it would be safe to say that the most popular message, the one most likely to succeed commercially, will not paint capitalism as a threat to world peace and prosperity. There are plenty of other examples of this tendency to rewrite or at least selectively remember history in American films. In the past, slavery was whitewashed or ignored (*Gone with the Wind*, 1939), even in the recent past (*Cold Mountain*, 2003). Lately, in a 180-degree turn on the subject, *Django Unchained* (2012) and *12 Years a Slave* (2013) stand the traditional narrative on its ear. The slaughter of Native Americans was for many years viewed as a triumph, only lately being depicted in a more nuanced manner.[8]

The most prominent determinants of a society's political culture are geographic, historical, temporal (point in time), and, for lack of a better term, cultural.[9] Geographic determinants such as location, resources, climate, and so on are vital determinants of a nation's development. In the case of the United States, its relatively large size, self-sufficiency, and isolation have contributed greatly to the American character. The history of the settlement of the American West is a significant totem in the American psyche that reflects our geographical heritage. Also, our relative isolation, buffered on both sides by vast oceans, has allowed our culture to develop in a unique manner, largely unsullied by the influence of Asian and European cultures. For example, while the world drifted into the totalitarianism of the 1930s, the United States remained relatively aloof.

The largely shared historical experiences of American citizens—most prominently, the immigrant experience, our relative isolation, our relative resource self-sufficiency, our struggle with slavery and its aftereffects, and our attempt to build a multicultural society—are all fundamental determinants of dominant attitudes in the United States. The status of the United States as a mature democracy with an advanced capitalist economy reflects the fact that there are widely shared notions of equality (and the meaning of equality) and justice.

Finally, while the ethnic diversity of the United States is quite remarkable, the dominant cultural influences at this time are the English language and European culture. In terms of religion, Americans are only somewhat devout but fairly unanimous in their support for the Judeo-Christian ethic (although that is changing). All of these factors add up to an exceptional and, given the diversity of our population, surprisingly homogeneous political culture.[10]

All of these environmental influences combine to delimit the range of policy options available to politicians in the American political system. And if feature films are reflective of the political culture, the political environment also delimits these films. As noted, it is hard to imagine that a film explicitly extolling the virtues of a centralized, state-controlled economy would have much commercial potential in the United States. By the same token, foreign films in the United States generally receive a quite limited release, which says something not only about the perceived marketability of those films but also about cultural sensibilities in the United States. Foreign themes and cultural eccentricities as depicted in films don't play well in the mall Cineplex. On the other hand, it is interesting to note that American films are widely accepted abroad and have thus become one of our country's most profitable and important exports.

HOLLYWOOD AND ITS EFFECT ON/BY AMERICAN POLITICAL CULTURE

By answering three general questions, we can analyze American films to trace the contours of American political culture. First, what are the special characteristics of American political culture represented in American films? As discussed, there is much about American culture that is exceptional. That exceptionalism is reflected in the films that are produced in the United States. For example, the plots of American films present us with explanations of who is responsible for what. In successful films, these are explanations that resonate and ring true. In looking for the politics of American films, we can look for the explanatory conventions. For example, is the criminal a "bad person" or the product of a deprived upbringing? Are people poor because they are lazy or because they are beset by disadvantages not of their own making? Are people successful because of their own individual efforts or because of the advantages they inherit or the opportunities provided to them by living within a nurturing community? In answering these questions and accepting those explanations as logical and just, we are told much about our American view of the world. And through repetition on television, in the theater, and on the news, these explanations become reinforced.

Second, does American culture dictate the content of American film, or is it the other way around? This is an important question. If film content is simply the plotting of an ideologically distant and isolated community ("Hollywood"), then films tell us nothing about the beliefs of the majority of Americans. However, if films are truly made to meet the demands of the consumer (and the consumer is a cross section of the American public), then the logic of the influence of film is simple: Filmmakers are businessmen and businesswomen. They want to make money. They make money by giving the public what it wants. Films then come to largely reflect the sensibilities of their audience. But even if that is true, the influence could work, in some limited sense, in the other direction as well.

Third, can films influence the behavior and perceptions? If films are simply made in service of demand, then most of this "top down" influence is simply the reinforcement of beliefs already held. Since films are made in the service of the market, the biases they reflect also become the biases they promote. For example, the recent *Pitch Perfect* (2012 and 2015) films portray a picture of college life that is hardly the norm. Nevertheless, the films are so attractive and pleasing that they can't help but influence behavior, as, say, *Animal House* (1978) did in an earlier generation.

What is just as interesting about this notion of the direction of causality is not only what it does to a domestic audience but also what it does to a foreign audience. After all, movie sales abroad constitute about 70 percent of American feature-film revenues, and what goes on in *Pitch Perfect* probably has very little to do with what happens at a university in Istanbul or Mexico City. And maybe such an influence is not so bad. One can only guess at how the perceptions (and perhaps the behaviors) of foreigners are influenced by this important American export. It should be noted, however, that *Pitch Perfect 2* is so culture specific that its foreign sales are far below the summer blockbuster norm. Watching *Pitch Perfect* in India must be like watching Bollywood (Indian films) in Pittsburgh.

AMERICAN IDEOLOGY: WHAT THEMES TO LOOK FOR IN AMERICAN FILMS

There are several core concepts of American political ideology that permeate feature motion pictures. Far and away the most dominant features of American political culture are the principles of its founding, classical liberalism. This is not the liberalism of Barack Obama, although that is part of it. Nor is it exclusively the philosophy of the Libertarian Party, although it is part of that too. Rather, liberalism, what I call *classical liberalism*, is the philosophy of the commercial middle class, those people who earn their living in the marketplace. Liberalism relies on the market to coordinate economic activity and leans toward the protection of private property. Liberalism, as an ideology, justifies a capitalist economic system and the American variant of democracy.[11]

According to these classical liberals, society is like the marketplace, where the value of ideas, people, and products are determined by the preferences of consumers. Those goods that are in demand will be valued, and those that are not, will not. Thus, the market for one's product determines one's worth—and the market delivers perfect justice. All of this should sound pretty familiar to the American reader since, in one way or another, most of us are classical liberals. Classical liberals will tolerate interference in the marketplace (and, thus, people's lives) only insofar as those limitations are imposed by a government, controlled through a democratic process that is respectful of basic human rights, often called "natural" rights. Thus, according to the classical liberal, it is appropriate for a government to provide police protection, enforce contracts, and provide for national defense. Strict adherence to classical liberalism will result in a limited government guided by democratic participation. There are some exceptions to the rule concerning government interference, such as in the areas of civil rights, social welfare, and so-called moral values. But even in these instances, Americans are deeply conflicted about the need for government to intervene.[12]

Democratic rule is important to classical liberals because democracy is as close to the absence of government as is possible without the actual absence of government. Through the democratic process we rule ourselves. Therefore, the laws imposed by a democratic government, in essence, are restrictions that we have placed upon ourselves. As long as the government respects the rights of individuals, citizens are obliged to obey the law (as if they were being true to themselves). However, when a government violates the rights of its citizens, citizens have a right and even an obligation to rebel. Thus, classical liberalism was an attractive justification for a Declaration of Independence and, ultimately, the design of our government.

Beside the essential role of democracy and capitalism in a liberal state is the notion of natural rights. John Locke, one of the founders of the liberal tradition, argues in his *Second Treatise on Government* that all persons by virtue of their humanity are deserving of certain "natural rights." The centerpiece of this Lockean notion of rights is the concept of property. Individuals, according to Locke, have the right to possess property free from the violation of those rights by individuals or the government. Locke defines property rights rather broadly. Property can be defined as a possession or as the "property" rights one has in one's own person. In other words, individuals in a just society should be free from assaults to their persons or possessions.[13]

The founders of the United States adopted this concept of natural rights more or less intact, as reflected in the words of the preamble of the Declaration of Independence.[14] According to Locke, all individuals have the right to life, liberty, and property (later written as "the pursuit of happiness" by Thomas Jefferson in the Declaration of Independence).

As prominent as Lockean (classical) liberalism is in constitutional design, it has persisted as an ideological strain throughout American history and is being reinforced still. Two important historical processes have served to lock the American body politic into an eighteenth-century philosophy in a twenty-first-century world. The fact that the United States has been predominantly settled by Protestant Christians has generally reinforced Lockean liberalism in the United States. Protestantism was born of a revolt against the Catholic Church. Among other things, Protestants believe that Christians can have a direct relationship with God, without the necessary intercession of a priest or the hierarchy of an official church. Along with the liberal rejection of strong hierarchical government, these beliefs mesh quite well with the individualism of Lockean liberalism, where the fate of the individual in the market is determined by his or her own actions.[15]

Besides religion and the tradition of Lockean liberalism, American individualism is reinforced by yet another widely shared American backdrop: the immigrant experience. For almost every American, with the exception of the Native American, there is a shared experience of flight. In almost every family tree in the United States is an ancestor who dropped a plow, waded out of a rice paddy, or swam the Rio Grande in search of a better life in the United States.

That shared history of flight reinforces the individualism of American political culture in a couple of important ways. First, the United States is, and continues to be, populated by the world's dispossessed. For those whose lives are comfortable and connected in the Old World, there is no need to flee. But for those who are persecuted or simply put at a disadvantage by the social hierarchy of the Old World, the United States offers a legitimate and desirable alternative. Thus, most immigrants who come to the United States have been and continue to be distrustful of governments and the established order. They desire that people be judged not by their origins but by their individual merits. More than anything else, they hope that the government will leave them alone. This is as true today for Vietnamese, Nigerian, or Afghan immigrants as it was one hundred years ago for immigrants from Poland, Ireland, or Italy.[16]

It is important to note that I intentionally include African Americans in this category (of immigrants) because so many fled the South to find work in the North and, in doing so, had the experience of flight. In addition, a large percentage of African Americans arrived well after the end of slavery, from Africa or the Caribbean, and have been exposed to more or less the conventional immigrant experience. Nevertheless, it would be impossible to argue that the black community has had a typical American historical experience. Thus, the current of Lockean liberalism does not run as strong in the black community—which is precisely the reason that in many ways the black community is more a distinct community than many others in the United States.

The immigrant experience is a recurring theme in many American films. *America America* (1963), *Hester Street* (1975), *Coming to America* (1988), *Moscow on the Hudson* (1984), *Gangs of New York* (2002), *The Godfather* (1972) series, and even the sci-fi comedy *The Coneheads* (1993) are just a few examples of what is a standard film plot genre in American political culture. These films resonate not only in the story they tell, a story to which most Americans can relate, but also in the metaphors they elicit. The immigrant is a risk taker, entrepreneurial and courageous. These are the positive traits of the immigrant that we admire and hope to emulate in this country.

However, there are traits in the immigrant that are also not so attractive, which are also part of the immigrant tradition (if not the myth), and thus American political culture. Immigrants are not a little hedonistic; they are loners, often abandoning their families and the other "problems" of their society. They are isolationist, insensitive to the plight of others, aggressive toward those who impinge on their freedom, and generally antisocial. It is this hedonism that was on display in the genocide committed against Native Americans, in the failure of the United States to join the League of Nations, and in the smallest per capita humanitarian assistance budget for any developed nation.[17]

Thus, the immigrant experience produces a relatively consistent and somewhat unique notion of "freedom." Freedom for Americans is the absence of constraint. This is in contrast to the freedom "to" as opposed to the freedom "from." In many other societies, freedom is evaluated in the functional sense: it is not enough for someone to have the right to do something, but they must also have the functional ability to do something as well. This is not generally true in the United States.

For example, in theory anyone can influence political decision making in the United States. In practice, however, there is a certain class bias in our American political system. More simply put, all things being equal, the rich have more influence than do the poor. Nevertheless, in the United States we are loath to define that as an insult to the freedom to participate. Thus, the freedom to participate as equals in politics exists in theory but not in practice. This concept of rights is important because it defines a wide range of story lines so popular in American films. For example, in many variants of the "rags to riches" story, characters overcome their disadvantaged circumstances to make good or be heard. Whether that is an accurate depiction of the American story is neither here nor there. The fact that the allegory of rags to riches persists and is constantly reinforced in our popular culture creates a reality of consciousness, if not a reality of fact.

Individualism, as opposed to communalism, is a powerful strain of

American political ideology. Consequently, socialism and fascism, ideologies that have on occasion been central to European politics, have never gained much of a toehold in the United States. The subjugation of personal preferences to the needs of the state in socialism and fascism are just too much of a violation of the American notion of freedom to resonate in the United States. Thus, story lines in praise of the rugged individual (Horatio Alger) and in support of the individual against the state (Ayn Rand) are a prominent and popular part of the American literary tradition and, thus, film tradition.

Of course, there are limits to even theoretical freedom. The actions of one person in society affect others. Thus, there is a constant conversation in American politics about the limits of freedom. For example, we witness the spirited debate in the United States over laws related to the possession of guns. Where these limits are is the source of endless and intense debate. These debates, which are intensely fought in Congress and the courts, are also a recurring theme in the literature of American political culture. But in many other political cultures, these issues would be irrelevant or beside the point.

What is not generally discussed in the American context is functional freedom. In theory, anyone can become president. However, is that functionally true? Judging by the past, about the only people who can qualify for the presidency are men. Of course, there is an equal opportunity for education or advancement in the United States. But in reality, do we live in a meritocracy or in an aristocracy based not on title but on wealth? This is an issue that is less explicitly debated. After all, such a discussion would tend to undermine the legitimacy of many of our politicians and business elite whose status is as much inherited as it is earned. Furthermore, an explicit discussion of the real opportunities available in American society would discomfit the moviegoing public. Nevertheless, when in *Mr. Smith Goes to Washington* (1939), or *Dave* (1993), or more recently *Idiocracy* (2006), regular guys find themselves in high office, they do so through a series of accidents and not through the more traditional route of winning an election. Thus, it might be surmised that it is almost inconceivable that a common person could otherwise attain political office (the implication also being that there is something inherently strange about people who do).

AMERICAN TALES

American political culture has generated a set of stories that serve as metaphors for American history. These American tales (designated as such in deference to an animated feature of the same name) provide a sort of oral tradition of American nationhood. In every community there is such an oral tradition. These stories exist to explain history, to condone some behaviors and condemn others, and to pass on the culture of the community from one generation to the next. In a complex, technologically advanced society such as ours, these tales are told and retold through the media. It is not up to the media to challenge these myths. In fact, to challenge these myths would be dangerous for media that in our country are so dependent on market success. The fact that much of what these stories say is true reinforces their credibility. But not everything in the American tales is true, or it is at least subject to question. And yet, these tales are repeated over and over, in one form or another, and go pretty much unquestioned in American film. Thus, American movies serve an important role in perpetuating and reinforcing our culture. There are several important American tales. Here is just a sample.

The Conquest of the West

One of the most enduring themes of American film is the conquest of the West. In this story, rugged individualists, overcoming all sorts of adversity, settle the virgin wilderness frontier and thereby spread American civilization from the Atlantic to the Pacific. There are so many films of this genre that it is nearly impossible to list even a representative sample. However, some of the classic favorites include *The Gold Rush* (1925), *High Noon* (1952), *My Darling Clementine* (1946), *The Searchers* (1956), *The Wild Bunch* (1969), *Little Big Man* (1970), *McCabe and Mrs. Miller* (1971), *Paint Your Wagon* (1969), *Unforgiven* (1992), and, of course, *Cowboys & Aliens* (2011). Naturally, there are some inaccuracies in this story as depicted in the movies. Much of the West was conquered by the American military in the Mexican-American and Indian wars. The West was hardly uninhabited anyway. The US government actively subsidized the railroads (built by slave and immigrant labor) that played such a significant role in the settlement of the West, and so on. Nevertheless, the conquest story is true enough to resonate whenever it is depicted in film. Besides, the conquest story reinforces the liberal notion of minimal government; individualism; and justice in hard work, enterprise, and true grit.

Kudos go to Clint Eastwood and the makers of *Unforgiven* (1992). In that excellent and Academy Award–winning film, we see a counter to the traditional western. All of the elements of the formula are there—the gunfighter, the sheriff, the sidekick, the apprentice, and the whore with a heart of gold—but what is missing is that none of them seem to play their assigned roles. The gunfighter is sensitive, disgusted with what he has been asked to do. The sheriff is brutal and lawless. The African American sidekick is every bit an equal to the protagonist, and so on. But, more to the point, as if doing penance for his previous work, Clint Eastwood depicts violence as shocking, with permanent and heartrending consequences. Is this film a more accurate depiction of the West? My guess is that the film is not much more historically accurate than *Shane* (1953). But what is different is that in this film the conversation about the West and its myths has changed. Thus, *Unforgiven* is a modern film about the West that tells us as much about America in the 1990s as in the 1890s.

The Cult of the Individual

The main focus for justice in a liberal society is the individual. To the greatest extent possible, individual rights are to be honored in the United States, even at the expense of the community. That is a core value of a liberal society. The cult of the individual as played out in movie plots goes something like this: a resilient, resourceful individual with personal courage and ingenuity overcomes the odds and succeeds without help, sometimes even against the grain of an oppressive environment often depicted as the government.

As noted, because the rights of the individual are so well respected in our country (even over the rights of the community), European and Asian communitarian traditions have never taken hold. Furthermore, the individualism of American society is constantly reinforced by the inflow of immigrants who generally share the core American values of self-reliance, thrift, and enterprise (the protestations of the nativist anti-immigration crowd notwithstanding). This focus on the individual is mainly all to the good. It promotes a dynamic, vibrant, and creative society. Thus, the benefits of individualism are constantly celebrated in the story lines of film, particularly American film. One of my favorite films in this regard is *Lonely Are the Brave* (1962), but there are many others, including much of the rags-to-riches genre—including *Joy* (2015), *Tucker: The Man and His Dream* (1988), *Conan the Barbarian* (1982), *The Jerk* (1979), *The Fountainhead* (1949), *Mr. Smith Goes to Washington* (1939), and *Mr. Deeds Goes to Town* (1936).

The problem with this point of view, however, is that the rights of the individual must sometimes be put into context. Unless you live in an uninhabited wilderness, what you do has consequences for other people. Since the Wild West no longer exists, the rights of the individual in this country are to a certain extent limited for no other reason than the shortage of space. Nevertheless, there may exist a disconnect between the ability of our society to protect individual rights (as we define them) and our sometimes ineffective attempts to address the problems of urban sprawl, environmental degradation, and other pressing problems. Collective action in response to these problems is hampered by our tendency toward deference to individual rights over community action, deference that is constantly reinforced by the repetition of this American tale. Thus, the movies affect public policy by reinforcing certain beliefs in our political culture.

Rags to Riches

There is a tremendous amount of controversy in the scholarly community in regard to the true nature of American opportunity. To what extent are the opportunities provided to us in this society functional as opposed to illusory? In other words, to what extent can individuals get ahead in our political and economic system?[18] The nuanced answer to this question is that, by and large, income disparity is increasing in the United States, but that is not the same as saying that the opportunity for the individual (to get ahead) isn't there.[19] Thus, it is not entirely inaccurate to suggest that, as the American literary tradition presented in the movies tends to reassure us, all holdings are earned and thus deserved and that we live in a meritocracy in the sense that hard work and perseverance are richly rewarded. One of the most time-honored and richly rewarded genres in American fiction is the tale of rags to riches.[20] In this story, those who are born poor have a real opportunity to overcome their disadvantage, and those who are wealthy have earned and thus deserve their prosperity.

Some would argue, however, that in general, people who are born poor tend to stay that way and that in order to counter that belief, Americans are fed a steady diet of films and literature that extol the virtues of our economy that are actually the exceptions to the rule. Nevertheless, some of the best films in this rags-to-riches genre are *Citizen Kane* (1941), *The Godfather* series, *The Getaway* (1972), *Mildred Pierce* (1945), *Stripes* (1981), and *Working Girl* (1988). In each of these movies, the protagonist is beset by a set of circumstances that make it nearly impossible to get ahead. In seeing these obstacles overcome, we come to believe that we, too, have a chance.

For example, in the enormously popular film *Pretty Woman* (1990), the best-looking, healthiest, most intelligent, nonaddicted streetwalker on the planet manages through pluck and charm to win the heart of a billionaire client. There are some real ironies in this story. The protagonist, rather than going to school or working hard at her job, manages to sleep her way to the top. While probably unintentional, this film can be seen as being basically anticapitalistic. Since the story is so preposterous, and because the "work" that the protagonist does involves performing sex for money, a viewer might well conclude that the film is a paean to Marxist Leninism—the suggestion here being that the only way a woman in her station can get ahead in our free market economy is to sleep with and marry money (as if that were going to happen anyway). But I don't think that is why the film was so popular. This weird story line (admittedly very nicely acted and produced) appeals to the underdog, rags-to-riches hopes of the moviegoer. But it doesn't tell us much about how getting wealthy can actually happen.

I am not going to argue that all holdings are inherited and thus in some sense are undeserved (at least from the perspective of a meritocrat). Much too much evidence suggests that real opportunity exists in the United States—with Bill Clinton, Steve Jobs, Ronald Reagan, Barack Obama, and Bill Gates being prime examples of those who have succeeded while coming from humble beginnings. Nevertheless, much of the wealth and privilege held in the United States is inherited, and much of the law in the United States is intended to keep it that way (making the lives of Clinton, Gates, Reagan, Obama, and Jobs all the more remarkable). It is this disconnect between the myth of a meritocracy and the actuality of an oligarchy of inherited wealth that makes this genre in American literature and popular entertainment somewhat distorted.[21]

If, according to the rags-to-riches tale, most wealth is earned and thus deserved, then poverty is earned and deserved as well. This myth is also highlighted in American popular culture. Throughout American history, not just in the history of American motion pictures, the poor and oppressed have often been depicted as deserving their fate. African Americans, particularly in the past, were disparagingly depicted as slow and lazy. Native Americans were traditionally depicted as primitive and brutal. Hispanics, Asians, and other groups in society have been subject to depiction through cultural and gender stereotypes that have been used at one time or another to explain and justify the existing hierarchy in society.

It is interesting to note that in recent times the rags-to-riches story often becomes a cautionary tale. In *Wall Street* and *The Wolf of Wall Street*, the protagonists end up either in exile or in jail. Even in *Fifty Shades of Grey*, the billionaire is actually a pervert. So the bloom is off the rags-to-riches story, especially after the Great Recession of 2008. Bank bailouts, failure to prosecute those who were responsible for the meltdown, and the increasing disparity of wealth in the United States have made the super-rich all the more suspect, especially to the middle-brow (and largely middle-class) audience for film.

Some cultural values and beliefs are rather consistent across time. The American commitment to democracy and the free market is pretty much bedrock solid. However, other values wax and wane. Thus, the timing of films is also important. The sensibilities of a film made in the 1950s were different from the content of a film made in the 1990s. In some cases, the myths have changed and so have the stories. At any point in American political culture, it is likely that a new set of stories is being told.

TIMING

It would be inaccurate to say that the movie industry is consistently insensitive to the plight of those who are less fortunate in society. As public attitudes change, so do audiences' tastes for entertainment. Times do change, and the movies change along with them. For example, many films have chronicled Custer's last stand. But there is a profound difference in the representation of General George Armstrong Custer's character in the 1942 film *They Died with Their Boots On* and the 1970 film *Little Big Man.* Certainly, historical facts did not change, but the attitudes of those who make and watch motion pictures reflected different sensibilities thirty years apart. The substantive equivalent of *Little Big Man* could no more have been produced and screened in the 1940s than *They Died with Their Boots On* could have been screened in the modern era. One of the most significant films and top-grossing films of all time, *The Birth of a Nation* (D. W. Griffith, 1915), is deeply troubling when viewed in the modern context, but it is also a window into the past.

Overall, the movie industry has been in existence for only a relatively short time. Even so, it has been in existence through some of the most tumultuous and significant changes in American history. What we see when we review the brief history of American motion pictures is a study of change in American political culture going through the twentieth into the twenty-first century. Some of the major events faithfully recorded in American film that profoundly influenced the United States in the twentieth century were the Depression, World War II, the Cold War, the Vietnam War, and the civil rights and environmental movements. The Depression, for example, as depicted in *The Grapes of Wrath* (1940) is presented as a deeply troubling and somewhat ambiguous failure of capitalism. The narrative of the film never really answers the central question of the film: Why are the Joads (the family at the center of the film) in the fix that they are in? Is the plight of the dispossessed family farmer a function of individual failure, systemic changes within a basically sound capitalist market, or a total and inevitable collapse of the capitalist system? The answer to that question is important because through the interpretation of history we determine solutions. If the Joads are simply shortsighted and inefficient, then all we can recommend is charity. If the Joads are in trouble through no fault of their own, maybe we should ease their transition into another line of work. But if the Joads fail because the system fails, we may need to change the system.

Not only is political culture reflected in historical film, but movies also often reflect modern sensibilities through metaphor. *Braveheart* (1995), the story of a medieval Scottish revolutionary, was seen by members of the House Republican freshman class as analogous to the Gingrich "revolution" of 1994, right down to the Democrats as the effete (and sometimes gay) English occupiers and the Republican moderate accommodationists as the Scottish nobles.[22] In fact, the more fantastic the setting of the film, the more freedom the narrative has to reflect contemporary concerns. In the

1950s, *The Thing* (1951) and *Invasion of the Body Snatchers* (1956) came to underscore the communist menace. *Invasion of the Body Snatchers* was remade in 1978, and it reflects some of the same, as well as some different, concerns mainly related to people's fear of loss of individuality. The *Planet of the Apes* series reflects the fear of nuclear war, *The China Syndrome* reflects concerns raised by nuclear power, and so on. Beyond being films with a message, these are films *of* a message. These are films that resonate with viewers not just as an escape but also as a release. In viewing our nightmares on screen, we confront our fears and put them into context. Sometimes these fantasies, such as the multifilm *Star Wars* saga or *Red Dawn* (1984), not only help us confront our fears of the evil empire (the Soviet Union) but also provide us with a cathartic release—the military and spiritual defeat of our adversaries.

CONCLUSION

This chapter is a brief examination of feature film as part of the feedback loop of politics. The entertainment media in a subtle way serves our political culture by repeating our stories, reinforcing our beliefs, and providing an emotional release for our fears. While some of the assumptions underlying the story lines in American film could at least be questioned, it is generally the case that American movies pretty much repeat the same themes in one context or another, over and over. Thus, I would argue that American films are nowhere near the corrosive influence that they are purported to be by cultural critics.

In the next chapter, I discuss the political economy of the American film industry. American film doesn't deviate from American core values because it is a business like any other. It cannot market products that will not sell. Thus, American films reflect rather than drive American culture, particularly in the modern context. More than ever before, films come to reflect rather than drive the sensibilities of the viewing public. However, several provisos must be added to this argument. Not everyone goes to the movies. Not all films accurately reflect the market. And a lot of filmmaking is just plain bad. I make each of those arguments in turn—but first to the political economy of American film.

Feature Film: *San Andreas*

Dwayne "The Rock" Johnson plays Chief Raymond "Ray" Gaines of the LA County Rescue Squad. He is the commander of a crew of life savers who have been together since serving in Afghanistan. Ray is a masterful helicopter pilot, but, as we find out early in the film, he is having problems at home. His wife, Emma, has left him for another man,

San Andreas, Warner Bros./Photofest, 2015

a wealthy real estate developer named Daniel Riddick (who is British). As we find out later in the backstory, Gaines's marriage broke up due to stress following a drowning accident when one of his two daughters was killed and he was uncharacteristically unable to save her.

In the meantime, we learn that Dr. Lawrence Hayes, a scientist at Caltech, has discovered a technique for predicting earthquakes, and there are all the signs that the "Big One" is coming along the San Andreas Fault.

So one bright, sunny day while Chief Raymond is out cruising in his helicopter (without his crew), the earthquake hits LA and all the special effects kick in. There is a lot going on in this sequence, so I'll cut to the chase: Gaines's wife, who is dining with her new boyfriend's bitchy sister on a rooftop restaurant in downtown LA, calls Gaines on her cellphone, and he heads off to save her.

The restaurant is in chaos; Emma tries to organize things as per Ray's instructions but nobody listens. In one of the movie's funniest sequences, Daniel's sister gets her comeuppance when she runs out of the room though a door that leads to oblivion.

Eventually Ray shows up and rescues his ex, and they head off to San Francisco to save their daughter. In the end, she is saved and the family gets back together. Daniel, as he abandons Emma's daughter, is conveniently and deservingly killed on the Golden Gate Bridge by a falling container that is being carried by a tsunami generated by the earthquake. He is smashed flat, presumably before he hears the message on the phone from Emma, who is breaking up with him. I guess the director spared him that.

I actually thought the movie was a lot of fun. I saw it in 3D and am starting to think that moviemakers are beginning to figure out how to integrate 3D into the medium. However, from the philosophical standpoint, I have some real problems with the film.

Does anybody notice that the minute disaster strikes, Chief Gaines abandons his responsibilities and heads off in a county helicopter to save his family? Inasmuch as his wife is in LA, I suppose it could be argued that Chief Gaines is not misappropriating county property by going off to save her. Of course, it's only right that she wait her turn. There are other people's ex-wives at risk as well. But when the couple heads off in the helicopter to San Francisco, they are no better than thieves. In fact, they are worse, because now LA County is down a helicopter that could be used for something else.

This is a classic example of one of the tropes of American political culture—the cult of the individual. While I root for Ray to save his family, I can't help thinking that if emergency personnel abandon their posts at the first sign of emergency, we are all in trouble. However, there is no real evidence to the effect that first responders actually act this way. That, to me, is what makes this film so unrealistic (and not the part about California falling off into the ocean).

EXERCISE

It's time to think like a cultural archeologist! Select a film that is leading in box office receipts and write a review about what that film tells us about the time in which the movie is shown.

SUGGESTED READINGS

Ball, Terence, and Richard Dagger. *Political Ideologies and the Democratic Ideal*, 9th ed. New York: Routledge, 2013.

Geertz, Clifford. *Myth, Symbol, and Culture.* New York: Norton, 1974.

Handlin, Oscar. *The Uprooted: The Epic Story of the Great Migrations That Made the American People.* Philadelphia: University of Pennsylvania Press, 2001.

Haskell, Molly. *From Reverence to Rape: The Treatment of Women in the Movies*, 2nd ed. Chicago: University of Chicago Press, 1987.

Levinson, Julie. *The American Success Myth on Film.* New York: Palgrave Macmillan, 2015.

Locke, John. *Second Treatise of Government.* Edited by C. B. Macpherson. Indianapolis, IN: Hackett, 1990.

Marubbio, M. Elise, and Eric L. Buffalohead, eds. *Native Americans on Film: Conversations, Teaching, and Theory.* Lexington: University Press of Kentucky, 2013.

NOTES

1. See David Easton, *The Political System: An Inquiry into the State of Political Science* (New York: Knopf, 1971).

2. It should be noted that President George H. W. Bush uttered these words ("read my lips") in an attempt to transmit not just an idea but also an image. President Bush labored under the general perception that he was somewhat removed on the basis of his privileged background from the problems and concerns of regular citizens. Using lines from a popular film, in this case a movie that also happened to embody a rather conservative perspective (*Dirty Harry*), Bush was trying to imply that he was a "regular guy" to a specific larger audience.

3. See Vivian C. Sobchack, "Beyond Visual Aids: American Film as American Culture," *American Quarterly* 32, no. 3 (1980): 280–300, or Todd D. Kendall, "An Empirical Analysis of Political Activity in Hollywood," *Journal of Cultural Economics* 33, no. 1 (2009): 19–47.

4. For a good discussion of the definition and nature of political discourse, see Harold Lasswell, *Politics: Who Gets What, When, How* (New York: Henry Holt, 1938).

5. Quoted From David J. Elkins and Richard E. B. Simeon, "A Cause in Search of Its Effect, or What Does Political Culture Explain?" *Comparative Politics* 11, no. 2 (January 1979): 127–45. Alexis de Tocqueville writes, "In order that society should exist and, *a fortiori*, that a society should prosper, it is necessary that the mind of all

citizens should be rallied and held together by certain predominant ideas." Tocqueville, *Democracy in America*, vol. 2 (New York: Knopf, 1945), 8, quoted in John Street, "Review Article: Political Culture–from Civic Culture to Mass Culture," *British Journal of Political Science* 24, no. 1 (January 1994): 95–113. See also Young C. Kim, "The Concept of Political Culture in Comparative Politics," *Journal of Politics* 26, no. 2 (May 1964): 313–36.

6. On this topic, see Neil Mitchell, Rhoda E. Howard, and Jack Donnelly, "Liberalism, Human Rights, and Human Dignity (in Controversies)," *American Political Science Review* 81, no. 3 (September 1987): 921–27; Robert Y. Shapiro and John T. Young, "Public Opinion and the Welfare State: The United States in Comparative Perspective," *Political Science Quarterly* 104, no. 1 (Spring 1989): 59–89; or Greg M. Shaw, "Changes in Public Opinion and the American Welfare State," *Political Science Quarterly* 124, no. 4 (2009): 627–53.

7. Andrew Sarris, *Politics and Cinema* (New York: Columbia University Press, 1978), 4–5.

8. See John A. Price, "The Stereotyping of North American Indians in Motion Pictures," *Ethnohistory* 20, no. 2 (Spring 1973): 153–71, or Ken Saldanha and Kay McGowan, "On Discussions of Westerns, Cowboys, and Indians: But Ought There to Be Included a Native American Perspective Too?" *International Review of Qualitative Research* 8, no. 3 (2015): 363–78.

9. For a discussion of the formation of political culture, see Samuel C. Patterson, "The Political Cultures of the American States," *Journal of Politics* 30, no. 1 (February 1968): 187–209; M. Margaret Conway, "The Political Context of Political Behavior," *Journal of Politics* 51, no. 1 (1989): 3–10; or Ronald P. Formisano, "The Concept of Political Culture," *Journal of Interdisciplinary History* 31, no. 3 (2001): 393–426.

10. For more on American exceptionalism, see Byron Shafer, ed., *Is America Different? A New Look at American Exceptionalism* (Oxford: Clarendon Press, 1991). See also Michael Kammen, "The Problem of American Exceptionalism: A Reconsideration," *American Quarterly* 45, no. 1 (March 1993): 1–43; Seymour Martin Lipset, *American Exceptionalism: A Double-Edged Sword* (New York: W. W. Norton, 1997); Deborah L. Madsen, *American Exceptionalism [Computer File]* (Edinburgh: Edinburgh University Press, 1998).

11. The classic text on this subject is Louis Hartz's *The Liberal Tradition in America* (New York: Harcourt Brace Jovanovich, 1955).

12. Stanley Feldman and John Zaller, "The Political Culture of Ambivalence: Ideological Responses to the Welfare State," *American Journal of Political Science* 36, no. 1 (February 1992): 268–307.

13. See John Locke, "Of Property," in *Second Treatise of Government*, ed. C. B. Macpherson (Indianapolis, IN: Hackett, 1980), chapter 5.

14. "We hold these truths to be self-evident, that all Men are created equal, that they are endowed by their Creator with certain inalienable Rights that among these are Life, Liberty, and the Pursuit of Happiness."

15. On this topic, see Michael S. Rabieh, "The Reasonableness of Locke, or the Questionableness of Christianity," *Journal of Politics* 53, no. 4 (November 1991): 933–57.

16. For a powerful rendition of the immigrant story, see Oscar Handlin, *The Uprooted: The Epic Story of the Great Migrations That Made the American People* (Philadelphia: University of Pennsylvania Press, 2001); and for a nuanced refutation, see Rogers M. Smith, "Beyond Tocqueville, Myrdal, and Hartz: The Multiple Traditions in America," *American Political Science Review* 87, no. 3 (September 1993): 549–66.

17. A solid repudiation of the notion that American liberalism is unsullied by retrograde nativism is authored by Rogers M. Smith, "The 'American Creed' and American Identity: The Limits of Liberal Citizenship in the United States," *Western Political Quarterly* 41, no. 2 (June 1988): 225–51.

18. Named in reference to the writings of Horatio Alger, a nineteenth-century novelist who supposedly extolled the virtues of and opportunities available in our capitalist economy. As it turns out, Alger's writings may have been misinterpreted, as noted in Michael Zuckerman's convincing "The Nursery Tales of Horatio Alger," *American Quarterly* 24, no. 2 (May 1972): 191–209. Nevertheless, the general perception is that Alger is the herald of justice of American capitalism, and the story is so often repeated that the perception has become reality.

19. For a classic discussion of this distinction, see Gabriel A. Almond, "Capitalism and Democracy," *PS: Political Science and Politics* 24, no. 3 (1991): 467–74, or Thomas Hill Green's "Lectures on the Principles of Political Obligation," in *T. H. Green: Lectures on the Principles of Political Obligation and Other Writings*, ed. P. Harris and J. Morrow (Cambridge: Cambridge University Press, 1986).

20. See Lisa A. Keister and Stephanie Moller, "Wealth Inequality in the United States," *Annual Review of Sociology* 26 (2000): 63–81, or Thomas Piketty and Arthur Goldhammer, *The Economics of Inequality* (Cambridge, MA: Belknap Press of Harvard University Press, 2015).

21. For example, see Clarke A. Chambers, "The Belief in Progress in Twentieth-Century America," *Journal of the History of Ideas* 19, no. 2 (April 1958): 197–224, for a disquisition on the illusory nature of American opportunism. Also see Larry J. Griffin and Arne L. Kalleberg, "Stratification and Meritocracy in the United States: Class and Occupational Recruitment Patterns," *British Journal of Sociology* 32, no. 1 (March 1981): 1–38; and Joseph P. Ferrie, "History Lessons: The End of American Exceptionalism? Mobility in the United States Since 1850," *Journal of Economic Perspectives* 19, no. 3 (2005): 199–215.

22. See Jeffrey Goldberg, "Adventures of a Republican Revolutionary," *New York Times*, November 3, 1996, section 6, 42.

2

Industry and Bias: The Political Economy of Film

In the previous chapter, I suggest that film content, indeed media content, can be influenced from both the top down and the bottom up. From the bottom up, the market influences the content of film through box office receipts. The film industry is a business, and as a business it must turn a profit. Therefore, in some sense, the market for films tells us about our interpretation of history because there are literally some stories we buy and others we don't.

From the top down, film content is shaped by regulation, available technology, and the people who make the product. As the film industry has evolved, there have been both internal and external pressures that have influenced film content. Government regulation is the most obvious case in point. Everything, from government prohibitions that can restrict certain economic activities to government subsidies that can encourage others, influences industrial products, including films. But besides the direct intervention of government, economic activities influence products as well.

The unfettered market—the free exchange of goods and services—is basically apolitical, but it can have political results. Consider the market for health care. In the free market, relatively scarce health care services will go to the highest bidder. But illness is egalitarian: it comes to us all. In a free market for health care, some people who are sick will not get treated because they don't have the money to pay. It is up to us as a society to decide whether this is a morally defensible state of affairs. If we believe, on balance, that it is more important to protect the rights of doctors, pharmaceutical companies, and the insurance industry to ply their trades without restriction than it is to guarantee health services, then some sick people will go untreated. If, however, we believe that health care is a right and not a privilege, then access to the free market by the aforementioned sectors can be restricted. This is not an either-or proposition. There are varying degrees of regulation. In the case of health care, doctors are licensed; pharmaceutical and insurance companies are regulated; and, under Obamacare, some patients are at least partially subsidized.

Superficially, it may seem that the politics of media control are not on a par with the importance of health care services. But upon further consideration, the media can have a profound influence on the way we think and behave. Advertisers certainly believe (and can prove) this to be true, as they spend billions on media to sell their products. Politicians spend billions, too, to influence how we think. So it stands to reason that the entertainment media influence how we view the world, a view that is crucial to the way that we behave and think in a democratic society.

In this chapter, I discuss the political economy of the film industry and how the economics of filmmaking produce the particular slant in the final product. The study of political economy can be defined as

> a branch of the social sciences that takes as its principal subject of study the interrelationships between political and economic institutions and processes. That is, political economists are interested in analyzing and explaining the ways in which various sorts of government affect the allocation of scarce resources in society through their laws and policies as well as the ways in which the nature of the economic system and the behavior of people acting on their economic interests affects the form of government and the kinds of laws and policies that get made.[1]

The central focus of this chapter is not only how the free market affects the content of film but also how the industry's structure, unique historical development, and interaction with government have shaped the content of films. It is fairly reasonable to assume that in an unfettered market, most films tend to appeal to the lowest common denominator. But that is clearly not the case. Many fine (and terrible) financially successful films have and are being made. This is true for three reasons. First, marketing isn't just the science of supplying consumers with what they want. Marketing is also the science of creating a demand for something consumers didn't know they needed—soft drinks, tissues, dryer sheets, Humvees, and video games come to mind. Therefore, the industry can shape the market—that is, quality films can be sold. Second, there are forces internal and external to the industry that expand the possibilities for making different types of films, regardless of the market. Furthermore, there are increasing technological opportunities (and limitations) in the making and marketing of commercial films. As we shall see, from time to time, technological limitations on the making of films, patents on technology, and availability of the raw materials for making film have all influenced the industry. Times have changed, and so has filmmaking.

THE THREE MONOPOLIES OF HOLLYWOOD FILM

Some critics argue that films are becoming ever more explicitly sexual and violent. It is hard to deny that the body count in the movies has been increasing. The question is: Why? While self-censorship has been the rule rather than the exception in the movie industry since almost the beginning, the effectiveness of that self-restraint in terms of limiting the pandering to prurient interests has been in decline since the 1960s. What changed between 1910 and 2015 is the film industry's loss of monopoly. Throughout much of its history, the film industry in the United States was structured as some form of monopoly—and the influence of monopoly on movie content was profound.[2]

Economists tell us that monopolies create distortions in the market in a couple of ways. First, monopolies create distorted pricing. Consumers pay more than the market-clearing price for monopoly goods. Second, in a related sense, monopoly industries are less sensitive to consumer demand. By definition, a monopoly for a product excludes alternatives. Because the movie industry was in one way or another a monopoly from the time it was created until about 1960, I argue that the movie industry was capable of controlling the content of its films, including the message of their films, up to that time. However, when the movie monopoly was challenged and more or less collapsed, the industry was forced to be more competitive. In this case, being more competitive meant more likely to appeal to the lowest common denominator. Thus, the movie industry changed its product not because the culture of Hollywood changed but because the economy of the entertainment market changed.

The First Monopoly: The Edison Trust

Still photography has been in general use since before the American Civil War. By the late nineteenth century, there were already some forward thinkers who had envisioned photographic moving pictures. In fact, the novelty use of drawings flipped past the eye in the pages of a book or on some kind of roller had been in use for quite some time. The problem for making moving pictures from photography, however, was that photographs were shot on individual plates with very slow exposure times. In order for action to appear seamless to the human eye, frames must be "flipped" at a minimum of about fifteen frames a second. As a practical matter, until the late nineteenth century, it was impossible to shoot action fast enough with the still photography of the day to capture actual events in motion.[3]

But then the technology changed. A much faster chemical-exposure process was introduced for film, and exposure plates were placed on continuous, flexible ribbons. Photographs could be shot on film. But there remained one major technological hurdle. Just because exposure times for film were faster—fast enough to shoot film at the minimum speed for the motion picture requirement of fifteen. frames a second—the camera to shoot the film had yet to be invented. The problem was that in photography, even shot at fifteen or the now standard twenty-four frames a second, photographs have to be shot as stills. In other words, a camera mechanism had to be invented that advanced the film, stopped the film, shot a picture, and advanced the film at a smooth, continuous rate, and it had to perform this process quickly. Such a "pull-down" device (now known as a rotary shutter) was invented in Europe and the United States in about 1895. The motion picture was then technologically possible.[4]

The final stage in the technological process was to devise a means for displaying this film. One of the earliest inventors of the film-display process was Thomas Edison. Edison envisioned motion picture display to be a logical extension of his phonograph technology. Therefore, when he designed a device for showing films, known as a kinetoscope, it was in some ways similar to the phonograph. The picture on a kinetoscope was meant to be seen by no more than a few persons, and it was designed as that for private viewing. Indeed, the kinetoscope had a successful introduction as a novelty in carnivals, sideshows, and pinball parlors. The films shown by kinetoscope lasted for only a couple of minutes, and the subjects were often what was considered in those days to be of a prurient nature. Thus, because of their subject matter and because of their marketing to some of the seamier segments of society, the film industry almost immediately garnered a reputation for being generally lowbrow and immoral.

On the other side of the Atlantic, however, the development of film projection went in a different direction. Projectors were designed using technology similar to the camera to project films on to a screen to a mass audience. Projection technology moved quickly back across the Atlantic, where the first film was shown in a theater in New York City in 1896.

After a series of patent disputes, Edison managed to make peace with his competitors by forming an alliance, a trust (monopoly) based on control of motion picture technology. The Motion Picture Patents Company that formed in 1908 was Edison's attempt to monopolize motion picture production and distribution. Since the Edison trust held the patents to most forms of motion picture technology of the day—and in agreement with the Kodak Corporation, the only supplier of film stock—the trust also held the key to film style and content. This technology cartel was doomed from the beginning and lasted only a few years. However, the creation of the Edison trust had the ironic effect of bringing outsiders, many of whom were immigrants, into the movie production business and, at the same time, encouraging technological development beyond the rather crude capabilities available at the time. Despite the fact that Edison and his cohort fought a vigorous rearguard action in the courts to protect their monopoly against patent infringements, a new, competitive movie industry was born.[5]

The strongest challenge to the Edison trust came from film exhibitors. Most of the films that were made by the cartel were short "one reelers," each with a running time of no more than a few minutes. In order to put together a half-hour screening, exhibitors were forced to prepare a program of as many as three one-reel films. That fact alone created a tremendous demand for the cartel's products. However, at the same time, the market for these films was limited. With a running time of only a few minutes, one-reel films had no capacity for the type of story line development that would attract a clientele better educated and classier (as well as better connected). On the midway of a carnival or in the amusement parlor, one-reel films were intended to pique the interest of the viewer in a few moments. Thus, films of this era tended to feature violence, chases, and/or nudity with little or no plotline. The unsavory content of early sideshow films attracted the attention of religious groups and thus local governments. Censorship boards were set up in a number of cities to screen and edit the content of films shown to the public.

At least one major exhibitor—Carl Laemmle, who owned a chain of nickelodeons and theaters in the Midwest—began to chafe at the supply-and-content restrictions imposed by the cartel. Furthermore, he feared the consequences of attempts by some communities to censor films and close down theaters. He began to explore other sources of films by dealing with independent film producers, who were not controlled by the cartel. At first, independent filmmakers were at a technological disadvantage. Film stock was generally unavailable, and to avoid discovery by the cartel and its lawyers (as well as its goons), independent films were shot covertly in what was then the film capital of the world, New Jersey. But with the introduction of new equipment, a new kind of filmmaking, and government antitrust prosecutions, the Edison trust began to crumble. In turn, this escape from monopoly led to a number of innovations in the film industry, not the least of which was the production of feature-length motion pictures.

Feature-length motion pictures had the effect of attracting a different and wider audience to the movie theater. Heretofore, in the United States motion pictures had been more or less a carnival sideshow. Because the decision makers in the Edison trust still had a limited vision of the future of motion pictures, the cartel refused to produce a more substantial product. But in Europe, filmmakers had already produced several feature-length films. The advantage was that the market for these films was much broader and much more respectable. After all, feature-length films didn't necessarily have to rely on titillation to attract an audience. Stories could be developed that would be compelling enough in their own right. Furthermore, feature-length films could be produced for a profit, a huge profit. When *The Birth of a Nation* (1915) was made for what was then the outlandish sum of $110,000 and returned by some estimates $100 million, the independents knew they had a business. The exhibition of feature-length films expanded the audience for movies to virtually the entire population. Movies became a mass medium and entertainment for the masses.

Thus, the movie industry was built from the bottom up. Exhibitors began to form their own production companies. Carl Laemmle founded Universal Studios; William Fox founded Fox Film, which was later purchased in a bankruptcy sale by Twentieth Century Pictures; Louis B. Mayer founded Metro Pictures, which later became Metro-Goldwyn-Mayer (MGM); the Warner brothers (Albert, Sam, Jack, and Harry) founded Warner Brothers Pictures; and Adolph Zukor founded Paramount Pictures. The retailers took over production, and they were not just any retailers. It just so happened that many of the movie moguls who built Hollywood were Eastern European Jews. In founding a new, completely unique business, they were able to make a fortune for themselves and their families, unhindered by the Protestant political and social establishment that dominated almost every other sector of the economy.

This pattern has been repeated constantly over the course of American history, as each new wave of immigrants becomes ensconced in some tiny corner of American business, the key being the ease of access. In many cities, even today, parking businesses, motels, nail salons, taxicabs, laundries, and corner grocery stores come to be associated with one ethnic group or another. In Los Angeles, Jews were associated with the nascent movie industry. That fact alone, as we shall see, has conditioned the content and public perception of the film industry even to this day.

The Second Monopoly: The Golden Age
of Hollywood Cinema

As exhibitors began to get into the filmmaking business, the monopoly character of the film industry began to change. From a film monopoly based on technology, the film industry moved to a monopoly based on distribution. Unlike the technology trust that was fragile from the beginning (because there is no way to restrain innovation in technology), the distribution monopoly was extremely resilient and was helped along by some lucky historical accidents.[6] The vertical integration of the film industry, control over production as well as distribution, almost guaranteed that small, independent film producers would have trouble screening their products without the support of the major studios. While this is even some-what the case today, it was even more so in the past.

During the so-called golden age of American cinema, in the 1930s and early 1940s, eight major studios had a virtual lock on the moviemaking industry. The majors owned or controlled not just the production of film but also practically every movie theater in the United States. Theaters owned or controlled by the big eight were permitted to screen only their own products. Beyond that, even theaters that were not owned by the majors were forced to display the works of the majors and the majors only. If they attempted to screen an independently produced film or balked at purchasing a package of films, a practice known as "block booking," they would simply be cut off from the source. And with no alternative, the majors (and a couple of secondary studios) were the only game in town.[7]

This worked to restrict the options of all who worked in the industry, as long as the studios agreed to collude and as long as there was no foreign competition. Furthermore, the Hollywood moguls caught a break when the film industry that had been thriving in Europe was halted by World War I and then, after a brief respite, by the rise of fascism, World War II, and the reconstruction of Europe. But the fact is that European filmmakers would have had trouble selling their wares in the United States in any event because of the distribution cartel.

The entire industry was therefore controlled from the top down by a few studio moguls—from the star system in Hollywood (in which stars were in essence "owned" by the studio to which they signed) to the collusive relationship between the studios and the film production labor unions to the distribution and screening of the final product. While this monopoly was stronger than the Edison technology trust, it too came under pressure as the industry was challenged under the antitrust laws by the Roosevelt administration.

In May 1948, the Supreme Court decided in *United States v. Paramount Pictures, Inc.* that the big eight studios were in violation of the Sherman Antitrust Act. The specific issue in the case was the practice of block book-ing. The big eight had virtually guaranteed a market for their products, no matter what the quality, by requiring theater owners to buy the good films with the bad by threatening to withhold blockbuster hits from operators who failed to cooperate. As a result of the court ruling, the Court ordered the studios to divest themselves of theater ownership. This remedy, how-ever, never really worked. The studios found ways to operate in the distribu-tion of film such that collusion still exists to this day, as the top studios still control the lion's share of the distribution market.[8]

During these halcyon years of the Golden Age, studios cranked out thou-sands of quality films, and many films that were not so good but nevertheless could be sold anyway through block booking. Because these films were produced in a truncated market, they tended to have a kind of industrial feel. The lack of competition that results from any monopoly generally stifles creativity. While the films of the golden era tended to be bright and sunny in outlook, they were also noncontroversial and bland. In the golden era, movies were produced as if they were any other industrial good. While there were subtle differences between the films produced by different studios—MGM was the class of the industry, Universal specialized in westerns and horror films, Paramount was known for its sophisticated comedies, and so on—there was a distinct (often quite fine) uniformity to their output.

Another influence on the industry in the golden era was the fact that the major studios (with the exception of Walt Disney Productions and Twentieth Century Fox) were mostly run by a group of first-generation immigrant Jews.[9] To understand why that is important is to understand what it was like for Jews in Europe during the late nineteenth and early twentieth centuries. Anti-Semitism was open and rampant. Jews were treated as the outsiders, even to a large extent in their adoptive United States. Therefore, the films of the moguls reflected not only their ethnic sensitivities but also their ethnic insecurities. Just as many immigrants had rejected the Old World to become almost caricatures of the new, most of the moguls tried hard to assimilate, and their effort was reflected in the conventions of their films. Add to that the US immigrants' natural affinity to the ideology of classical liberalism, and the films of the golden era became as American as apple pie, even if at the same time their producers were as native as a potato knish.

Thus, when the movie business was mainly a sideshow attraction at a carnival or in a storefront and literally a nickel-and-dime business (hence the term *nickelodeon*), the ownership of the business was really irrelevant to the rest of society. However, by luck, accident, and hard work, the movie business became a major industry, almost overnight. At that point, the ownership of the business became an issue. Unlike other major industries, the moviemaking industry was clearly dominated by a population of ethnically uniform and religiously unrepresentative "new money"—that is, from predominantly non-Protestant backgrounds. Besides the Jews, the industry was well populated with Italian immigrant Catholics and followers of the Greek Orthodox Church.

American culture has always harbored an unattractive distrust of immigrants, especially immigrants from non-Protestant religious backgrounds. Thus, it was natural that the American political establishment came to have, and continues to have, a love-hate relationship with the film industry. The public loves the product, but they are vaguely distrustful of the crowd that produces it.

The film industry has certainly contributed to this love-hate relationship.

The purpose of the film business is entertainment. One way to entertain is to titillate. It was sometimes the case that filmmakers in the early years of the second monopoly violated the sensibilities of the general public—gangster films in the 1920s were particularly alarming. Furthermore, the film industry has a way of creating instant millionaires who just happen to be very much in the public eye. The lives of Hollywood actors, producers, and directors, many of whom were accumulating money for the first time in their lives, were glaringly exposed. The perception was that Hollywood was an isolated bohemian enclave outside of the American mainstream. Certainly to the extent that its community was wealthy, living on the West Coast, and ethnically diverse, Hollywood *was* different. But were its members less moral than, say, the average real estate, railroad, steel, or oil tycoon of the time? It is difficult to say. They were certainly more exposed.

The Hollywood community was definitely sensitive to these criticisms. Jews in particular have been constantly conscious of being a minority in an environment that can turn hostile at a moment's notice.[10] Thus, the movie moguls of the golden era of Hollywood film were more than willing to accede to the demands of those who would censor film content. The production code, as it came to be known, was written in 1930 and later was strictly enforced by an organization called the Catholic Legion of Decency (under the threat of a boycott), implemented by the Production Code Administration (PCA), and willingly adhered to by the film moguls of the second monopoly, who saw the code as providing a veneer of respectability for their products.

The code required that the PCA approve every new script and changes to scripts in production. Even today, at the beginning of most American films produced before about 1960, one can still see the production code "bug" (the cursive letter *a*) signifying approval by the PCA. The production code was quite intrusive. It regulated not just nudity and violence but also plotlines. While the censorship board was often arbitrary, movie plots were forbidden if they allowed criminals to get away with their crimes or couples to engage in romance without getting married. Note, for example, that during most of the years governed by the code, couples would never be shown in bed together without at least one foot on the floor.[11]

Films that did not conform to the code were simply not exhibited; they were subject to a boycott by the Legion of Decency and thus never made. This applied not just to films with prurient content but also to films that might be considered subversive—critiques of capitalism, the church, and traditional values. The studio executives willingly practiced this form of self-censorship not just because they were intimidated but also because they were indeed capitalists themselves who had been richly rewarded by the American system. Their view of America was honestly that of Horatio

Alger. The films of the golden era of Hollywood cinema overwhelmingly conformed to the code that reflected such a perspective.[12]

This was truly a halcyon era of film when content and message of the movies was mainly about all that is good and right about American society. What eventually eroded this foundation of the production code was the bust of the movie distribution trust and the entry into the entertainment market of new competitors for the audience's attention. Starting with the government's efforts to force the big eight to divest themselves of their distribution monopoly, and ending with the advent and general popularization of television, the film industry began to change—and so did the content of film. As television began to siphon away the movie audiences and as foreign filmmakers emerged from the recovering economies of Europe and Japan, foreigners began to export a new and more adventurous class of films. Hollywood had no choice but to respond in kind. Picking up on a trend begun in the late 1930s, Hollywood produced in the 1950s a whole new genre of films that skirted the edge of the written and unwritten production code.

This second monopoly, commonly referred to as the golden era of Hollywood film, was relatively short-lived, and its fall—albeit briefly delayed by World War II—was facilitated by the forced divestiture of theater chains controlled by the studios, the advent of television, and competition from outside and inside the industry. Thus, modern-day calls for a return to the golden age of Hollywood cinema really are calls for the return to ownership of the studios by executives long since dead and a return to an economic monopoly that could only be reproduced by more or less getting rid of television and foreign films. It is remarkable that many of the current attacks on the politics and profile of the film industry are so out of date. The problem of subversive film content to the extent that it now exists is a function of the third monopoly of Hollywood film—the monopoly of money.

The Third "Monopoly": The Marketization of Hollywood

Even before the end of World War II, producers and directors began to skirt the edge of the production code. Film classics such as *Citizen Kane* (1941), *Double Indemnity* (1944), and *The Big Sleep* (1946) spawned a whole genre of film that explored a darker aspect of American society. This film genre came to be known as film noir. As one author describes it, "What film noir was, what was so revolutionary about it, was its inherent reaction to decades of forced optimism."[13] The themes and indeed the techniques explored in these films were edgy and innovative and viewed by some as more than a little subversive. It is not surprising then that in combination with the latent aversion toward the otherness of the Hollywood moguls at the end of World War II, when the Soviet Union and world communism came to be viewed as America's primary threats, Hollywood was ripe for attack. The McCarthy-era blacklist attacked not so much the communist threat in the industry—it is now fairly clear that most of those who were blacklisted were not communists or even particularly political—as it did the departure from the mainstream of American political culture.[14] In that sense, the McCarthy-era blacklist reflected and carried on in practice a general, historical distrust of the entertainment industry.

Thus began, in at least the economic sense, the darkest days of Hollywood cinema. Despite the fact that in the 1950s some fine feature films were made, the studios were reluctant to air what could be construed to be subversive themes, even as they were slowly losing market share to television. The studios tried to compensate by offering technological innovations such as widescreen cinemascope and 3D special effects, by filming elaborate musicals borrowed from Broadway, and by exploring more mainstream and upbeat themes. But despite a steady stream of biblical epics, Broadway musicals, mainstream westerns, war movies, and frothy bedroom farces, the audience hemorrhage continued. Given their limitations on content, censored by the code, and intimidated by the blacklist, what could the studios offer that the viewer couldn't get with less bother and expense on television at home?

In some ways, this was a repeat of the pattern that brought to an end the first monopoly, except now for their intransigence it was the moguls' turn to be outsmarted. Because movie executives refused to embrace the possibilities of television or were prevented from moving into television production by the federal government because of antitrust concerns, they were overtaken by the new technology and its new potential for profit.[15] For example, not recognizing the value of their extensive film libraries, the studios sold the rights to movies for much less than their market value. After all, who would want to watch a rerun of a film such as *Casablanca* on television? Who indeed? Many people did, and the individuals who bought these film libraries made a fortune. What emerged from this second monopoly was a third monopoly of corporate ownership and independent production.

By the late 1960s, all the major studios began to fail and were forced to sell out, most often to large corporate conglomerates. Gulf and Western (commodities) bought Paramount, which was in turn briefly owned by Coca-Cola; Transamerica (insurance and Budget Rent a Car among others) bought United Artists; Kinney National Services (funeral homes and parking lots) bought Warner Brothers; and so on. To the corporations who bought them, the studios were little more than the sum of their component parts. This is generally the case in corporate fire sales. The acquiring companies see value in the bankrupt company's component parts. Kirk Kerkorian bought MGM for its film library and apparently for its brand (Kerkorian built the MGM Grand Hotel in Las Vegas). The former production backlot of Twentieth Century Fox was bought for its real estate value and converted into a glittering office, hotel, and retail complex now called Century City. Only the shells of the studios survived. The actual production of films was passed on to independent production companies such as Orion, the Ladd Company, Tri-Star Pictures, and New Line Cinema.

The advent of television was a devastating blow to the movie industry. To compete, the film industry had to change. What could the film movies offer that was not available on the television screen, and what new audiences could be tapped to make up for the loss of audiences who stayed home?

The answers to these questions tell us a lot about why film content is what it is today. First, to make up for a loss in domestic viewership, the film industry began a much more aggressive pursuit of foreign audiences. Depending on the exchange rate for the dollar and the release of blockbuster films, such as *Titanic* (1997), foreign sales of American films can constitute up to 70 percent of the American film industry's annual revenues. As a percentage of sales abroad, American films are crowding out foreign domestic producers. Fully 70 percent of all admissions to theaters in the European Union market are to American films. In 2000, Hollywood's share of the world market was twice what it had been in 1990.[16]

Second, the film industry began to look for new ways to distribute its product. Instead of trying to beat television, the film industry decided to join it. By the end of the 1950s, most of the major studios began to get into the television production business. Ultimately, the spread of cable television allowed film producers to market their products on television cable outlets, such as on the so-called superstations, on movie channels, and on pay-per-view television. Finally, the development of home videocassette and then DVD playback allowed filmmakers to directly market their product for viewing at home. In the United States in 2014, some $7.5 billion in consumer spending was generated from home video sales and rentals (including streaming video) while movie ticket sales amounted to slightly more than that amount ($10.4 billion). Many films have no theatrical release at all and go straight to pay per view. Indeed, the functional distinction between television and motion picture production has begun to disappear, as television networks and cable outlets produce original films and miniseries that can be rented in video stores and purchased online or through services such as Netflix or Amazon Prime and are on a par in quality with any feature film. By the same token, film franchises such as the *Fast and Furious* series are prepared for theatrical release on a more or less regular schedule.

Third in the evolution of the film industry is the creation of a new star system. In the days of the golden era, studios owned stars the way that sports teams owned athletes (although that system has gone away as well), the one difference being that they could "loan" their contract players out to other studios. With the collapse of the studio cartel, movie stars became free agents. That is both good news and bad news for the film-acting profession. On the one hand, actors and actresses in demand can command enormous salaries. Dwayne "The Rock" Johnson received $15 million for *San Andreas*, and Jennifer Lawrence got $10 million for the first *Hunger Games* movie. But depending on the fee structure, actors can earn a lot more. Robert Downey Jr. earned about $70 million for *Iron Man* (2008), mainly because he had a 7 percent stake in the gross.

The bad news is that with so much of the fate of a film dependent on bankable stars, the work and salaries available for other fine actors is limited. For example, in *The Wolf of Wall Street* (2013), Leonardo DiCaprio made about $25 million, while Jonah Hill, the second lead, made $60,000 (but he did win an Oscar for his role).

In the studio system, careers were nurtured, and there was plenty of work available for actors to hone their craft; for example, Ward Bond, regular sidekick to John Wayne, has 273 acting credits on the Internet Movie Database (IMDB).[17] In the modern market, promising careers are often stillborn. Thus, actors who succeed have control over their own careers in a way that would have been inconceivable in the studio era. For example, Mel Gibson had the money and clout to play *Hamlet* (1990) and to produce his own interpretation of *The Passion of the Christ* (2004). Other actors, such as Tom Hanks, Clint Eastwood, and George Clooney, have been able to produce and direct and star in movies of their choice because they, themselves, are franchises.

Fourth, as the Hollywood film industry passed on from privately held to publicly held, corporate management (ownership by diversified publicly owned corporations), the film business took on attributes more or less common to any industry. The first thing that the corporate managers of the new Hollywood did was cut costs by divesting themselves of many of the ancillary activities of the studios under the second monopoly that had the movie executives involved in everything from contracting and developing talent to providing schooling for child stars. It should come as no surprise to anyone who works in, say, the automobile industry that outsourcing, one of the quickest ways for a business to cut costs, was instituted in the film industry starting in the late 1960s. In that way, manufacturers pay piecework wages for labor. And while hiring Spielberg to direct or Brad Pitt to act may be expensive, it is nothing compared to having Spielberg and a lot of less successful directors (and actors, writers, editors, and other technicians) on the payroll while paying for their development.

To further cut costs, studios have moved a large portion of film production overseas. According to the US Department of Commerce, in 1990, 29 percent of all US-developed film projects were shot overseas; by 1999, 37 percent were. Again, according to the Department of Commerce, the main reason that these productions were moved overseas was not for creative purposes (to shoot on location) but to cut costs.[18] Just like many other American manufacturers, the film business is taking its production overseas. But lately this trend has stabilized and sometimes been reversed as American state governments have begun to allow for generous tax breaks to attract movie production companies. Besides, there are costly inconveniences in shooting abroad as well.

Finally, the nature of corporate ownership of the film industry has changed. There was never a lot of natural synergy linking sales of Coke, insurance, parking lots, funeral homes, or rental cars and the movie business. In the latest transformation of the movie industry, giant media conglomerates have been formed to take advantage of the synergies between film and related technologies and entertainment outlets. For example, *Time* magazine bought out Warner Brothers Pictures. Later, CNN was added to the mix. This means that films produced and distributed by Warner Brothers can be promoted "in house" both in print and on television without going into the commercial market for advertising. The same can be said for Twenty-First Century Fox, which is owned by News Corporation, with its enormous holdings in newspapers and television. In the future, should the Justice Department allow it, media conglomerates will acquire streaming services to allow the screening of their vast film and video libraries that are now being marketed on pay-per-view outlets such as Netflix and Amazon Prime.

There may be problems, however, with this sort of media ownership. The entertainment divisions of these corporations may come to be indistinguishable from their journalistic outlets. Consider this one small problem. While the news divisions of these corporate giants are supposed to be hermetically sealed from their entertainment divisions, it is hard to imagine that film reviewers working for newspapers, magazines, or media outlets can be totally objective in reviewing films produced by their own corporations or those of others. It is already the case that sporting events such as the NBA Finals and the World Series when purchased by the sports division of, say, NBC become promo platforms for NBC television series as the stars of those series often turn up at these events.

At the same time, the film production business has become more segmented and specialized. The studios are more a financier, coordinator, and distributor of production than a genuine factory for the production of films. The actual creative process is contracted out to powerful talent agencies and independent production companies (that themselves have become specialized). This is not to say that the creative process is completely out of the control of the studios. Rather, creative control has passed from the studio executive to the market.

And the market is an ever-changing place. With the advent of streaming video and pay per view, the market itself is also highly segmented. Films that once would have never been made because they would never turn a profit can now be made and marketed to discrete segments of the viewing audience such as gays, Latinos, and senior citizens. The shelf life of a film can be extended as well. In foreign markets or on pay per view, a film can get a second life after its theatrical release.

What this last transformation of the movie industry has meant is simply that the film industry must now appeal to either a new lowest common denominator or a very specialized segment of the viewing public. To justify the costs of big-budget blockbusters, film producers must aim to attract the largest possible domestic and now international audience with films of a lowest common denominator that avoid complex dialogue, plot development, and ethnocentric themes. Complex and ethnocentric themes simply do not translate well in foreign markets.[19] On the other hand, to make a film for a specialized audience, filmmakers must keep their production costs low enough to recoup their expenses on a limited number of screens and through nontheatrical release outlets.

The film industry is no longer even a shadow of the monopoly it once was. Independent film producers have a multitude of outlets for their product. And while it is difficult for independent film producers to get the financing and distribution of their films without the support of the major studios, it is not impossible. In fact, the market for independent filmmakers seems to be expanding for the last decade or so as more theaters exhibit such work.[20] Thus, because of the new outlets for independent films, independent producers are more likely to be able to produce modestly profitable films for niche audiences.

Consequently, the balance of power has changed in the film industry—from the executives in Hollywood to the market. Any recent changes in the content of films, therefore, are more a product of market demands than of a "degenerate" culture of Hollywood. In fact, with the corporatization and the internationalization of Hollywood, there really isn't still a Hollywood at all. Hollywood exists as only shorthand for an increasingly national and international film industry as a whole.

So what has changed in the content of film? The product has changed because the industry has changed. Clearly, a massive increase in foreign viewership has influenced motion pictures in several ways. One is the general subject matter of film. Complex plots, what may be viewed as subversive abroad or ethnocentric themes that may lose something in the translation, are much riskier enterprises for Hollywood producers. For example, black actors, writers, and directors have leveled charges of racism against the entertainment industry.[21] However, big-budget films that are meant to appeal to an Afrocentric audience are less likely to do well in the foreign market and are thus not as willingly financed by the major studios. This may say something about the racial intolerance of film consumers, but it doesn't necessarily reflect the proclivities of the producers themselves.[22]

On American television or as part of a segmented domestic audience, African American viewers are such a large share of the audience that networks can devote entire prime-time programming slots to black-oriented television shows (and even advertisements). By the same token, while the international markets may demand the lowest common denominator for blockbusters, lower-budget films appealing primarily to black audiences can turn a profit.

This homogenization of the blockbuster movie market and this heterogeneity of the domestic entertainment market have led to a two-track film-production environment. Big-budget Hollywood spectaculars must appeal to an international audience in order to attract the attention and financing of the Hollywood majors. At the same time, there exist in the domestic market quite a few niche audiences who will support the small-scale, relatively low-budget production of independent producers. In addition, there are many more outlets besides the mall multiplex cinema for independent productions, including art house screenings, DVD, and streaming video. In addition to a substantial market for African-American-oriented cinema, there are viable markets for family-oriented films, religious films, gay-themed films, and so on.

It would be easy for one to draw the conclusion from watching blockbuster releases of the major studios that film content is becoming more un-American, more violent, less complex in terms of plot development, and more graphically sexual. And this conclusion is probably true. The question is: Why the change, and what, if anything, to do about it?

The answer to the first question (why the change in movie content?) requires a two-part response. First, the audience for American films has changed. In the twenty-first century, with 70 percent of revenues coming from foreign markets (the percentage for blockbuster films is higher), producers must pay attention to the bottom line. The safest and most easily financed projects are those that take the fewest risks in terms of content. In other words, filmmakers must respond to a new lowest common denominator. If kung fu action films sell well in Asia, then including at least one martial arts sequence in our version of the kung fu action film—for example, the *Fast and Furious* series—is the safest bet for American producers. In addition, there are certain themes that are almost certain to create trouble abroad. Besides specialized topics that have little relevance for foreigners, such as the plight of the African American in the United States, there are also plotlines that are downright subversive in a foreign context. How would the Chinese, Saudi Arabian, or Zairian governments react to *Mr. Smith Goes to Washington*? The case of *The Interview* at the beginning of this book is instructive. This film and others like it would almost certainly be banned in authoritarian countries. This is a sad comment on the state of the world, but it is hardly a condemnation of Hollywood.

Has this multifaceted market improved the quality of American films? The answer is yes and no. Many more films and many different types of films can be made and expected to turn a profit. In that sense, there is a lot more variety, and there is the actuality and potential for some terrific films. Terrific films, however, may be hard to find. Even though there is so much product, theater owners will still be reluctant to take a chance on films without brand-name directors and actors and cookie-cutter plots. Cineplex theaters still tend to enforce a de facto monopoly. From their perspective, theater owners will want to book the film with the highest sales. Even excellent films with a little-known cast and director may not make money. Without a large advertising budget, word-of-mouth films may take a long time to catch on, well beyond the carrying capacity of an average multiplex theater. Thus, independent films produced by unknown directors with unknown actors may only receive theatrical release in the largest cities. With luck, those films will receive good reviews and attendance. Eventually, such films will percolate down through the distribution system to smaller and smaller markets. *Sling Blade* (1996) was such a film. Even so, despite its acclaim, the film was hard to find in the suburban multiplexes of my hometown, Atlanta.

Furthermore, because the market is so segmented, the studios are much more reluctant to invest in blockbuster, expensive productions without the participation of high-profile, well-established writers, actors, and directors. This is a good news–bad news story. Worthy projects proposed by relative unknowns will not receive blockbuster funding. Nevertheless, there is a way that low-budget films can be produced and turn a profit.

Thus, the marketization of Hollywood cinema has been mostly for the good. While it may be difficult to find a particular movie or get to the theater before the film closes, there are a variety of interesting films for a variety of tastes available on the market. And most of those films, if not booked in the local theater, can now be viewed at home on streaming video television.

Of course, blockbuster, high-profile films with large advertising budgets and wide releases may tend to be formulaic and brain-dead, more dependent on technology and the reputations of the producer, director, and cast than on the quality of the product. But it is just as likely that they will be exceptionally well crafted and entertaining for the largest possible audience. *Titanic* was such a film. This production behemoth, which is really a pretty good film, was the seventh-highest grossing film of 1997 in less than two weeks of theatrical release and has to date grossed $2.1 billion worldwide, more than ten times its production costs of about $200 million.[23]

One also has the possibility of walking into the wrong film. Michael Medved, a conservative film critic, panned the film *Snowpiercer* (2014) (zero stars out of four) for its "Marxist" allegory and gory content.[24] I think it is fair to say that the audience for Medved's reviews is not the audience for this film. And I think Medved plays an important role in warning his audience off going to see the film. However, the film is generally regarded as a stylish piece of science fiction, with a 95 out of 100 rating on Rotten Tomatoes, with the gory parts being no worse than other films that have an R rating. The fact is that this is not a bad film. But with its Marxist subtext it would be the last film that a conservative would want to see.

The third monopoly of American film is therefore not so much a monopoly as it is the final marketization of American cinema. Now that the film industry has begun to outsource and export, compete with foreigners, and justify its operations to millions of stockholders, it is more or less just another industry. More to the point, the audience now for Hollywood films is not just the one sitting in theaters but also the one sitting in boardrooms and the stock market. This is where conservative (and some liberal) critics of Hollywood tend to miss their mark. The problem with the film industry today is not that it is immoral but that it is *amoral*. But that is a problem of business in a free market in general. The violence, the nudity, and the muddled messages of many of today's films are produced not as much as a reflection of the subversive visions of a film industry elite out of touch but as a marketing strategy for filmmakers in a market increasingly competitive for entertainment dollars. To the extent that the film industry is a monopoly at all, it is not the artistic talent that is in control but the financiers, distributors, and exhibitors.

Feature Film: *Furious 7*

As discussed in an earlier review of a feature film, movies are a flexible medium for the discussion in metaphor of matters of contemporary concern. Without making reference to actual problems that exist in our society, this film highlights several current political debates that have received attention in the headlines. For one thing, this film is about cyberterrorism. The defection of computer programmer Edward Snowden to the Russians and his pirating and release of classified information has highlighted two related and contradictory problems associated with national security. On the one hand, terrorism of the traditional and cyberterrorism kind has to be defended, but at what cost? Do we have to sacrifice our personal privacy to fight terrorists, and is government monitoring of our phone calls and the Internet one step toward an authoritarian regime?

Furious 7, Universal Pictures/Photofest, 2015

Furious 7 is the seventh installment in the *Fast and Furious* series and, by far, the most successful. As of its tenth week of release, *Furious 7* has made $1.5 billion on a $190 million budget. Some 76 percent of its revenues have come from abroad. This is truly an international phenomenon.

The *Furious* formula is as old as the automobile. Car chases have been the staple of the movies since the gangster movies of the 1920s and have a long history of success in American film from *Bullitt* to *The French Connection* to the *Smokey and the Bandit* series. And just when you thought the car chase genre had been done to death, *Furious 7*, so to speak, reinvents the wheel.

For me, a car is what I use to get to work. My idea of driving excitement is to not be in traffic. But even I enjoyed most of the car chases in this movie. Who can't be impressed by cars dropped from planes, cars flying between skyscrapers, and cars shooting down helicopters? That's Hollywood!!!

Oh, and then there's the plot. I confess I haven't seen the other *Furious* films, but it didn't take me long to figure out that this is an ensemble film. However, unlike the *Avenger* series, none of the group seems to have a distinct "superpower." Interestingly, comic relief is provided by Tyrese Gibson. This seems to me to be a dangerous choice, as black actors often played the role of the stereotyped clown in movies of the golden era. However, Gibson's role is balanced by the more serious Ludacris—go figure. Otherwise, the *Furious* crew led by Vin Diesel is very diverse but down one Asian, which no amount of kung fu fighting can replace. I wouldn't be surprised if a young Jackie Chan (or the same) shows up for the next installment.

Anyway, the plot has something to do with a terrorist threat that comes from two quarters. Jason Statham, a rouge black ops agent, is seeking revenge against, I guess, everyone for the maiming of his brother by the police. He creates a lot of mayhem and hurts a lot of innocent people for no good reason. If I were him, and had the ability to disappear, I would disappear and leave it at that. But that wouldn't make it a good movie.

In the meantime, the US government is fighting a terrorist organization that has developed some really powerful software that can trace anyone, anywhere on the planet. For some reason they can't go get it themselves, so they (in the person of the venerable Kurt Russell) recruit Vin Diesel and his crew to kidnap the programmer Ramsey, who turns out to be a really good-looking girl.

Several car chases later, they get the program (and the programmer) and capture the bad guy, who, I am sure, will be back. Now the US government has the "God's Eye" program. Heaven help us!!!

In what is a twist, the end of the film is obviously altered to pay homage to Paul Walker, who died in an automobile accident during the filming of the movie. Walker was the passenger in a car traveling at speeds in excess of 80 miles an hour on a residential street in LA. The publicity surrounding his death certainly provided unintended publicity for the film, and the tribute in the film is very tastefully handled. However, one has to wonder whether the kind of driving that got him killed, even as a passenger, makes Walker a hero.

EXERCISE

Trace the history of race relations in the United States as depicted in film. Start with the film *The Birth of a Nation* (1915) and contrast that to the film that is currently leading in annual box office receipts.

SUGGESTED READINGS

Black, Gregory D. *Hollywood Censored: Morality Codes, Catholics, and the Movies.* New York: Cambridge University Press, 1994.

Cousins, Mark. *The Story of Film*, 2nd ed. New York: Pavilion Press, 2013.

Gabler, Neal. *An Empire of Their Own: How the Jews Invented Hollywood.* New York: Anchor, 1988.

Goldman, William. *The Big Picture.* New York: Applause, 2000.

McDonald, Paul. *The Star System: Hollywood's Production of Popular Identities.* London: Wallflower, 2000.

Medved, Michael. *Hollywood vs. America.* New York: Harper Collins, 1993.

Miller, Toby, Nitin Govil, John McMurria, and Richard Maxwell. *Global Hollywood.* London: British Film Institute, 2001.

Rosenbaum, Jonathan. *Movie Wars: How Hollywood and the Media Conspire to Limit What Films We Can See.* Chicago: Cappella, 2000.

Sikov, Ed. *Film Studies: An Introduction.* New York: Columbia University Press, 2010.

Thomson, David. *The Big Screen: The Story of the Movies.* New York: Farrar, Straus and Giroux, 2012.

NOTES

1. From the online edition of "A Glossary of Political Economy Terms," by Paul M. Johnson, Auburn University, http://www.auburn.edu/~johnspm/gloss/political_economy (accessed December 29, 2015).

2. Literally, a "single seller"—a situation in which a single firm or individual produces and sells the entire output of some good or service available within a given market. If there are no close substitutes for the good or service in question, the monopolist will be able to set both the level of output and the price at such a level as to maximize profits without worrying about being undercut by competitors (at least in the short run). Johnson, "Glossary," http://www.auburn.edu/~johnspm/gloss/monopoly (accessed December 29, 2015).

3. For an excellent introduction to the invention of motion picture photography, see Martin Quigley Jr., *Magic Shadows: The Story of the Origin of Motion Pictures* (Washington, DC: Georgetown University Press, 1948), chapter 11.

4. To read a much more detailed account of the invention of the movie camera, see James Monaco, *How to Read a Film: Movies, Media, and Beyond: Art, Technology, Language, History, Theory* (New York: Oxford University Press, 2009), chapter 2.

5. For a detailed account of this process, see Lewis Jacobs, *The Rise of the American Film: A Critical History* (New York: Harcourt Brace, 1939), particularly chapter 6.

6. For the story of the development of one of these distribution behemoths, see Douglas Gomery, "The Movies Become Big Business: Public Theatres and the Chain Store Strategy," in "Economic and Technological History," *Cinema Journal* 18, no. 2 (Spring 1979): 26–40.

7. Block booking means that "a studio would sell its films in packages on an all-or-nothing basis—usually requiring theaters to buy several mediocre pictures for every desirable one. Because the studios made mass-produced films, they also sold them in bulk." J. A. Aberdeen, "Block Booking: The Root of All Evil in the Motion Picture Industry," Society of Independent Motion Picture Producers, http://www.cobbles.com/simpp_archive/blockbook_intro.htm (accessed December 29, 2015).

8. Erwin A. Blackstone and Gary W Bowman, "Vertical Integration in Motion Pictures," *Journal of Communication* 49, no. 1 (1999): 123–40.

9. For an excellent history of the Jews in Hollywood, see Neal Gabler, *An Empire of Their Own* (New York: Anchor, 1988).

10. See Harold Brackman, "The Attack on 'Jewish Hollywood': A Chapter in the History of Modern American Anti-Semitism," *Modern Judaism* 20, no. 1 (2000): 1–19, or, for a discussion of a movie about this sort of thing, see Philip Hanson, "Against Tribalism: The Perils of Ethnic Identity in Mamet's *Homicide*," *Clio* 31, no. 3 (2002): 257–77. *Humanities International Index*, December 29, 2015.

11. For an excellent book-length examination of the production code, see Gregory Black, *Hollywood Censored: Morality Codes, Catholics, and the Movies* (New York: Cambridge University Press, 1994). See also, by the same author, a discussion of the anti-Semitic seeds of the movement to impose the production code, *The Catholic Crusade against the Movies, 1940–1975* (New York: Cambridge University Press, 1998).

12. For a discussion of the content censorship enforced by the production code, see Ruth Vasey, *The World according to Hollywood, 1918–1939* (Madison: University of Wisconsin Press, 1997).

13. Jon Tuska, *Dark Cinema: American Film Noir in Cultural Perspective* (Westport, CT: Greenwood, 1984), 152. See also Alain Silver and and James Ursini, *Film Noir Reader* (New York: Limelight Editions, 1996), in four volumes.

14. Dorothy Parker once commented that "the only ism adhered to in Hollywood is plagiarism."

15. For a discussion of Hollywood's risks in a venture into television production, see Jack Howard, "Hollywood and Television: Year of Decision," *Quarterly of Film Radio and Television* 7, no. 4 (1953): 359–69; William Boddy, "The Studios Move into Prime Time: Hollywood and the Television Industry in the 1950s," *Cinema Journal* 24, no. 4 (1985): 23–37; or J. A. Aberdeen, *Hollywood Renegades: The Society*

of Independent Motion Picture Producers (Los Angeles: Cobblestone Entertainment, 2000), chapter 14.

16. Data cited in Toby Miller et al., *Global Hollywood* (London: British Film Institute, 2001), 4–5.

17. http://www.imdb.com/name/nm0000955/ (accessed December 29, 2015). For an excellent history of the star system in Hollywood to date, see Paul McDonald, *The Star System: Hollywood's Production of Popular Identities* (London: Wallflower, 2001).

18. US Department of Commerce, http://selectusa.commerce.gov/industry -snapshots/media-entertainment-industry-united-states.html (accessed December 29, 2015).

19. See M. Mehdi Semati and Patty J. Sotirin, "Perspectives: Hollywood's Transnational Appeal," *Journal of Popular Film and Television* 26, no. 4 (1999): 177; Allen J. Scott, "Hollywood and the World: The Geography of Motion-Picture Distribution and Marketing," *Review of International Political Economy* 11, no. 1 (2004): 33–61; or Mary C. Beltrán, "The New Hollywood Racelessness: Only the Fast, Furious, (and Multiracial) Will Survive," *Cinema Journal* 44, no. 2 (2005): 50–67.

20. Scott Sochay, "Predicting the Performance of Motion Pictures," *Journal of Media Economics* 7, no. 4 (1994): 15; Corinn Columpar, "Contemporary American Independent Film: From the Margins to the Mainstream," *Film Quarterly* 60, no. 2 (2006): 68–69; Greg Marcks, "The Rise of the 'Studio Independents,'" *Film Quarterly* 61, no. 4 (2008): 8–9.

21. See Vincent F. Rocchio, *Reel Racism: Confronting Hollywood's Construction of Afro-American Culture* (Boulder, CO: Westview Press, 2000); Brian D. Behnken and Gregory D. Smithers, *Racism in American Popular Media: From Aunt Jemima to the Frito Bandito* (Santa Barbara, CA: Praeger, an imprint of ABC-CLIO, LLC, 2015).

22. Sharon Willis, *High Contrast: Race and Gender in Contemporary Hollywood Film* (Durham, NC: Duke University Press, 1997), would disagree, but not very convincingly in my opinion.

23. Box Office Mojo, "Titanic (1997)," www.boxofficemojo.com/movies/?id=ti tanic.htm (accessed December 30, 2015).

24. See http://www.michaelmedved.com/wp-content/uploads/SNOWPIERCER .mp3 (accessed December 30, 2015).

3

Who Makes 'Em and Who Watches 'Em

I often walk out of the movies shaking my head. "Who," I wonder, "thought that one up?" Who felt it necessary to explore the lives of a brother and sister who dress up as John and Jackie Kennedy, re-create the president's assassination, and have sex—with each other (*The House of Yes*, 1997)? Some of what we see in the movie theater is pretty twisted and strange. But then again, we also see the remarkable and the reflective. The opening sequence of *Contact* (1997) says more in three minutes than an hour's lecture in astrophysics. The film then goes on to intelligently muse on the relationship between man and God and between faith and science, which brings us to the subject of this chapter: How do producers decide what films to make?

If, as social conservatives argue, films are made without regard to the sensibilities of their audience, then we can argue that films are "art" (and sick art at that). If films are made with the sole purpose of turning a profit, then we can argue that film is just another product, like laundry detergent or furniture, and the content of film simply reflects the demands of consumers. Are the movies art or product? Does the market drive the content of films, or is content driven by a bunch of beatniks/capitalists in California?

Art is a form of human expression that often disregards the marketplace.[1] It represents the personal vision of the artist. It is sometimes revolutionary in the sense that good art stretches our senses. Good or at least compelling art is something that we haven't seen before and, in the best case, gives us a new perspective on color, light, sound, or the human condition. Product, on the other hand, is a function of the market. Product is manufactured to meet some real, perceived, or stimulated need of the consumer. Something of an intersection exists between art and the market in the sense that artists sell their wares to survive and manufacturers use art to manufacture demand. Nevertheless, good art (well regarded in retrospect) generally doesn't follow the market, and good capitalists don't get too far out in front of the consumers. A good many of the greatest artists in history have died broke, and a good many of the greatest capitalists in history have died rich.

Therefore, we generally assume that businesspeople, regardless of their personal beliefs, will endeavor to produce marketable products, and that artists, regardless of their financial status, will strive to produce their art. It doesn't make a lot of sense, then, to assume—as do so many of the critics of the American film industry from both the Right and the Left—that studio executives, producers, actors, theater owners, and everyone else involved in the film business are not capitalists, that filmmakers in their desire to promote their personal beliefs disregard market realities. At least one author goes so far as to argue that the movies are neither liberal nor conservative but "contested terrain, and that films can be interpreted as a struggle over representation of how to construct a social world and everyday life."[2] It is simply not enough to demonstrate that one segment of the film industry, the creative (manufacturing) "elite," are overwhelmingly liberal and then assume that films will be the same way. There is a causal connection here that is missing. What difference would it make if, say, the engineers at Ford Motors were frustrated sculptors and their creative energies were held in check by stockholders, management, financiers, and, most important, the market for Ford automobiles? It is therefore somewhat perplexing that film critics who are devoted capitalists throw their core economic beliefs out of the window when it comes to the entertainment industry.

Why would studio executives, regardless of their beliefs, consciously turn out a product that, because of its unpopular and weird appeal, is likely to fail? Now there is such a thing as a bad businessperson—one who fails to recognize the market. But for the bad capitalist, market retaliation is swift and terrible. One who is bad in business will not be in business for long. Unless critics of the film industry can demonstrate that there exists within it some sort of market distortion, we must assume that the market itself is the driving force. Unless our understanding of capitalist economics is seriously mistaken, it cannot be otherwise.[3]

In the last chapter, I suggest that there did exist at certain periods of time in Hollywood a market distortion in the form of a monopoly—first in technology (the Edison trust) and later in the vertical integration of the industry (the golden era of Hollywood cinema). The product of that second monopoly was commercial film produced according to a strict production code. But now that the film industry monopoly has been broken, all bets are off. The Motion Picture Association of America (MPAA) rating system is a mere shadow of what the production code once was. If modern films appeal to the lowest common denominator, or if they appeal to a particular politics or to prurient interests, the reason is that they are largely driven by the market, which brings us to two recent scholarly examinations of the film industry.

Until now, much social film criticism has been based on several articles of faith that have yet to be thoroughly examined. In two recent books on the political economy of the film industry, the authors survey mostly filmmakers from mainly the creative side of the industry. Specifically, in *Risky Business: The Political Economy of Hollywood* and in *Hollywood's America*, the authors conduct a survey of film professionals and come to the conclusion that Hollywood filmmakers as a group are more liberal and more Jewish than are other groups of businesspeople. Whether that fact is relevant to the content of modern motion pictures, however, is debatable. Commentators from both the Left and the Right assume that the ethnic, political, and class backgrounds of the production side of the movie industry constitute a slam-dunk case for a particular political bias in entertainment content. But it would probably make more sense to assume that because the film industry is a business that Hollywood movies are largely product, not art. Therefore, film content is no more a reflection of the filmmaker's beliefs than an automobile is the reflection of the automobile engineer's frustrated desire to be a sculptor. Thus, attempts to promote the big conspiracy theory of media are in reality an attempt by two groups in society, either conservative social critics or the radical Left, to assert their control over media content and so restrict our general constitutional rights. Consequently, this discussion of the political economy of the film industry is more than academic—it is a discussion of the politics of control.

WHAT IS THE "FILM INDUSTRY"?

In *Risky Business: The Political Economy of Hollywood*, Professor David Prindle interviews thirty-five "studio heads, presidents of artists' unions, trade association leaders, editors and publishers of trade papers, leaders of interest groups, and various industry people who were active in social and political organizations."[4] He finds that his sample, from mainly the creative side of the movie industry and the west side of Los Angeles, is significantly more liberal, less likely to be identified with the Republican Party, and more likely to be Jewish than the general public. In summarizing his results, he states, whatever the explanation, artistic liberalism seems to exert a strong influence over the general political outlook of Hollywood. It is not, however, the only force for left-wing politics. Hollywood contains a much higher percentage of Jews than does American society as a whole. Hollywood was virtually founded by Jews (the only important early industry business figure who was not Jewish was Walt Disney), and its important decision-making positions have been dominated by them ever since. Five out of six studio heads that make up the MPAA are Jewish.[5]

Nevertheless, he concludes that, regardless of their ideological or ethnic profiles, executives in the industry are primarily motivated by economic concerns. But not all observers arrive at the same conclusion. Another author writes, in summary, that Jews, both on screen and off, span the entire history of Hollywood cinema. As producers, screenwriters, directors, composers, and actors, they have been a dominant force in the industry and provide for its creative sustenance.[6]

While it is probably true that on the production side Hollywood filmmakers are more liberal (and Jewish) than the population as a whole is, it is not clear that it is liberals and Jews who "dominate" Hollywood. In fact, liberals and Jews may not have dominated Hollywood for a long time—maybe even from the time of the imposition of the production code.[7] It is essential to reiterate that even during the golden era of Hollywood cinema, when the studios were privately held, the production code was imposed on the Hollywood moguls from the outside. Consequently, even during the second monopoly, the moguls were not completely masters of their own house.

The fact is that even a representative survey of filmmakers in Southern California is not representative of the industry. It would be more accurate to rethink what we mean when we talk about "Hollywood" in the modern era. It is probably more accurate now to think of Hollywood as not so much a place as an abstraction. As an industry, Hollywood is no longer dominated by the moguls but by the market. If those market forces are distorted at all, they are influenced by the large, integrated media corporations that make decisions influenced by the requirements posed by their corporate structures.

The six companies that constitute the MPAA are responsible for the production and release of films that generate about 90 percent of all domestic box office receipts.[8] All of these studios are part of corporations that are publicly held, meaning that their stock is traded on the open market. Twentieth Century Fox is a wholly owned subsidiary of Twenty-First Century Fox, with Rupert Murdoch as CEO. Universal Studios is owned by Comcast, through its subsidiary is NBC Universal, with Brian Roberts as CEO. Comcast is the largest broadcast and cable company in the world. Paramount Studios is a wholly owned subsidiary of Viacom, the second-largest media conglomerate in the world (Executive Chairman Sumner Redstone). Walt Disney Studios is a subsidiary of the Walt Disney Company, which, after Comcast, is the second largest broadcasting and cable company in the world (CEO Bob Iger). Columbia Pictures is a subsidiary of Sony, a Japanese corporation (CEO Kazuo Hirai). Time Warner (CEO Jeff Bewkes), the third largest media corporation in the world, owns Warner Brothers Entertainment, and it is also a member of the MPAA. While there are prominent Jews in management—Redstone, Iger, and Roberts are Jewish—the suggestion that they dominate the industry is subject to challenge. Nor are all these CEOs particularly liberal. To the contrary, Murdoch is an unabashed conservative, and Redstone was a strong supporter of the reelection of President George W. Bush.

Furthermore, as publicly held corporations, these studios are required by the Securities and Exchange Commission to submit quarterly statements to their shareholders. While they may hold large positions in the stocks of companies they manage, CEOs are managers, not owners. Murdoch and any one of the CEOs listed here would not be in compliance with their fiduciary responsibilities were they to allow an underperforming subsidiary to lose money because of its penchant to embark on ideological crusades. For one thing, their stockholders would not tolerate it.

It is also worth noting that the persistent focus on the ethnic and political background of movie executives may reflect at least some of the vestigial anti-Semitism that has dogged the industry from its beginnings. In different times, anti-Semitism against Hollywood manifested itself in different ways: first, in the form of nativist distrust of the "foreigners" who founded the industry, then in the imposition of the production code by the Legion of Decency, after that by isolationist elements in the lead-up to America's entry into World War II, after that in the vigorous pursuit of antitrust investigations against the industry, then in the blacklist and communist witch hunt of the McCarthy era, and now in the rabid attacks on "Hollywood" by the conservative Right.[9]

But in reality, there is no more "Hollywood." Decisions about film production are ultimately approved in corporate boardrooms in New York, Tokyo, Paris, and only sometimes in Los Angeles. Consequently, it is fascinating that so much attention is paid to the ethnic backgrounds of members of the media—liberal journalists and all that—as though it makes a difference. And if it does, why aren't the ethnic backgrounds of bankers, politicians, general officers in the military, and other corporate and societal leaders examined with the same rigor? It wouldn't be accurate to say that the personal backgrounds of journalists or filmmakers make no difference at all in the content of films, entertainment, or the news. But it could be more than plausibly argued that the influence of their personal backgrounds is overrated because of the influence of a much more powerful force—capitalism. To suggest otherwise is to suggest that the employees (or contractors) in the film industry are more important to corporate decision making than the owners are. Not only is that suggestion hard to believe, but there is also no incontrovertible evidence to that effect. Again, unless it can be demonstrated that there exists some sort of market distortion, such as a monopoly or government regulation, the argument that a bunch of liberal Jews are corrupting the youth of America is hard to accept. The movie business is now a free-for-all, and, as a result, capitalism is a much more powerful force and feature films are more product than art.

In *Hollywood's America: Social and Political Themes in Motion Pictures*, Stephen Powers, David J. Rothman, and Stanley Rothman attempt to be more systematic in their survey of their movie "elite." They draw a random sample from "a list of writers, producers, and directors of the fifty top grossing films made between 1965 and 1982."[10] Their final sample size is 96, with a response rate of 64 percent, out of a pool of 150 candidates. While their sample is somewhat larger and more systematically drawn than that of the Prindle survey, the authors find that, again, the Hollywood elite is different from other elites but not radically so, except to the extent that the former is much less religious than the latter and much more liberal in some respects. According to Powers and colleagues, the liberalism of the Hollywood elite is cultural (and not economic), meaning that Hollywood filmmakers, on average, are more tolerant of alternate sexual lifestyles, divorce, and a broad range of freedom of expression. In other words, they are more cosmopolitan. But the influence may be not industry specific but geography specific—that is, the same result might be expected if researchers were to interview a group of, say, lawyers, bankers, or real estate brokers all from west Los Angeles.

On economic matters, however, moviemakers are almost as much capitalists as are other economic elites. They are only slightly more liberal on economic matters than are other businesspeople. Nevertheless, even these modest differences in economic liberalism would probably be washed out if the authors controlled for the regionality of their sample. Thus, their study indicates that Hollywood filmmakers are just as interested in making a buck as any other businessperson. Consequently, if this survey is a modestly accurate sample of Hollywood filmmakers, even on the creative side, would they be willing to suppress their personal political preferences when it comes to making a film for popular consumption? Furthermore, were we to include in the sample those who finance the films or show the films in their theaters, would we find that the influence of cultural liberalism overall among those who make and market commercial feature films is minor indeed?

I believe that critics of Hollywood liberalism, in a manner of speaking, have been seduced by Hollywood. In defining the producers of feature films as part of the "cultural elite," too much credit is given to the editorial influence of the creative side of the business. Filmmakers would like to think of themselves as artists and are anxious to convince anyone within earshot of such. It has to do with their self-image—Hollywood filmmakers like to think of themselves as artists. But to take Hollywood filmmakers at their word is to ignore some of the verities of capitalism. In feature films, more often than not, art does not sell. Art certainly doesn't sell well enough to justify a $100 million investment. While there is a certain amount of art in the execution, the producers of the *Iron Man* series, the *Star Wars* series, the *Jurassic Park* series, and *San Andreas* are consummate capitalists.

They are masters of their craft as well. But the fine craftwork of their films hardly makes them artists. The stars of *Transformers: The Age of Extinction* (2014), the Autobots, are a technological achievement, to be sure, but they are no more a work of art than a dishwasher or Cuisinart. Thus, in parsing their sample in such a way as to separate the creative side from the business side of the movie industry, Powers and colleagues create a problem—the liberalism of the cultural elite—by constructing a study that merely compares the political beliefs and lifestyles of liberals and conservatives without considering their effect on the movie business as a whole. What is missing here is a causal connection.

While their surveys regarding the attitudes of one segment of the movie-making industry are no doubt accurate, critics of Hollywood liberalism err in drawing conclusions from unrepresentative samples. Surveying film-makers from the creative side of the business biases results in favor of that side of the industry. However, we should also consider the input of corporate CEOs, financiers, distributors, and consumers, who are at least as much a determinant of the content of movies as are moviemakers. To assume that the opinions of writers are on a par with those of producers is to equate the power of those who write screenplays with those who seek financing for production.

According to someone who ought to know (Martin Scorsese),

In the old days the director dealt with moguls and major studios; today he faces executives and giant corporations instead. But there is one iron rule that has never changed: every decision is shaped by the moneymen's perception of what the audience wants.[11]

To his credit, conservative social critic and commentator Michael Medved, in his critique of Hollywood, *Hollywood vs. America* (1993), confronts the economic argument head-on.[12] He does not ignore the economic verities of capitalism but instead argues that Hollywood filmmakers ignore the capitalist impulse to produce broadly popular films because of peer pressure. In seeking the acceptance of their peers, Medved argues, Hollywood filmmakers will ignore the dictates of the market.

Psychologists suggest that peer acceptance is a powerful motive in group decision making. Groupthink is a powerful dynamic that can drive decision making in small groups in all sorts of weird directions.[13] That is particularly true for decision making that takes place outside of democratic control or market incentives. Thus, we need to guard against the degenerative effects of groupthink in the decision-making processes of bureaucracies or other nonprofit institutions, but in a for-profit business, the penalty for flawed decision making of the groupthink variety is swift and terrible. Hollywood peers may give awards to fellow travelers, but they can't pay for a $100 million film. The desire to have the respect of one's peers or to live north of Sunset Boulevard (the toniest address in Los Angeles) is an important motivation, but it is not a moneymaker. Making films that sell is all that matters, unless there exists some kind of market distortion.

Medved goes on to suggest that there is indeed a market distortion in modern-day Hollywood. He argues that a kind of monopoly exists in Hollywood in the sense that certain films simply will not get made because of the nepotism and insularity of the industry. In other words, family-oriented films are less likely to receive backing because of the degeneracy of the self-perpetuating Hollywood elite. To a certain extent, it is hard to argue with this logic. Almost all businesses resort to some degree of nepotism to promote people into positions of responsibility. Indeed, Jews and other immigrants got into the movie business in the first place because it was a new industry and thus without an existing hierarchy and the informal barriers to entry that go with a nepotistic structure. It is not difficult to understand why Michael Douglas or Jane Fonda (to name only two) had an edge in getting jobs in the movie business—they had connections.

There can be several responses to this argument. First, the insularity of Hollywood does limit the types of themes that are explored, but only to the extent that the industry may be slow to react. While Hollywood filmmakers may be cultural outliers, they are still rabid capitalists. Any market-driven industry will have a lag between market changes and product development. Nevertheless, unless there exists some sort of market distortion, an industry that fails to adapt to changing market conditions will experience falling profits. That has certainly not been the case for what has been a very profitable time for the movie industry.

Second, if there exists a monopoly in Hollywood based on nepotism, it must be a fragile monopoly indeed. This is not OPEC. For a monopoly to exist, there must be some sort of centralized control over the means of production and the marketing of a product. Furthermore, the demand for the product itself has to be nonelastic, meaning that the product is an absolute necessity for which there are no substitutes, such as oil. This hardly describes the film business. Theater ownership is no longer integrated with film production. Film producers are no longer guaranteed screens for their products. In addition, production facilities are readily available for rent, and there are literally tens of thousands of out-of-work actors, directors, and producers who will make a film practically for free. Furthermore, feature films themselves are extremely elastic goods. Going to the movies is not essential for life. Finally, there is a lot of product out there—not just in the theater but also on cable, the Internet, and pay per view. Therefore, Medved vastly overemphasizes the monopoly of nepotism in Hollywood because of the overall indefensibility of his argument, which ignores the basic tenets of economics.

If there is a market for films more sensitive to conservative social values, it will be developed, even in Hollywood. There is, in fact, a small but vibrant market for commercially produced, Christian-themed films. The blockbuster in this class was *The Passion of the Christ* (2004), which grossed $670 million on a $30 million budget. There has never been another film of that magnitude in the space before or since. However, there are still produced a number of Christian-themed films that when made on a modest budget can produce a modest return. More typical are a pair of quite successful films produced in 2014—*God Is Not Dead* (2014) grossed $63 million on a $9 million budget, and *Heaven Is for Real* (2014) grossed $101 million on a $22 million budget. Neither film sold well abroad.

These numbers are relatively small change for corporate Hollywood, and the market is not expanding. Right now, religiosity is on the decline in the United States. But this doesn't mean that in the current environment these films can't be made and can't be distributed at a modest profit. What Medved didn't take into account when he published his book in 1993 (and, in fact, couldn't have taken into account) was the transformative effect of a change in media broadcast and production technology.

The fact is that the movie business is ever changing. Much of this change has historically been, and is currently being, driven by technological developments that have, in turn, changed the audience for film. The development of VCRs, then DVDs, and then on-demand, streaming video has transformed the market for motion pictures. This means that there is now a huge market for feature films outside the movie theater. There is now an audience for feature films that, if production costs are kept down, can be shown to segments of the population who are less likely to go to the theater because of, say, mobility problems, financial constraints, or small children at home.

When the market for feature films was primarily the audience that would go to the theater, films were geared toward generally younger audiences without children. Times have changed, and so have films. In the much more segmented market that now exists, there *are* more films made that are oriented to a stay-at-home audience.

Television in particular has been on the cutting edge of this transition. In the last decade, there has been an explosion in television content, particularly in the form of serials.[14] In a programming space that had once been the very modest province of PBS and *Masterpiece Theatre*, a variety of content and broadcasting companies, such as Netflix, Amazon, HBO, AMC, and even Xbox have become production companies. This resembles the progression in the birth of Hollywood itself. The Edison trust was broken by theater owners who began to make their own films. In the same way, modern exhibitors have gotten into the production business.

This is not to say that slasher, car chase, and sexually explicit films are still not being made and won't, to a certain extent, continue to dominate feature films in theatrical release (for reasons to be discussed later in this chapter). The first-run theater box office continues to be a more lucrative source of income for moviemakers than that of pay-per-view rentals. Nothing is going to change the fact that religious people and parents with small children in particular are busy on the weekends doing something other than going to the movies. The teenager, out of school, with some extra money in his or her pocket is still the market for films in large-scale theatrical release. But it is interesting to note that even blockbuster films in theatrical release have often adopted a variant of the serial format.

MARKET-DRIVEN FILM INDUSTRY: EVIDENCE

In the following section, I provide evidence to support my assertions that the film industry is basically market driven. First of all, allow me some disclaimers. What I am talking about here is a general trend. There are individual cases that contradict my overall analysis. However, I cannot respond to arguments based on anecdotal evidence or to survey analyses not based on representative samples. Furthermore, what I am discussing here is causality. If one thing causes another, it may also be the case that the direction of causality may be reversed. For example, the demand for a product is in part intrinsic and in part driven by advertising.

This is a basic problem of marketing. Is it enough to simply identify and serve the market, or can a market for a product be created? The general rule of thumb is that it is easier to serve an existing market than to create a new one. A market for a product not in demand is usually nonexistent for good reason. Therefore, it would be reasonable to assume that, on balance, the market for feature motion pictures is driven by intrinsic demand rather than by a demand created by advertising (or the films themselves). In truth, marketing is a combination of the two, but the tendency toward serving an existing demand or adopting a tried-and-true formula is particularly pervasive in the film industry, where industry executives must attract millions of dollars of investment in commercial films that each have basically a one-shot, two-week window for success.[15]

My contentions are that film content is market driven and that the personal profile of filmgoers is unique enough to drive film content in a direction that may seem out of the ordinary (especially to the social conservative). More specifically, I argue that the audience for movies is significantly more socially liberal and less religious than the population as a whole and that filmmakers make movies intended to satisfy the intrinsic demands of that audience. Furthermore, there are some practical reasons that cultural conservatives, older people, and families with children don't go to the movies. This I call the *crowding-out effect*. There is only so much time in the day. Older people have restricted mobility, and religious people or families with children are busy doing other things. The film industry is less anxious to serve this market because it is a less lucrative market. While this situation may have changed to a certain extent due to the expanded market of American cinema, with the advent of VCRs, pay per view, and cable television, the main audience for American film is still foreign, younger, and more culturally liberal. Hollywood industry executives aren't changing their tune, not because they are out of touch, but because they are in touch in a way that only the market can enforce. Furthermore, there really isn't much of a prospect for a huge expansion of the production of films for cultural conservatives because they are the type of people who for some very understandable reasons don't go to the movies.

FILM ATTENDANCE AND
POLITICAL AFFILIATION

The data presented here are the results of a national survey of over four thousand adults commissioned by the Motion Picture Association of America. The time frame for the latest survey was January 8 through January 25, 2015, for moviegoing in the year 2014. The MPAA has been conducting an annual survey for several years. Thus, we can track the progression of movie attendance over time.

Some of the key findings of the survey include the following:

- Global box office for all films released in each country around the world reached $36.4 billion in 2014, up 1 percent over 2013's total, due to an increase in international box office ($26 billion). Growth was driven primarily by the Asia Pacific region (+12 percent). Chinese box office ($4.8 billion) increased 34 percent in 2014, becoming the first international market to exceed $4 billion in box office.
- Cinema screens increased by 6 percent worldwide in 2014 to over 142,000, due in large part to continued double-digit growth in the Asia Pacific region (+15 percent). Over 90 percent of the world's cinema screens are now digital.

United States/Canada

- In 2014, US/Canada box office was $10.4 billion, down 5 percent from $10.9 billion in 2013. The 3D box office ($1.4 billion) comprised 14 percent of total box office, two percentage points less than the previous year.
- Admissions, or tickets sold (1.27 billion), and average tickets sold per person (3.7) both declined 6 percent in 2014. The average cinema ticket price increased by four cents (less than 1 percent) in 2014, less than the rate of inflation in the economy.
- More than two-thirds of the US/Canada population (68 percent)—or 229.7 million people—went to the cinema at least once in 2014, comparable to the previous year. Frequent moviegoers who go to the cinema once a month or more continue to drive the movie industry, accounting for 51 percent of all tickets sold in the United States/Canada. Despite an increase in frequent moviegoers in 2014, total tickets purchased by frequent moviegoers and occasional and infrequent moviegoers all decreased in 2014 compared to 2013.
- In 2014 the share of tickets sold to forty-to-forty-nine and fifty-to-fifty-nine-year-olds were at all-time highs, while the share of tickets sold to sixty-plus-year-olds (13 percent) was at its highest level since 2011. Moviegoer demographic shares remain relatively stable from 2013 to 2014, with twelve-to-seventeen, eighteen-to-twenty-four-year-olds, and Hispanics especially continuing to oversample in tickets sold versus their proportion of the population.
- Frequent moviegoers tend to own more key technology products than the general population of adults eighteen years and older. Over two-thirds of all frequent moviegoers (73 percent) own at least four different types of key technology products, compared to 55 percent of the total adult population.
- Films released by MPAA member studios increased for the first time in five years, reaching 136 in 2014. Total films released and films by non-MPAA member studios also increased from 2013 (up 7 percent and 5 percent, respectively).
- Among the top five highest-grossing films in 2014, *Guardians of the Galaxy, Captain America: The Winter Solider, The LEGO Movie,* and *Transformers: Age of Extinction* attracted majority male audiences, while *The Hunger Games: Mockingjay Part 1* showed the strongest female attendance of the top five films, with 57 percent of box office revenue coming from women. *Transformers: Age of Extinction* drew the most ethnically diverse audience, earning 38 percent of its box office from Caucasian audiences, 22 percent from African American audiences, 26

percent from Hispanic audiences, and 14 percent from the Asian/Other audience group.[16]

What these results tell us is that the audience for American film is 72 percent foreign and growing (up from 66 percent in 2010). Overall, the industry is growing, about 3 percent a year, and all the growth in revenues is from abroad. The largest market for growth is in China and the Asian region in general.

Domestically (still a $10 billion market), the demographics of the audience are beginning to change. While the youth market for film is overweighted, and has been for some time, the fastest-growing audience for film domestically are older adults, in their late middle age, who are probably empty nesters. After all, at $15 a ticket, taking a family to the theater can get pretty expensive (when compared to the cost of pay per view). However, once the kids are out of the house or old enough to fend for themselves, one of the enduring date-night activities of choice is going to the movies. But domestically, overall, the movie business is what is called a mature business, meaning that its days of explosive growth are over.

It should be noted that children (people below the age of eighteen) were not interviewed in this survey, and yet there is pretty good evidence to suggest that teenagers in particular are frequent moviegoers. The problem is that it is difficult to survey people below the age of consent. Parents tend to object to the practice of strangers asking their children personal questions. Thus, this survey is not entirely representative of the population of moviegoers. Consider, however, that movie distributors and theater chains suffer the same problem in doing their own marketing studies. They can survey children at the theater simply by seeing who attends, but in terms of doing broader comparative surveys of the population they are "flying blind." That may be one of the reasons that children's programming (not just in the movies but also on the television) is so scarce and sometimes inappropriate. Producers of children's entertainment have little information to go on and thus either make mistakes (by screening unsuitable material) or avoid the market altogether. As far as this survey is concerned, it is inaccurate in a representative way. That may sound like an oxymoron, but in fact, in using these data we are working off the same kind of information available to the producers of entertainment themselves.

With that and other holes in the data in mind, filmmakers must adjust the content of their films to the available information they have about their audience. If film content is really market driven, and if the audience for feature motion pictures is more culturally liberal than the norm, then film content will reflect a point of view that is more culturally liberal than the norm.

In their 2014 survey, the MPAA determined that 11 percent of the population in Canada and the United States over the age of two are *frequent* moviegoers. A frequent moviegoer is defined as someone who goes to the movies on average once a month or more in a calendar year. Frequent moviegoers are particularly important to film distributors for three reasons. First, they are responsible for 51 percent of all ticket sales to the movies. Second, because of the revenue-sharing arrangement distributors have with theaters, the lion's share of the revenues from theater admissions goes to the distributors in the first few weeks of a film's release (on a sliding scale). Finally, frequent filmgoers are more likely to see a film in its first few weeks of release. Consequently, frequent filmgoers are the most likely to establish the "buzz" for a film in its first couple of weeks. A film that gets a positive "buzz" is said to have "legs," which means it will play in more theaters for longer than other films and will have a greater potential in the DVD and pay-per-view market.

In figure 3.1, we see the age demographics of frequent filmgoers. What is most apparent from this chart is that the largest demographic among frequent filmgoers is the age group from eighteen to thirty-nine. However, that age group is also shrinking the fastest. The fastest-growing audience for film in this group is the over-sixty age category. This may be due to contextual conditions; younger people may spend more time playing video games or communicating on social media, or the change may be due to the aging of the population or some combination thereof. Regardless of the cause, the market for films in this segment of the audience is getting older.[17]

In addition, the gender mix and the ethnicity of the frequent moviegoer population is a virtual mirror of the population as a whole. Thus, the operative difference between the general population and the frequent moviegoing audience is age. There are niche markets in other sectors of the

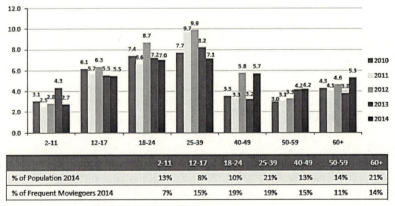

Figure 3.1. Frequent Filmgoers by Age

population, to be sure, but the largest audiences for films are to be located in certain age categories. It is important to remind that this refers to the domestic market only; the foreign market is a bit trickier.

Now let us examine the politics of these groups. One way to measure political attitudes is to look at response rates by party affiliation. Party labels are generally used as a surrogate for complex ideological beliefs. For example, a political candidate's identification as a Republican or Democrat tells the potential voter a substantial amount about the positions that will be adopted by that candidate if elected to office. This is particularly the case in the last few years, as the parties have proceeded to polarize on the right and left sides of the political spectrum.

In figure 3.2, we see party identification by age.[18] Note that in the most important age category for film producers, eighteen to thirty-nine, individuals are more likely to identify as Democrats by a large margin. However, past that point, and especially in the fastest-growing segment for frequent filmgoers, the audience gets more conservative. Thus, we might expect that in anticipation of a changing audience for films (in domestic release), filmmakers will have to be more sensitive to a more conservative audience.

But what kind of conservatism? Conservatism in the United States is an admixture of conservative social attitudes and free market liberalism. What kind of conservatives will filmmakers want to cater to?

Figure 3.3 breaks down age cohorts by political attitudes.[19] In addition,

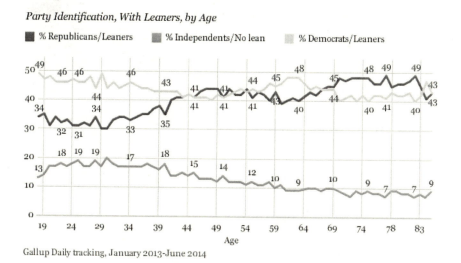

Figure 3.2. Party Identification by Age

Political Typologies Shift with Age

Percent of Americans in each age bracket who are...

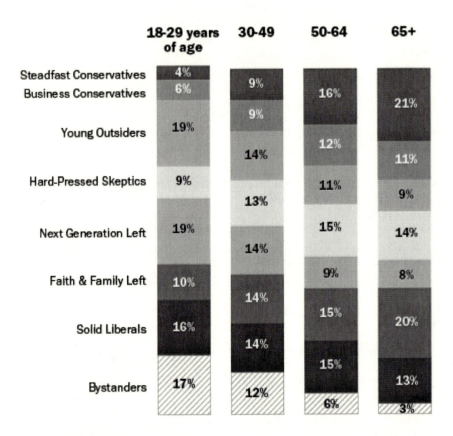

Source: 2014 Political Typology
PEW RESEARCH CENTER

Figure 3.3. Political Typologies Shift with Age

it is important to note that studies have shown that, on average, political attitudes are relatively stable.[20] The attitudes of younger individuals are likely to remain the same throughout their lives. Thus, the attitudes of a particular age cohort travels through the population across time, pardon the analogy, like a rat going through a snake. Thus, the chart above is a snapshot of political attitudes across demographic groups at a particular point. It would be tempting to suggest that individuals get more conservative as they age. But by and large, that is not the case. Thus the "art" of filmmaking may not be so much in the placement of the camera or the construction of a plot but in trying to figure out where to find an audience for a film, and that, as we can see, is not an exact science.

Of course, all of this market research depends on the assumption that film content is market driven. If film content is basically market driven, a movie producer will not care whether their audiences are Republican or Democrat, black or white, Martian or human, as long as they pay to see a film. As noted above, the most important consumer is the one who goes to the movies more frequently. Film content should then be geared toward the frequent moviegoer, especially if the frequency of film attendance by a few far outstrips the less frequent attendance (or less lucrative video rentals) of the many.

The political profile of the most frequent movie goers (eighteen-to-thirty-nine-year-olds) is as follows:

45 percent identify with the Democratic Party (31 percent is the national average)

33 percent identify with the Republican Party (25 percent is the national average)

18 percent are Independents (41 percent is the national average)

In other words, if party identification can act as a surrogate for American ideology, frequent moviegoers are more likely than the national average to identify with the Republican Party and *much* more likely to identify with the Democratic Party. Thus, they are more partisan, and they are more liberal.

But what kind of liberalism? According to the more nuanced Pew Foundation survey of political attitudes, frequent moviegoers are much less likely than the population as a whole to be religious (motivated by religion to either traditional values or progressive policies) and are much more likely to be apolitical. Surprisingly, the percentage of self-identified liberals in the population is fairly consistent across demographic groups. Consequently, if filmmakers are out to attract a broad-based domestic audience and are market driven, they will stick to themes that are generally apolitical, and if they are political, they will lean to the left side of the political spectrum.

I think this pretty much describes the character of American film at the moment. And this tendency to stay away from politics is reinforced by the large and growing market for American films abroad. Foreign audiences are not interested in the problems of American politics and may find themes associated therewith downright subversive.

The obvious response to these survey results is that conservatives don't go to the movies because they have nothing to see. This is a "chicken and egg" problem. What causes what? First, in the demographic sense, because older audiences are not as likely to go to the movies as younger audiences, it wouldn't make sense for filmmakers to make films for older audiences. Furthermore, as a general rule in marketing, it is much safer in a financial sense for a producer to serve an existing market than to create a new one. Certainly, marketing firms that work for the film studios have gotten pretty much the same results as these surveys have. Consequently, the safest bet for financiers is to serve an existing audience. There are usually some valid reasons that a market for a particular product does not exist, which leads to our next analysis.

Primarily because of the crowding-out effect, cultural conservatives (many of whom are Republicans) have other things to do when it comes to their spare time and are therefore less likely to go to the movies. Specifically, because religious people are otherwise occupied, particularly on the weekends, they will be less likely to go to the movies. We would assume for people who are serious about their religion that no amount of content change in the movies is going to make them shortchange their church-related activities in favor of going to the movies.

In August 2015, a Christian-themed film, *The War Room* (2015), briefly surpassed *Mission Impossible: Rogue Nation* (2015) for leadership in box office receipts. Eventually the film went on to gross $67 million on a $3 million budget. The success of this film points up both the potential and limitations of films made for religious audiences. While there is an audience for religious-themed films, it is limited in size. Even a wildly successful film in the genre (with the noted exception of *The Passion of the Christ*, which most observers think was a "one off") is unlikely to net large enough profits to attract the major studios. Furthermore, if the demographics of movie audiences are any indication, the market for film is getting less, not more, religious. *MI: Rogue Nation* grossed $682 million on a $150 million budget.

Finally, it may well be the case that cultural liberals, besides being higher per capita filmgoers, are also more profitable for filmmakers. There are a number of ways that people can go to the movies. They can go to the local Cineplex, or they can watch films at home on commercial television, subscription cable, pay per view, or on their VCRs and DVDs. For the film industry, the most lucrative audience by far is the one that pays full admission at a first-run movie house. In a typical distribution deal, the distributor receives up to 80 percent (the theater owner, 20 percent) of the admissions revenue for the first two weeks that a film is screened. The distributor "take" begins to decline after that on a sliding scale. That makes high-gross box office features extremely profitable for the distributor (and long-running features extremely profitable for the theater owner). Thus, the most lucrative audiences for feature films are independents, Democrats, and the apolitical, in that order.

FILM CONTENT AND THE MARKET: SOCIETAL CONCERNS

If film content is market driven, it will tend to reflect rather than drive societal attitudes. In other words, film content will tend to lag behind changes in public opinion or, to be more precise, the opinion of the audience for film. Because of the vagaries of public opinion polling (especially in terms of political attitudes) and evaluating film content, this is a difficult relationship to illustrate. Nevertheless, in certain areas of film content—specifically in regard to violence, and gun violence—there is some fairly reliable public opinion data.

Let us test the proposition that movie violence reflects (rather than drives) the movie audience. First the facts: according to a recent study in the journal *Pediatrics* (2013), since 1950 the rate of violence in movies has more than doubled.[21]

After 1985, when the current film rating system was introduced, the rate of *gun* violence more than tripled in PG-13 films (and stayed the same or declined in R- and G-rated films). The PG-13 rating warns but does not prohibit teenagers from attendance.[22] PG-13 films are responsible for more than half the ticket revenues of Hollywood cinema. The authors conclude:

> The effects of exposure to gun violence in films should not be trivialized. Even if youth do not use guns, the current research suggests that because of the increasing popularity of PG-13–rated films, youth are exposed to considerable gun violence in movie scripts. The mere presence of guns in these films may increase the aggressive behavior of youth.[23]

The results of this study were covered fairly widely in the press, which sparked calls for a "more responsible" film industry.

According to the article, there is a spike in film violence after 2010. Without that spike in violence (and a similar spike in gun violence as well), the authors would have had to draw an entirely different conclusion. Thus, this analysis invites the question of what exactly happened in 2010 to cause a spike in film violence. The answer to that question is fairly obvious. Figure 3.4 lists the top-grossing films of all time.[24] The three films from 2015 are still, as of this writing, in theatrical release and stand to gain a bit more in sales. But one thing stands out in this list: nine of the ten films listed date from 2011 on, with three out of the top ten films in 2015 alone. It is also important to note that these top-grossing films *average* 70 percent of their revenues from abroad.[25]

Clearly, in 2010, Hollywood hit upon a formula that leads to massive profitability. This formula, as researchers have pointed out, obviously involves a spike in violence in the narrative. But that is where the usefulness of the research on movie violence begins to lose its relevance. As noted above, the authors of this study, with no real evidence, try to impute some kind of corrosive effects on teenagers of exposure to all this movie violence. However, the preceding study does nothing to support that conclusion.

As I have noted, this recent spike in movie violence (which, when averaged into the data, affects the entire trend, which up until 2010 was basically flat) is the result of the introduction of a new business model. That is not to say that movie violence has no effect on the behavior of those who watch it. However, that conclusion begs a more nuanced assessment of the effects of movie violence on the audience.

Furthermore, most of the audience for these films comes from abroad. If we look at the list of the top ten domestic grossing films (see figure 3.5),[26] we find, first, that American filmgoers are beginning to be left behind in favor of international audiences. The release dates for these top ten films on this list predate, on average, the films on the worldwide gross list. Second, American audiences have a preference for many of the same films that inter-

Rank	Title	Studio	Worldwide	Domestic	/ %	Overseas	/ %	Year^
1	Avatar	Fox	$2,788.0	$760.5	27.3%	$2,027.5	72.7%	2009^
2	Titanic	Par.	$2,186.8	$658.7	30.1%	$1,528.1	69.9%	1997^
3	Marvel's The Avengers	BV	$1,519.6	$623.4	41.0%	$896.2	59.0%	2012
4	Furious 7	Uni.	$1,511.7	$351.0	23.2%	$1,160.7	76.8%	2015
5	Jurassic World	Uni.	$1,472.9	$595.6	40.4%	$877.2	59.6%	2015
6	Avengers: Age of Ultron	BV	$1,388.7	$455.4	32.8%	$933.3	67.2%	2015
7	Harry Potter and the Deathly Hallows Part 2	WB	$1,341.5	$381.0	28.4%	$960.5	71.6%	2011
8	Frozen	BV	$1,274.2	$400.7	31.4%	$873.5	68.6%	2013
9	Iron Man 3	BV	$1,215.4	$409.0	33.7%	$806.4	66.3%	2013
10	Transformers: Dark of the Moon	P/DW	$1,123.8	$352.4	31.4%	$771.4	68.6%	2011

Figure 3.4. Worldwide Grosses (All Time—No Inflation Control)
Courtesy of BoxOfficeMojo.com, a division of Internet Movie Database

Rank	Title(click to view)	Studio	Lifetime Gross	Year^
1	**Avatar**	Fox	**$760,507,625**	2009^
2	**Titanic**	Par.	**$658,672,302**	1997^
3	**Marvel's The Avengers**	BV	**$623,357,910**	2012
4	**Jurassic World**	Uni.	**$611,174,000**	2015
5	**The Dark Knight**	WB	**$534,858,444**	2008^
6	**Star Wars: Episode I - The Phantom Menace**	Fox	**$474,544,677**	1999^
7	**Star Wars**	Fox	**$460,998,007**	1977^
8	**Avengers: Age of Ultron**	BV	**$456,009,000**	2015
9	**The Dark Knight Rises**	WB	**$448,139,099**	2012
10	**Shrek 2**	DW	**$441,226,247**	2004

Figure 3.5. Domestic Grosses (All-Time—No Inflation Control)
Courtesy of BoxOfficeMojo.com, a division of Internet Movie Database

national audiences enjoy, with the exception of *Shrek*, the *Star Wars* series, and *The Dark Knight* or modern Batman series. This list hardly highlights a unique American propensity for violence. However, it should be noted that a screening of *The Dark Knight Rises* was the scene of a shooting in Aurora, Colorado, resulting in twelve people killed and seventy injured. However, that one incident does not reflect a trend toward lower rates of violence in the United States. According to the FBI, between 1993 and 2013 the rate of violent crime has dropped 75 percent in the United States. During the same period, even firearm violence was down (albeit not significantly in the statistical sense).[27] Where are the effects of this spike in film violence?

In conclusion, the rise in violence in film is, if anything, more of a threat to people abroad and is the result of a business decision that has yielded outstanding profits. That is not to say that there are not deleterious effects of violence on viewing audiences, although even that assertion is subject to dispute. In the next chapter, I will discuss some of the latest evidence in regard to the effects on viewers of filmed, fictional violence. Is this new model in the marketing of film a dangerous precedent?

Feature Film: *Avatar*

Avatar, Twentieth Century Fox Film Corporation, 2009

Imagine a film in which an evil government/mining consortium backed by the military conspires to uproot an indigenous people in pursuit of industrial gain. In the end, the indigenous people, in tandem with traitors from the corporation, defeat the military and send the mining concern on its way. The indigenous people then celebrate by thanking their "earth god," which manifests itself in the form of a giant tree.

The plot of this film sounds like something dreamed up in a 1960s ashram in Big Sur, California. But this is in fact the plot of a film that was shot in Hollywood and distributed by Twentieth Century Fox, a division of News Corp, with archconservative Rupert Murdoch at the helm. If there were ever an example of the principle that, to capitalists, money isn't red or blue, this is it.

Avatar is the top-grossing film of all time. It is also one of the most expensive. For the most part, its box office boffo is well deserved. *Avatar* is a combination of stunning visual effects and a very interesting plot. One doesn't usually lead to the other, as special effects are often used a crutch to compensate for a subpar script. But as blockbuster releases go, *Avatar* is something special.

Avatar is about a paraplegic ex-marine, Jake, who is brought to the planet Pandora by something called the Resources Development Administration that, apparently, is an agency of the American government. It turns out that before being wounded and losing the use of his legs, Jake had fought bravely in Venezuela (the enemy flavor of the month under the now deceased Hugo Chávez). So it is pretty obvious that while at this point the United States has managed to negotiate interstellar travel, the same can't be said for world peace.

The RDA has been dispatched to Pandora to mine the substance "unobtainium," which has the potential to supply an unlimited source of power to Earth. The problem is that Pandora has a hostile environment with an atmosphere that is lethal to humans. Furthermore, the native population of the planet, the Na'vi, while essentially peaceful, lives on top of the largest deposit of unobtainium. It is Jake's job to inhabit the avatar and either talk the Na'vi out of their homes or scout their weaknesses for the military.

Through a series of contrivances, Jake meets and falls in love with a Na'vi girl. It is my understanding that the couple, well, couples Na'vi style, but that scene was cut for the PG rating. Ultimately, Jake goes native and adopts the Na'vi traditions and ends up fighting against the human invasion. In the end, the humans retreat Vietnam, Iraq, and, I suspect, one day Afghanistan style, and the Na'vi get to keep their world. What we do about energy after the withdrawal, I'm not entirely sure.

The plot of this film is surprisingly New Age, with the Na'vi cast as the "noble savage." Their reverence for the planet has obvious Native American and green policy undertones. While it is never entirely clear who the master of the RDA is, the Earthen government, Earthen commercialism, and Earthen military come under some pretty serious scrutiny. The fanatical commander of the Earthen military is a kind of Custer on steroids, and the fact that the demand for resources outstrips the concerns of their fellow "man" is played as pretty much the human condition. Furthermore, the Na'vi religion bears little resemblance to the Earthen deist tradition (and looks like a heck of a lot more fun).

As noted above, this film made a lot of money. And if a celebration of the victory of an indigenous people over the US military garners an all-time high gross, then maybe Lenin was right when he said, "The Capitalists will sell us the rope with which we will hang them."

EXERCISE

Pick a major feature film that has been a commercial disaster. Analyze why it did so poorly in relation to its target population of moviegoers. Why was this film made in the first place? What were they thinking?

SUGGESTED READINGS

Balio, Tino. *Hollywood in the New Millennium*. London; New York: Palgrave Macmillan on behalf of the British Film Institute, 2013.

Burke, Liam. *The Comic Book Film Adaptation: Exploring Modern Hollywood's Leading Genre*. Jackson: University Press of Mississippi, 2015.

Curtin, Michael, Jennifer Holt, and Kevin Sanson. *Distribution Revolution: Conversations about the Digital Future of Film and Television*: Berkeley: University of California Press, 2014.

Keating, Gina. *Netflixed: The Epic Battle for America's Eyeballs*. New York: Portfolio/Penguin, 2012.

McDonald, Paul, and Janet Wasko. *The Contemporary Hollywood Film Industry*. Malden, MA; Oxford: Blackwell, 2008.

Parenti, Michael. *Make-Believe Media: The Politics of Entertainment*. New York: St. Martin's Press, 1991.

Powers, Stephen, David J. Rothman, and Stanley Rothman. *Hollywood's America: Social and Political Themes in Motion Pictures*. Boulder, CO: Westview, 1996.

Prindle, David. *Risky Business: The Political Economy of Hollywood*. Boulder: Westview, 1993.

Rafter, Nicole. *Shots in the Mirror: Crime Films and Society*. Oxford: Oxford University Press, 2006.

Tryon, Chuck. *On-Demand Culture: Digital Delivery and the Future of Movies*. New Brunswick: Rutgers University Press, 2013.

Webster, James G. *The Marketplace of Attention: How Audiences Take Shape in a Digital Age*. Cambridge, MA: MIT Press, 2014.

NOTES

1. While there are many definitions of "art," the key distinction between art and product, from the perspective of many, lies in the motives of the artist. This point

of view is well summarized by one author, who writes, "While the concept of art *in* industrial civilizations has broadened to an extraordinary degree in terms of medium and content, it has, at least implicitly, narrowed in terms of use, function, and meaning, a narrowing of the relation of art *to* its context. This is the concept of art as being purely for esthetic contemplation, art for art's sake, pure art, and the necessity of the uselessness of an object *to* be called 'art.'" Evelyn Payne Hatcher, *Art as Culture: An Introduction to the Anthropology of Art,* 2nd ed. (Westport, CT: Bergin & Garvey, 1999), 8–9.

2. Douglas Kellner, "Film, Politics, and Ideology: Reflections on Hollywood Film in the Age of Reagan," *Velvet Light Trap* 27 (1991): 9–24.

3. For an important and thorough discussion of the business of Hollywood, see Edward Jay Epstein, *The Big Picture: The New Logic of Money and Power in Hollywood* (New York: Random House, 2005).

4. David F. Prindle, *Risky Business: The Political Economy of Hollywood* (Boulder, CO: Westview, 1993), 90.

5. Prindle, *Risky Business,* 98. Prindle notes that Hollywood "would still be a liberal community even if it contained no Jews" (99).

6. Patricia Evans, "Jews in American Cinema," in *Political Companion to American Film,* ed. Gary Crowdus (Chicago: Lakeview Press, 1994), 223.

7. See Steven Alan Carr, *Hollywood and Anti-Semitism: A Cultural History up to World World War II* (Cambridge: Cambridge University Press, 2001), particularly chapter 9.

8. Box Office Mojo, "Studio Market Share," http://www.boxofficemojo.com/studio/ (accessed December 31, 2015).

9. See John E. Moser, "'Gigantic Engines of Propaganda': The 1941 Senate Investigation of Hollywood," *Historian* 63, no. 4 (2001): 731–51; *Academic Search Complete,* December 2015; and Harold Brackman, "The Attack on 'Jewish Hollywood': A Chapter in the History of Modern American Anti-Semitism," *Modern Judaism* 20, no. 1 (2000): 1–19. For a current illustration of this, google the term *degenerate Hollywood* on your computer.

10. Stephen Powers, David J. Rothman, and Stanley Rothman, *Hollywood's America: Social and Political Themes in Motion Pictures* (Boulder, CO: Westview Press, 1996), 252–53. For a somewhat more recent version of this study with the same basic results, emphasizing among other things the overrepresentation of Jews in the "cultural elite," see Stanley Rothman and Amy E. Black, "Media and Business Elites: Still in Conflict?" *Public Interest* 143 (2001): 72.

11. Martin Scorsese and Michael Henry Wilson, *A Personal Journey with Martin Scorsese through American Movies* (New York: Hyperion, 1997), 20.

12. Michael Medved, *Hollywood vs. America* (New York: Harper Collins, 1993). For a less nuanced but more recent version of this argument, see Ben Shapiro, *Primetime Propaganda: The True Hollywood Story of How the Left Took Over Your TV* (Northampton, MA: Broadside Books, 2012).

13. For a thorough discussion of the groupthink phenomenon, see Irving L. Janis, *Groupthink,* 2nd ed. (Boston: Houghton Mifflin, 1983).

14. The distinguishing characteristic of the serial form is the fact that the segments must be viewed in sequence from beginning to end, in order to follow the

narrative. This sort of programming is only possible when there is easy access to video recordings and, even more convenient, view on demand.

15. See Michael Bywater, "They're Not Selling Movies to You, They're Selling You to the Movies," *New Statesman* 126, no. 4321 (1997): 42; for a technical discussion of the marketing of film, see Sanjeev Swami, "Research Perspectives at the Interface of Marketing and Operations: Applications to the Motion Picture Industry," *Marketing Science* 25, no. 6 (2006): 670–73, or Jeff Ulin, *The Business of Media Distribution: Monetizing Film, TV, and Video Content in an Online World,* 2nd ed. (Waltham, MA: Focal Press, 2013).

16. Motion Picture Association of America (MPAA), "2014 Theatrical Statistics Summary," 2, http://www.mpaa.org/wp-content/uploads/2015/03/MPAA-Theatrical-Market-Statistics-2014.pdf (accessed January 2, 2016).

17. MPAA, "2014 Theatrical Statistics Summary," 12.

18. Gallup Organization, http://www.gallup.com/poll/172439/party-identification-varies-widely-across-age-spectrum.aspx (accessed January 2, 2016).

19. Pew Foundation, *Political Typologies Shift with Age,* http://www.pewresearch.org/fact-tank/2014/07/09/the-politics-of-american-generations-how-age-affects-attitudes-and-voting-behavior/ (accessed January 2, 2016).

20. Jon A. Krosnick, "The Stability of Political Preferences: Comparisons of Symbolic and Nonsymbolic Attitudes," *American Journal of Political Science* 35, no. 3 (1991): 547–76; Markus Prior, "You've Either Got It or You Don't? The Stability of Political Interest over the Life Cycle," *Journal of Politics* 72, no. 3 (2010): 747–66.

21. B. J. Bushman et al., "Gun Violence Trends in Movies," *Pediatrics* 132, no. 6 (2013): 1014–18, http://pediatrics.aappublications.org/content/pediatrics/132/6/1014.full.pdf (accessed January 2, 2016).

22. Bushman et al., "Gun Violence Trends in Movies," figure 1.

23. Bushman et al., "Gun Violence Trends in Movies," figure 1.

24. Box Office Mojo, *Worldwide Grosses,* http://www.boxofficemojo.com/alltime/world/ (accessed January 2, 2016).

25. It should be noted that the worldwide grosses listed above are *not* controlled for inflation. The three top-grossing films for all time, when controlling for inflation, are *Gone with the Wind* (1939; this film is *The Birth of a Nation* [1915] "lite"), *Star Wars* (fighting aliens again), and *The Sound of Music* (singing and running away from the Nazis).

26. Box Office Mojo, *Domestic Grosses,* http://www.boxofficemojo.com/alltime/domestic.htm (accessed January 3, 2016).

27. US Government, Federal Bureau of Investigation, *Uniform Crime Reports,* https://www.fbi.gov/about-us/cjis/ucr/crime-in-the.u.s/2013/crime-in-the-u.s.-2013/tables/1tabledatadecoverviewpdf/table_1_crime_in_the_united_states_by_volume_and_rate_per_100000_inhabitants_1994-2013.xls (accessed January 3, 2016).

4

Film Content: Cause or Effect?

In this chapter, I examine the issue of causality. In a book on the relationship between film and politics, it is important to study the issue of causality at two levels. First, if it can be demonstrated that film and, in a larger sense, the media create some kind of undesirable behavior, then media content becomes a cause for political action. Calls for censorship, boycotts, or voluntary industry controls would have little meaning if there were no direct relationship between media depictions and behavior. At another level, the issue of causality is also important to the central theme of this book, that media and film content is a reflection of the sensibilities of at least some segments of our society.

In chapter 3, I present evidence to the effect that the most lucrative audience for films is generally less political and more socially liberal than those who don't go to the movies. In combination with the fact that the international market, one that is not that responsive to American domestic politics, has become the most important market for American film means that film content will be generally apolitical unless it is slated for a domestic audience. *Selma* (2014), for example, a film based on the life of Martin Luther King Jr., was a very political film and generated a lively political debate, but it generated almost nothing in foreign sales (and was no more than a mediocre performer domestically). The same could be said for *American Sniper* (2014), which was the top-grossing domestic film for the year but didn't make the top ten internationally.

Thus, to a large extent, film content seems to be the consequence of a conscious decision to market films abroad. And in that effort, the result is a higher body count. But does that spike in violence have an effect on behavior?

It appears to many that the body count in movies contributes to crime

93

rates or that relaxed sexual attitudes on film drive increases in teenage preg-nancy rates. As one set of authors sums it up,

> In research on aggressive behavior, it is generally believed that exposure to vio-lent images such as those typically found in horrid fiction is capable of produc-ing certain short-term responses through activation of cognitive structures semantically related to hostile action. In the same way that byproducts of priming can impact the development of social perceptions, activation of vari-ous cognitive structures may also influence displayed social behavior. Follow-ing exposure to materials with violent images or expressions, additional aggressive thoughts, scripts, and schema can be primed.[1]

But in this charge are a number of assumptions and alternative explana-tions that need to be examined. Also, it is quite unlikely that cause and effect in this case is simply unidirectional, or not influenced by other inter-vening variables such as the nature of the message or the degree of parental involvement.[2]

First, the influence of movies on socialization and behavior is probably the least significant of any of the entertainment media, and the entertain-ment media are probably not a terribly important influence on the behav-ior of individuals in general. The fact is that many studies of socialization, political and otherwise, suggest that the most significant variable in de-termining media influence is reinforcement, or the repeated and intense exposure to an influence.[3] Furthermore, age and maturity seem to be determinant factors as well.[4] The more mature the individual, the less likely the exposure is to have a lasting impact on an individual's beliefs or behavior.

Because the age of the viewer and duration of exposure are such impor-tant variables, feature films are an unlikely source of many socialized behaviors and beliefs, if for no other reason than that moviegoing is a dis-crete experience. While viewing a film may be an intense experience, it is not a long-lasting one. Furthermore, the context of viewing a film, the movie theater, cannot be mistaken for anything but make-believe. In addi-tion, while television shows such as the news can be watched continuously over long periods or video games played for hours on end, it is uncommon for a filmgoer, even an enthusiastic one, to see a film more than a couple of times. Finally, the rating system, albeit imperfect and spottily enforced, does at least keep the youngest children out of adult films. It is true that films can now be streamed by almost anyone and that there are fewer ways to limit the viewing of a rented film, but the fact remains that serial con-sumption of media is more likely to occur via the television or the video game. In addition, while in the relatively distant past, feature films were the most prominent form of media entertainment, in the modern context, films are but one of many competing forms of entertainment. Finally, as we have seen, the audience for film is getting older. Thus, to single out movies as harmful or even enormously influential is to ignore the multitude of other, stronger influences on behavior.

To the extent that films have any influence at all on the socialization of children and young adults, they seem to reinforce existing beliefs. In one study, a researcher found that among young adults ($N = 709$), those who were already predisposed toward conservative ideology were repelled by what they perceived as liberal attitudes in feature films and that the only effect a film had on those youngsters was, if anything, to harden their conservative predisposition. By the same token, young people who were predisposed toward liberal beliefs were repelled by film messages that they perceived as being objectionable, such as violence against women, but were otherwise unaffected by the liberal lifestyle characteristics portrayed in films.[5]

Therefore, because children generally have their most sustained and profound contact with their parents, the home is the most important influence on a child's socialization. Other institutions besides the family that may influence a child's socialization are school, church, peers, and the media, probably in that order of importance. Despite some notable instances in which a link was made between a particular movie and a particular event, the connection is so tenuous and so many other factors are at work that it would be impossible to draw a direct causal connection. For example, the gunmen in the tragic Columbine High School shootings were said to have modeled their crime after an incident portrayed in the movie *The Basketball Diaries* (1995). However, so many other factors were involved—the perpetrators' being bullied in school, their circumvention of gun laws, their being influenced by other media (such as violent video games)—that to pin the blame on any one factor would be impossible. In fact, for lack of evidence, federal courts in a couple of cases dismissed lawsuits filed against film producers and video game distributors by the parents of some of the victims of Columbine and another school shooting in Kentucky.[6]

Since Columbine there have been a couple of mass shootings in movie theaters. On July 20, 2012, James Eagan Holmes shot up a Cineplex theatre in Aurora, Colorado, killing twelve and wounding seventy others. The film that was screening at the time was *The Dark Knight Rises* (2012), part of the Batman serial. Holmes does reference the movie once in his notebook that was released during the trial. The reference, which doesn't make much sense, reads, "Embraced the hatred. The Dark Knight Rises."[7] However, it does not appear that he actually saw the movie, as it was released that day. Instead, he probably chose the theater because it was likely to be crowded and it had the kind of configuration he was looking for. But to say there was any direct connection between the content of *The Dark Knight Rises* and the Aurora shooting doesn't seem to make sense.

The next major movie theater shooting was in Lafayette, Louisiana, on July 23, 2015, when a man opened fire in a crowded movie theater, killing two people before he, himself, was killed. The movie that was screening was *Trainwreck* (2015), a romantic comedy.

There are always exceptions to any general rule. Certain individuals, no matter what their age, are so disturbed as to be susceptible to violent or antisocial behavior portrayed in film. However, it is hard to act on such an assumption. What restrictions should we place on the content of film to prevent the rare incident, and would it make any difference anyway? How can we predict what a disturbed individual will do when exposed to even the most innocuous film message or plot variation taken out of context? What, if any, is the predictable causal relationship between film and behavior?

The answer to this question is not as obvious as it may seem. Some politicians and pundits are fond of arguing that movies and the media in general are a terrible influence on American society. However, implicit in this statement are a number of assumptions that need to be addressed, primarily related to the issue of causality. The nature of causality is always difficult to outline in the social context. To demonstrate, for example, that violent movies cause violent behavior is fraught with methodological peril.

First of all is the question of the direction of causality. To say that one thing causes another is to go beyond a simple correlation. The sun rises and the rooster crows: the relationship is close and consistent, but to say that the rooster's crowing causes the sun to rise is a jump in logic and is inaccurate as well. Thus, the statement that movie violence causes actual violence is a statement that assumes a relationship that is not supported by mere correlation. Nevertheless, it is an empirical, testable proposition. In the last chapter, I argue that because the film industry is a business in a free market, the market generally drives film content. Thus, the content of film more likely reflects our society (or, more accurately, the tastes of the audience for movies) than the other way around.

Second, and just as difficult to demonstrate, is the degree and nature of causality within a given context. It is not enough to argue that because the incidence of violence coincides with the release of a violent film that one thing causes another. In the parlance of the methodologist, the relationship could be totally spurious.[8] Causation in this relationship implies that in the absence of violent movies, violent behavior would be less likely. However, since film viewing is such a universal experience and has been so for most of this century, it is difficult to know what would have happened in the absence of film. Nevertheless, we can examine this proposition by looking at things from a comparative perspective. Is violence less prominent in societies where American films are not screened, or was violence less evident before the advent of the movies?

In the twentieth century, the three greatest genocides committed were by regimes in states where American movies were heavily censored or strictly forbidden. Hitler's Germany, Stalin's Russia, and Pol Pot's Cambodia were hardly influenced by American film. The same can generally be said for states where the slaughter of citizens is more or less sanctioned by the government—for example, in the former Yugoslavia, Rwanda, Red China, Afghanistan, Syria, and so on. Even the most cursory examination of the list of states involved in wholesale slaughter of civilians indicates that the operative factor leading to violence in those countries may be the absence of democratic rule or some other factor, not the screening of *Taxi Driver* (1976). Furthermore, it is difficult to argue that before the advent of film society was a less violent place. How many assaults, rapes, and murders went unreported in the South before the end of slavery? If *12 Years a Slave* (2013) is anywhere near an accurate depiction of the treatment of people held as slaves in the South, and it is based on a journal of the actual experiences of an individual, then pre-media violence in the South was ubiquitous. The fact that we now define the killing of a black man in Mississippi as murder doesn't necessarily mean that there are more murders per capita now in Mississippi than there were one hundred years ago. The murders now are just reported more often.

But what I am referring to here is mainly organized violence. What about the influence of film on criminal interpersonal violence? While the United States has one of the highest incarceration rates in the world, it has an average intentional murder rate (111 out of 218; Honduras is number one).[9] Thus, at least from the comparative perspective, the presence of a free and unfettered media seems to make no difference in the rate of violent crime in the United States.

In fact, free media may actually be associated with a lower rate of criminality and violence. It should be noted that many authoritarian states have rates of crime lower than that of the United States—Iran and Russia, for instance. The crime rate in either society, however, is not a good indicator of the amount of violence it experiences. Russia is a state in which the peace maintained is the peace of the authoritarian state. Iran is a "peaceful" place, where the state has issued an execution order for the author Salman Rushdie that could best be described as an officially sanctioned contract for murder.

Another way to use the comparative approach to test the proposition that film violence causes actual violence is to look at crime from the regional perspective. It is fairly clear that criminal violence varies greatly within the United States from one locality to another. To demonstrate a definite link between film violence and real violence, we would have to show that, all things being equal, moviegoing is much more common in the poorer neighborhoods of South Central Los Angeles, East Saint Louis, or the South Bronx, which happen to have higher-than-average rates of crime. Besides the fact that there are virtually no movie theaters in those locales, this argument may suggest that poverty leads to crime (and the other way around), but not that movies lead to crime.

Nevertheless, besides violent crime, films may stimulate other types of interpersonal behavior that is objectionable—for example, in the United States, the decreasing age at which teens engage in sexual activity or the frequency with which they engage in sex. In sum, since about 1995 (to 2010), rates of teenage pregnancy, abortion, birth rates, and sexual activity have actually been on the decline, dropping by about one-third.[10] Also, in the 1990s the ages at which children and teens were arrested for violent crimes and the vicious character of those crimes seemed to be changing for the worse. But that trend began to reverse as well.[11]

While it is difficult to say exactly why this drop occurred, arguing that the media has much of a part in this, in either the promotion or the reduction of undesirable behavior, is a stretch. At the very least, if there is a connection, then the media must be given credit for the good as well as blame for the bad. Furthermore, there is certainly a plethora of alternative, plausible explanations for the undesirable behavior of the young—such as the ready availability of guns, the higher rates of poverty among the young, and a lack of parental supervision with the economic necessity of having both parents work outside the home.

CAUSE OR EFFECT: MOVIES AND THE BEHAVIORAL APPROACH

The question of whether film content drives human behavior is an important focus of investigation by behavioral scientists. Consequently, there are literally volumes of research on the topic of media content and behavior. As noted above, however, it is not enough to simply point out a simultaneous increase in actual violence and on-screen violence and then declare that movies cause violence. If I have a cup of coffee every morning, that certainly does not cause the sun to rise—likewise for movies and violence. The former does not necessarily cause the latter. In fact, it could be the other way around. In a previous chapter, I present evidence to suggest that public attitudes drive film content and not the other way around—which is a theory that is supported not only by the evidence presented here but also by pretty much everything we know about classical economics.

First, it is important to state the obvious. A significant amount of evidence suggests a kind of relationship between media violence and aggressive behavior. In a statement before a subcommittee of the Senate Judiciary Committee in October 1984, John P. Murray, testifying on behalf of the American Psychological Association, pretty much summed up the massive body of evidence in regard to the relationship between television violence and behavior:

> The first question raised the issue of whether viewers of televised violence are more aggressive than other people. On the basis of research evidence, I conclude that the answer to this question is emphatically yes. Children and adults who more frequently watch violent programs tend to hold attitudes and values which favor the use of aggression to resolve conflicts. They also tend to behave more aggressively. That does not necessarily mean that television causes this aggression but at least these studies show that there is a link between the two.
>
> The second question is: "Does television violence produce aggressive behavior?" The answer to this question, again, seems to be yes—based on studies conducted both in laboratories and in naturalistic settings observing preschool children, school age youngsters, college students, and adults. The experimental evidence seems to support the notion that viewing violence does lead to aggressive behavior in these settings and that there seems to be a long-term relationship between viewing violence and behaving aggressively.[12]

Nothing that I can find in more recent studies seems to undermine the basic premise of this statement that people who are predisposed toward violence tend to watch violent programming and that the viewing of that programming tends to reinforce existing tendencies.[13] However, in one study, the authors suggest that in the short and medium term (three weeks), the release of a violent film actually coincides with *a reduction* in violent crime, perhaps as violent people are actually, in watching a movie, busy doing something else.[14]

There is a wide-ranging and lively debate over media violence and cause and effect. There is in the field of the social sciences an intramural debate over the value of looking at society from the behavioral perspective as opposed to the structural perspective. This refers to the fact that behaviorists start with the premise that the sum of society's parts (individuals) are equal to its whole, whereas structuralists believe that the whole is greater than and different from its parts. More simply put, according to behaviorialists— who come mainly out of the field of psychology (although the subfield of social psychology is a bridge to the structuralist school)—if a phenomenon can be observed at the individual level, then that behavior will presumably register at the societal level as well. Thus, if it can be demonstrated that individuals respond with actual violence to viewing violence on screen, we can assume that film violence begets actual violence. This seems like a pretty commonsense approach to looking at human behavior. However, it is, when examined more closely, a flawed and even preposterous point of view.

Structuralists (also known as institutionalists) believe that behavior is largely a function of setting. In other words, a person's behavior results from societal pressure. A husband remains faithful to his wife because of the constraints imposed by the institution of marriage. He may remain faithful because the Bible tells him so, and he believes that he will be punished by God if he cheats on his wife. Or he may come to believe that by remaining faithful to his wife, he serves society and his family. Or he may remain faithful to his wife because he loves her and prefers her to other women. Or other women may find a married man to be a less attractive partner, and so on. The least likely explanation for his faithfulness is that the act of marriage leads to a physical diminution of sexual desire for women. The institution of marriage mediates and redirects those desires. Thus, if a study of married men was to show that most husbands still lusted after other women (a result that would be quite likely), we still could not assume that men would be generally unfaithful to their wives. The institutional explanation for the tendency of husbands to remain faithful to their wives is probably more accurate.

The structural explanation is probably more accurate in other settings as well. People act, dress, and behave in ways that are largely dictated by circumstance. This is not to say that people never act inappropriately; rather, it can be said that inappropriate behavior is a mistake committed by a normally rational person, the irrational response of an irrational person, and/ or the result of some other, mediating factors. So it is with violence and other undesirable behaviors. We all may have a certain capacity for violence. In general, however, the institutions of society—such as the family, religion, and the law—mediate our tendency toward violence.

Much of the evidence-based arguments in favor of some sort of restriction of film and television content rely heavily on the research of behavioral scientists.[15] That being the case, therefore, much of the criticism of film content suffers from what methodologists would call the ecological *fallacy*, or the unjustified assumption that the sum of the whole is equal to its parts. The argument that movie violence causes societal violence may fail simply because of the societal constraints on violence, such as the law, the family, and the church.

Just as it is true that most studies examining the link between media violence and aggressive behavior have supported that theory, it is also true that the relationships demonstrated are fairly weak (albeit statistically significant). The person influenced by violent film content is also influenced by a myriad of other internal and external factors, such as societal constraints and personal inhibitions. Thus, if the link could be tested in the larger macro sense, then, all things being equal, there would be virtually no significant link between societal violence and media violence. Remember that in the analysis in the previous chapter, movie violence lags societal violence and not the other way around. Therefore, the direction of causality at the societal level, where it really matters, is in the opposite direction than the one assumed by those who on the basis of behavioral research make the mistake of ignoring the ecological fallacy. At worst, media influence is a reinforcement of existing behavioral tendencies. But those tendencies, in all but the most extreme cases, are compensated for by societal and other pressures. Even if it might be possible to demonstrate that there exists a relationship between media violence and aggressive behavior, this does not mean that a crime will be the result.

Furthermore, we would have to assume that just as media-depicted acts of violence stimulate corresponding behavior, so too do media-depicted acts of heroism, kindness, and generosity. Certainly, those who argue that violence and sex in the movies have pernicious effects on society because they influence behavior would also have to take into account the positive influence of graphic screen generosity and kindness. This fact, the good messages of film, would have a countervailing effect on screen violence at both the individual and the societal level that would offset much or all of the damage.

There has been so much research done on the relationship between screen and actual violence that it is now possible to summarize these results through meta-analyses. A meta-analysis is a collection and integration of any number of studies on the same general topic that controls for differences and samples. In one such meta-analysis, Susan Hearold summarizes the results of some 230 studies on the relationship between televised and actual violence. Her study produced three important findings: first, the more fantastic the setting of the violence depicted (cartoon violence, for instance), the weaker the relationship between viewing and actual violence; second, programs designed to produce prosocial behaviors had a stronger effect on positive behaviors than violent programs had on negative behaviors; and third, the relationship between media and actual violence was stronger for males in their adolescent years than it was for comparatively aged females. Thus, it seems that positive messages and context in fact can mediate the message of broadcast violence.[16]

In another, similar meta-analysis, Haejung Paik and George Comstock summarize the results of 217 studies. While their results are again quite similar to those of Hearold, the authors also found that the strength of the relationship between depicted and actual violence was over twice as strong when produced in the laboratory as opposed to that demonstrated in more naturalistic settings. Thus, laboratory results are misleading if for no other reason than the fact that they overstate the relationship between screened and actual violence.[17]

Nevertheless, there are quite a few studies in the laboratory and using survey research that show a distinct relationship between viewed and actual violence among children. In 1963, psychologist Leonard Eron began to follow the development of a group of children from one small New York village. In that study, he evaluated television-viewing habits, family settings, peer evaluations, and other relevant environmental data. In following the maturation of these children across time, he found a distinct relationship connecting television-viewing habits at age eight, violent behavior at age eighteen, and criminal behavior at age thirty.[18] This study has lots of potential methodological problems; yet there still seems to be plenty of evidence to show at least some relationship between viewing violence and perpetrating actual violence, albeit mediated by other factors.[19]

Presumably, then, the most impressionable segment of the population—children—is the most vulnerable to the messages sent to them through the media. These children are "most impressionable," meaning that because of their youth and inexperience they are to a certain extent "blank slates" that can be imprinted by what they see in real life or fiction. If that experience involves the use of violence for the resolution of conflicts, children will absorb that lesson, which in turn will be reinforced by the programming they choose to watch and so forth. For adults, particularly those who are not predisposed toward violence, they will choose not to watch violent programming, which in turn will not reinforce any violent tendencies that they already have.

What all this suggests is that we have to be careful about corrupting our youth. In fact, everything from voluntary movie and television-rating codes to the Federal Communications Commission's regulating children's programming to the mandatory V-chip, that can be used to set the parameters of ratings of shows children are allowed to see, has been an effort to protect children and probably the rest of us from violent programing. Nevertheless, with the advent of streaming video and the decline of "broadcast" television (usually carried by cable), parental control has again been challenged. However, Netflix and Amazon Prime can be password protected, and parents can monitor Internet use.

But to go beyond regulating the media to protect children is not only of questionable constitutionality but also of questionable value. In the same studies noted above, it appears that other factors mediate the effects of televised violence, such as intelligence, genetics, gender, levels of self-esteem, and even ethnicity (blacks seem less negatively affected by violence than whites). There is an inverse relationship between intelligence and the effects of televised violence. Women are less susceptible than males, and low levels of self-esteem correlate with the negative effects of media violence.

It would be very difficult and, in fact, impossible to select for IQ and levels of self-esteem, not to mention gender, in the screening of a movie.

Media audiences tend to be self-selecting. People who want to watch violence will watch violence. Even if we censor the content of adult cinema or television to control for violence, what do we do about other violent programming in the media? Can we order news organizations to stop reporting on violent crime or war on the supposition that such reporting encourages violent behavior? And what about art? Should *Hamlet*, a play that ends in a bloodbath, be performed for adults only?

What these examinations of over four hundred studies on the relation of media violence to actual violence show is that there is really very little actual scientific evidence to support popular and widely held assumptions about the effects of media on violence at the societal level.[20] This is not to say that the evidence is fairly solid at the individual level that media depictions influence behavior. But at the macro level, the evidence is not there. In fact, the opposite may be true. According to at least one researcher,

> Claims that the persistently high levels of violence in mass media, mostly television, are largely responsible for violence in society represent narrow views of very large issues. These narrow views overlook essential elements of both phenomena—violence and media. Direct models of interpersonal violence in families and in the community probably give rise to more violent behavior than indirect models in media. Disinhibitory and provocative aspects of media probably do as much or more to trigger violent behavior than violent narratives and violent actions. Comprehensive meta-analysis indicates that prosocial messages on television can have greater effects on behavior than antisocial messages. These data support the contention that mass media can play a strong and positive role in alleviating some of the distress of victims of community violence, and in redirecting the behavior of some of its perpetrators so as to protect the children.[21]

The contradiction between the perceived and real role of media effects at the macro level suggests that most "evidence" purporting to demonstrate a relationship between media (particularly film media) and undesired behaviors at the societal level is probably science with an agenda. And for those studies that do purport to establish a relationship between entertainment media and undesired behaviors, media scholar David Gauntlett cautions us to be just as worried about the pernicious influence of media effects studies as we are about the effects of media.[22] He suggests that we look for any of ten possible flaws in studies that purport to support a causal relationship between media and undesirable behaviors:

1. *Researchers attack the problem based on faulty but generally accepted assumptions.*
   If researchers assume that there is a relationship between media and behavior and then study the relationship between media and behav-

ior, they are making an unjustified assumption. For example, if we assume that marijuana smoking leads to heroin addiction (since most heroin addicts have smoked marijuana), we might be tempted to look for links between marijuana smoking and heroin use without considering that most marijuana smokers don't graduate to heroin. Without taking this last fact into consideration, we may establish a relationship between marijuana and heroin use that is completely spurious.

2. *Researchers treat children as blank slates.*

To say that media influences children is one thing, but to assume that media *causes* children to act in a particular way is a jump in logic. Children can and do discern on their own right from wrong. That means they can withstand certain types of messages (even mixed ones) without any harm. General assumptions to the effect that children cannot decipher and discard certain types of messages have to at least be qualified.

3. *Researchers have an ideological axe to grind.*

Any study not subject to rigorous professional peer review is likely to be biased at best and flawed at worst.

4. *Researchers fail to define what they are studying.*

To say that media violence causes violence begs the question of what type of behaviors researchers are trying to explain. There is violence in crime, violence in war, psychological cruelty, doing violence to the truth, violence officially sanctioned by the state, spanking children, beating wives, and so on. What actions are related to what consequences?

5. *Results of studies in a laboratory may not be transferable to the world at large.*

As noted, meta-analyses suggest that laboratory experiments tend to exaggerate effects. Subjects are often subject to stimuli that they wouldn't encounter in the real world (they are shown films, for example, that they wouldn't normally go to see) and are then asked to react to situations that they wouldn't encounter in real life. It is difficult, if not impossible, to extrapolate from that kind of test what people will do in real life, not to mention within the context of society as a whole.

6. *The methodology of media effects studies can be profoundly flawed.*

While there are many problems with these studies, such as the ecological fallacy, the main problem (as stressed) is the use of correlations to impute causality. Just because two events co-vary does not support a causal relationship. Professional researchers would probably not make these kinds of mistakes (and still get their work published), but nonprofessionals in support of a particular point of view can misinterpret and misapply academic research.

7. *The definition of undesirable behaviors serves a particular ideological perspective.*

Incidents such as the police shooting in Ferguson, Missouri, of an unarmed African American man can be viewed by different people and, in fact, different communities in different ways. If in a study of media effects, undesirable violence or sexual activities, or political or lifestyle choices, are narrowly defined to proscribe some behaviors and allow for others, then there may be researcher bias. To say that sexual relations outside marriage is a depiction of an undesirable behavior is to make an ethical statement, but such an ethical judgment cannot be made within the context of a scientific experiment without compromising the results. Apparently, for many people sex outside of marriage is not immoral, which brings us to our next point.

8. *Researcher selection bias takes on the aspect of a public censor.*

A viewer may not care for televised wrestling matches. A viewer may not agree with certain political opinions. If that viewer defines, for the purposes of a study of media effects, some kind of show or behavior as being undesirable, then the researcher sets oneself up as a public censor. As noted, self-described conservatives are more likely to object to media content. They themselves are not influenced by that content. But if their dissatisfaction results in public policy or regulations that delimit the media behaviors or messages they don't like, they are effectively acting as public censors.

9. *Studies of media effects are not grounded in theory.*

To say that one thing causes another is not to say *why* one thing causes another. We may be able to show that media violence has an effect on children, but the more interesting question may be *why*. If, for example, children who are most likely to be affected by media messages are those who come from broken homes, the answer may not be to shield all children from certain types of programming but to encourage better parenting at home. But in doing research that is not well grounded in theory, "we may be kicking the dog because the cat scratched the furniture."

10. *Research does not attempt to understand the meanings of the media.*

Most of us can divine the subtle meaning in complex story plots, even if those stories contain what might be seen, when taken out of context, as disgusting or despicable behavior. A number of studies have shown that audiences are able to discern nuanced meanings from subtle plotlines.[23] And thank goodness they can. What would literature and entertainment be without the author being able to assume this ability on the part of the audience?

It is crucial to this discussion of cause and effect to expand on this last point—that is, to demonstrate that even if there are messages or events in film that, when taken out of context, are hard to understand or tolerate, most of us (adults) are capable of making up our own minds.

VIOLENT PROGRAMMING IN CONTEXT

The fact is that we live in a violent world and a violent society. We have plenty of opportunities beyond the cinema or entertainment television to view violence—UFC martial arts, football, and boxing, for example. We also have many legitimate outlets for engaging in and celebrating violent behavior. The cinema or television are certainly not the only, and probably not even the primary, sources of violence in our society.

The suggestion here is that there is not even a consensus as to what constitutes "violence" in the meaning of film critics. Most of us would agree that under some circumstances violence is an acceptable option. In time of war, in the application of the death penalty for murder, or in the pursuit of self-defense, the use of violence is sanctioned by society. Sometimes the violence in films is even presented in such a way as to be emulated. In *Sands of Iwo Jima* (1949), lots of people are killed, most of them Japanese, and within the context of the film that is acceptable. Even when the main character, played by John Wayne, is killed, the death is heroic, one to be emulated. Were we to evaluate the film's violence in context, most of us would regard it as acceptable violence as opposed to unacceptable violence. If we were to apply that standard, one that takes into account the "eye of the beholder," we would almost certainly find that films are a lot less violent than what we are led to believe.

Let us consider some of the many types of film violence. *Braveheart* (1995), for example, has lots of violence, almost all of which is placed in the appropriate context. English atrocities are dutifully recorded to put the Scottish rebellion into context. How could the viewer identify with the Scottish rebellion without feeling the sense of rage of the occupied toward the occupier? Furthermore, the battle scenes, which feature some of the best kill scenes in film history, capture the brutality, confusion, and heroism of hand-to-hand combat.

Other films demonstrate "cartoon" violence. *RoboCop* (1987) has, in my opinion, the best kill scene in history. A bad guy is doused with toxic waste, and, as he begins to melt, he is hit by a car that explodes him like a bowl of Jell-O. His remains are then wiped off the car with the windshield wipers.

Now that's cinema! It is hard to imagine that any adult with even a shred of sanity would take this scene seriously, much less go out and imitate it. However, within the context of this film, which is remarkably good, this sort of violence has internal consistency, so to speak.

Violence that is unjustified, however, is not uncommon in the modern cinema. The production code used to dictate that no act of evil, including the use of violence, could go unpunished. Now that the production code is no longer in effect, it is true that an act of unjustified violence can go unpunished with or without implications. Nevertheless, this sort of thing goes on a lot less often in the movies than we think. If for no other reason than that unpunished or nonconsequential violence is a hanging plotline, the "bad" type of violence is pretty rare. Furthermore, most of the bad type of violence is the result of brain-dead plot development or muddled thinking that went into the writing of films. Therefore, unjustified violence, as rare as it is, is probably more an act of omission rather than commission.

As noted at the beginning of this chapter, there has been a spike in the incidence of film violence that corresponds with an increasing reliance on foreign markets. Of necessity, films intended for a foreign market have to "translate" well into multiple cultures. The best way to do that is to limit dialogue, excise topics that are American centric, and have plenty of action. But one thing of note and one thing that is different about this violence targeted for foreign audiences is the care with which filmmakers avoid controversial topics. Resorting to violence in fighting aliens from outer space (*The Avengers*) or rampaging dinosaurs (*Jurassic World*) or international terrorists of the right kind (*Furious 7*) is unlikely to ruffle the feathers of audiences abroad. Thus, the modern blockbuster, while violent, is hardly culture specific. So, for example, this week the top-grossing film in the world is *Avengers: Age of Ultron* in every country except Australia and New Zealand (*Pitch Perfect*), Japan (*Cinderella*), China (*Furious 7*), and North Korea (with no American films). Therefore, what is lost in academic studies that track film violence from one era to the next is the subtle shift in the types of violence recorded.

Furthermore, American audiences are no more prone to movie violence that those filmgoers in other countries. In the previous chapter, I highlighted the top-grossing films of 2015 (worldwide). The top *domestic* grossing films (in order) in 2015 are *Jurassic World, Avengers: Age of Ultron, Furious 7, Inside Out,* and *Minions.* Besides the two animated movies, the only man-on-man violence in this lineup is violence against international terrorists. Just to compare, before 9/11, the top *domestic* grossing films for 1995, exactly twenty years ago, were (in order) *Toy Story, Batman Forever, Apollo 13, Pocahontas,* and *Ace Ventura: When Nature Calls.* By and large, this is a pretty wholesome lineup. The only film in the top ten domestic list that would qualify as a particularly disturbing film would be *Se7en,* which finished in 1995 at number nine. In the relative harmlessness of this collection of films, one characteristic stands out. When compared to the international lineup of top-grossing films for those years, the American list is relatively peaceful compared to the rest of the world. If that, then, is the case, complaints about violence in film or other types of undesirable messages are related to films that are not even that popular at home. Now it may be that video games or television are the offending media, but certainly not the movies.

ONE OTHER POINT: MOVIES IN CONTEXT

Up until now, we have generally conflated the behavioral effects of television and the cinema. Television viewing is much more ubiquitous. The average television viewer may watch as much as forty hours a week of television, while even a frequent filmgoer, who is in the minority of even filmgoers, will probably spend somewhat fewer than ten hours a week viewing movies in the theater. Thus, the cumulative effect of movie content will likely be less substantial, if for no other reason than that, for the average viewer, the amount of time spent viewing movies is less than that spent viewing television. Furthermore, going to the movies requires more of an effort than simply sitting down in front of a television set. To a large extent, film viewers are probably more selective about the films they see than the television they watch. Children aren't even allowed into many adult-themed movies. Thus, the negative effect of film violence is somewhat mitigated by the structure of the theatergoing experience.

Nowadays, it is the case with the advent of streaming video that access to movies and television shows with violent and sexual content is much more ubiquitous than before, even for children to watch. Nevertheless, the moviegoing experience, which is much more intimate, is much more likely to stimulate some kind of inappropriate behavior. Watching television, on a small screen with the distractions of modern life, is a very different and much less provocative experience than watching a movie in a theater.

Consequently, we are generally at a loss as to how to predict, much less act on, the information that purports how some films may motivate some individuals to violence. The behavioral studies in this regard, as numerous as they are, are hazy. It is true that John Hinckley watched *Taxi Driver* at least fifteen times before deciding to attempt to assassinate President Reagan in order to impress Jodie Foster. However, at the Hinckley trial, the prosecution's chief psychiatrist, Park Dietz, suggested that Hinckley probably didn't realize the movie's import to his motivations until he explored the issue in sessions with a psychiatrist while preparing for his trial.[24] If even Hinckley didn't know what motivated him to act, how can we? Furthermore, we have no idea how many others were obsessed with, and identified with, Travis Bickle (the main character in *Taxi Driver*) without trying to assassinate the president.

CONCLUSION

In this chapter, I examine the relationship between film content and societal behavior from the perspective of a social scientist rather than a psychologist. That is to say, that I am not willing to take the leap from the study of individual behavior to societal consequences. There is just too much more going on. In an earlier chapter, I present evidence to the effect that societal attitudes are much more of a determinant of film content than the other way around. This conclusion contradicts much of the criticism of film content that has emanated from conservative (and leftist) political circles. For those from the political Right, this conclusion means that to attack movies and their producers for their content is to miss the point. The causal relationship between film content and behavior is much more likely from the bottom up (audience demand to the producer) than from the top down (producer bias to the audience). But to blame filmmakers for doing what comes naturally to businesspeople and then to suggest that because one, say, ethnic group or another is "overrepresented" in Hollywood and thus the cause of a distortion is to miss the point in a rather ugly way. If film content is a problem (and I think it is not), both the patron who views feature films and the capitalist system that translates that demand into product may be in need of reform. In any other business, Protestants or Catholics or conservatives or liberals would do the same thing—respond to the market to serve their customers—or they wouldn't be in the business for long. For moralists, the options are not all that daunting. If they think that films made for primarily religious audiences will make money, there is a whole wide world of filmmaking for them to explore on their own nickel (as Mel Gibson has done with great success). But asking businesspeople to carry the word without compensation is un-American. Such a policy might be more appropriate in Iran.

From those on the Left who criticize film content for being too much in the service of the economic elite, pretty much the same response applies.[25] The public consumes what it wants to consume. The viewing public may be misguided in wanting to be entertained by films that trumpet the benefits of American democracy and its capitalist economy, but that is their choice. The Left has the same access to the economy as anyone else. Independent filmmakers can make and market their products on a shoestring—and make a bundle provided that there is an audience for their product. For example, consider the success of liberal filmmaker Michael Moore's production *Fahrenheit 9/11* (2004), which grossed $119 million with a production budget of $6 million.[26] While this may somewhat misrepresent actual access to the market, it is worth a try.

Is the shortage of progressive films a function of the capitalist system that suppresses dissent, or is it the failure of the political Left to put its money where its mouth is? Parenthetically, the Hollywood production crowd cannot be classified as part of this political Left. Hollywood money may be a big source of funding for the Democratic Party, but that does not mean that Hollywood money is socialist money. The movie production class is as capitalist as they come.

Finally, I have taken issue with behaviorialists or, more to the point, those who misuse behavioral studies to support their political agenda. The behavioral approach is limited to studying phenomena at the individual level. Influences on the individual, however, may not translate into large-scale influences on society. Furthermore, film violence needs to be viewed in context. While media violence may have an influence on aggressive behavior, so do other messages, many of which are countervailing.[27]

Much of what we see in movies can also be an affirmation of what is good and wholesome in America. Thus, it would make no sense to argue that the same Hollywood culture that produced *It's a Wonderful Lift* (1946) and *Mr. Smith Goes to Washington* (1939), wildly popular films that celebrate mainstream America, also produced *The Human Centipede I–III* (2009–2015), films that have to be the most disgusting of all time. Either the culture of Hollywood has changed or the films it produces reflect both the good and the bad (taste) in society.

What we have here is not so much a controversy about whether violent films cause actual violence; I argue that what we have here is no more than a matter of taste. But it is not enough for some to argue that many films and television shows are in bad taste. Because there are those in society who wish to censor films that are in bad taste and because they know that the First Amendment stands in their way, they have tried to invent a case for the negative public health consequences of lousy films. But in the end, lousy films are just that—lousy. We should be alarmed that people are so undemanding of the shows and movies they watch that they tolerate so much drivel. But that dynamic has more to say about the tastes of the public than it does about the degeneracy of Hollywood.

In the next chapter, I discuss what a bad film is—not what I think a bad film is (except for the purposes of illustration), but what for the individual viewer can be a standard for declaring a film good or bad. In this era of the third monopoly, the chances of walking into the wrong film or purchasing the wrong film on Netflix are substantially higher than what they have been in the past. As I have said, this is a good news–bad news story. There is a lot to see out there, and there is also a lot more trash. Use the next chapter, as you will improve your chances of enjoying the movies.

Feature Film: *Taxi Driver*

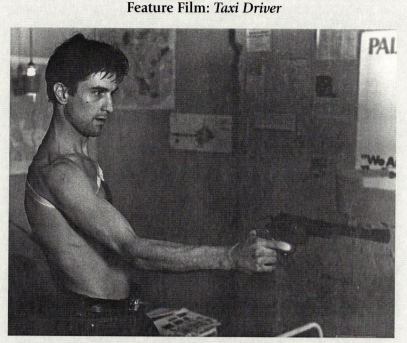

Taxi Driver, **Columbia Pictures, 1976**

Besides being regarded as one of the best films of all time—ranking eighty-second in the Internet Movie Database's top 250—this movie is also famous for having supposedly inspired John Hinckley to shoot President Ronald Reagan. If ever there were an example of the clash of First Amendment liberties and the public good, this is it. Does the artistic value of films such as this and their audience appeal outweigh the potential harm? If not, what should we do about it?

This is a film about a feeling. It may seem to be a film about a person, Travis Bickle, a disaffected Vietnam veteran who now works as a taxi driver. But this is in fact a film about alienation. Some people become so estranged from society that they cease to function as normal human beings. This was particularly a concern of the 1970s, as a huge number of Vietnam vets returned from the war without necessarily physical wounds but psychological wounds once known as "shell shock" but now diagnosed as PTSD, or post-traumatic stress disorder. A few years after every war, it seems, we have to deal with a cohort of young men whose lives were set off course by their service in war. *Taxi Driver* is simply an earlier rendition of the same drama that takes place later and in different ways in the recently released film *American Sniper* (2014).

In this film, Bickle, as portrayed by Robert De Niro, practically writhes with pain. And the thing that seems to eat at him the most is his gnawing loneliness. He is no longer capable of ordinary human contact. While that feeling is hard to describe, Martin Scorsese (the director) and De Niro capture that loneliness beautifully. Ultimately, Bickle's frustration boils over in a paroxysm of violence. After first failing to shoot the presidential candidate for whom the object of his affection (Betsy, played by Cybill Shepherd) works, he shoots his way into a brothel and frees from the bonds of child prostitution the other object of his affection (Iris, played by Jodie Foster). While we are never completely sure why he opts for this route of violence, it makes sense within the context of the film. He has to do something, or he will implode. It just so happens that the thing that he manages to do is generally for the good. But he could have just as easily gone the other way. Furthermore, by the end of the film we are never entirely sure that he isn't a ticking time bomb ready to go off again.

The violence in this film is horrendous. And that may have set John Hinckley off. I rather suspect, however, that the seduction scene is probably more to blame. In that scene, Harvey Keitel, playing a pimp, seduces young Iris. The scene is at the same time mesmerizing and in many ways just as horrifying as the violence that takes place later (even though the consummation takes place off screen). Despite the scene's emotional impact and the strong performances of Foster and Keitel, I don't recall that watching it made me want to shoot the president.

Besides Hinckley's crime, I wonder what other behaviors the film might have inspired. Did someone go nuts and try to get better mental health benefits for veterans? Did somebody go insane and try to get more stringent gun laws passed? Did somebody go off their rocker and try to stop the international trade in child prostitutes? Well, probably not. You have to be insane to be moved to action by this movie. Or maybe this movie isn't influential enough.

Don't agree? What do you think?

EXERCISE

After watching a film, write down what prevailing social behaviors are depicted in the film. Are the behaviors within the context of the film treated positively or negatively or without comment? Do you agree with the overall philosophy of the film as reflected in the treatment of political issues, social relations, and violence? How much violence is in the film, and how would you define it? Most important, do you think that the film has moved you to act in a way you normally wouldn't act?

SUGGESTED READINGS

Dill, Karen E. *How Fantasy Becomes Reality: Seeing Through Media Influence.* Oxford; New York: Oxford University Press, 2009.

Gauntlett, David. *Moving Experiences: Media Effects and Beyond.* Eastleigh, UK: John Libbey, 2005; Bloomington, IN: Distributed in North America by Indiana University Press, 2005.

Gentile, Douglas. *Media Violence and Children: A Complete Guide for Parents and Professionals,* 2nd ed. Santa Barbara, CA: ABC-CLIO, 2014.

Graber, Doris A., and Johanna Dunaway. *Mass Media and American Politics.* Thousand Oaks, CA: CQ Press, an imprint of Sage, 2015.

Groseclose, Tim. *Left Turn: How Media Bias Distorts the American Mind.* New York: St. Martin's Press, 2011.

McChesney, Robert Waterman. *Rich Media, Poor Democracy: Communication Politics in Dubious Times,* 2nd ed. New York: New Press, 2015.

Postman, Neil. *Amusing Ourselves to Death: Public Discourse in the Age of Show Business.* New York: Penguin Books, 2006.

NOTES

1. Ron Tamborini and Kristen Salomonson, "Horror's Effect on Social Perceptions and Behaviors," in *Horror Films: Current Research on Audience Preferences and Reactions,* ed. James B. Weaver and Ron Tamborini (Mahwah, NJ: Erlbaum, 1996), 186.

2. See E. Jo and L. Berkowitz, "A Priming Effect Analysis of Media Influences: An Update," in *Media Effects: Advances in Theory and Research,* ed. J. Bryant and D. Zillmann (Hillsdale, NJ: Erlbaum, 1994), 43–61; Jeanne Rogge Steele, "Teenage Sexuality and Media Practice: Factoring in the Influences of Family, Friends, and School," *Journal of Sex Research* 36, no. 4 (1999): 331–41; or Barbara J. Wilson, "Media and Children's Aggression, Fear, and Altruism," *The Future of Children* 18, no. 1 (2008): 87–118.

3. For example, see Marc J. Hetherington, "The Media's Role in Forming Voters' National Economic Evaluations in 1992," *American Journal of Political Science* 40, no. 2 (1996): 372–95, or Karen E. Dill, *How Fantasy Becomes Reality: Seeing Through Media Influence* (Oxford; New York: Oxford University Press, 2009).

4. See Jeffrey Jensen Arnett, "Adolescents' Uses of Media for Self-Socialization," *Journal of Youth and Adolescence* 24, no. 5 (1995): 519–33.

5. See David J. Jackson, *Entertainment and Politics: The Influence of Pop Culture on Young Adult Political Socialization* (New York: Lang, 2002), chapter 4.

6. *Sanders v. Acclaim Entertainment Inc.,* 188 F. Supp. 2d 1264 (D. Colo. 2002); *James v. Meow Media Inc.* (02–740); *James v. Meow Media Inc.,* 300 F.3d 683, 696 (6th Cir. 2002).

7. Will C. Holden and Carly Moore, "Aurora Theater Shooting Notebook Details Aired for First Time at Trial," Fox 31, Denver, May 26, 2015, http://kdvr.com/2015/05/26/raw-video-theater-shooting-notebook-details-aired-for-1st-time/ (accessed July 24, 2015).

8. Darrell Huff, *How to Lie with Statistics* (New York: Norton, 1993).

9. UNDOC, *Global Study on Homicide*, https://www.unodc.org/gsh/ (accessed July 27, 2015).

10. Heather Boonstra, "What Is Behind the Declines in Teen Pregnancy Rates?" *Guttmacher Policy Review* 17, no. 3 (2014).

11. US Department of Justice, "Trends in Juvenile Violent Crime," OJJDP Statistical Briefing Book, http://www.ojjdp.gov/ojstatbb/crime/JAR_Display.asp?ID = qa 05201 (accessed January 5, 2016).

12. Senate Subcommittee on Juvenile Justice, *Oversight on Alleged Media Violence as It May Affect Children*, 98th Cong., 2nd sess., 1985, 47.

13. See Faith McLellan, "Do Violent Movies Make Violent Children?" *Lancet* 359, no. 9305 (2002): 502; Brad J. Bushman and Craig A. Anderson, "Media Violence and the American Public: Scientific Facts versus Media Misinformation," *American Psychologist* 56, nos. 6–7 (June–July 2001): 477–89; J. Garbarino, "Violent Children: Where Do We Point the Finger of Blame?" *Archives of Pediatric Adolescent Medicine* 155 (2001): 13–14.

14. Gordon Dahl and Stefano DellaVigna, "Does Movie Violence Increase Violent Crime?" *Quarterly Journal of Economics* 124, no. 2 (2009).

15. See, for example, Committee on Public Education, American Academy of Pediatrics, "Media Violence," *Pediatrics* 108, no. 5 (November 2001): 1222–26.

16. Susan Hearold, "A Synthesis of 1043 Effects of Television on Social Behavior," in *Public Communication and Behavior*, vol. 1, ed. G. Comstock (Orlando, FL: Academic, 1986), 65–133; for a more recent discussion to this effect, see Douglas Gentile, ed., *Media Violence and Children: A Complete Guide for Parents and Professionals*, 2nd ed. (Santa Barbara, CA: ABC-CLIO, 2014), particularly chapter 14, as well as George Comstock, Erica Scharrer, and Jack Powers's "The Contribution of Meta-Analysis to the Controversy over Television Violence and Aggression," chapter 13 of the same book (381–412).

17. Haejung Paik and George Comstock, "The Effects of Television Violence on Antisocial Behavior: A Meta-Analysis," *Communication Research* 21 (1994): 515–46.

18. L. D. Eron, "Parent-Child Interaction, Television Violence and Aggression of Children," *American Psychologist* 27 (1982): 197–211.

19. For example, see Jessica Taylor Piotrowski and Patti M. Valkenburg, "Finding Orchids in a Field of Dandelions: Understanding Children's Differential Susceptibility to Media Effects," *American Behavioral Scientist* 59, no. 14 (2015): 1776–89, or Joseph A. Schwartz and Kevin M. Beaver, "Revisiting the Association between Television Viewing in Adolescence and Contact with the Criminal Justice System in Adulthood," *Journal of Interpersonal Violence* (2015): 0886260515576970.

20. Nevertheless, in November 2004, one of the most recent, albeit dated, polls on the subject, 62 percent of those in the general public who were surveyed believed that "Hollywood was lowering moral standards." *CBS News/New York Times* Poll, http://pollingreport.com/media.htm#Content (accessed January 8, 2016).

21. B. Z. Friedlander, "Community Violence, Children's Development, and Mass Media: In Pursuit of New Insights, New Goals, and New Strategies," *Psychiatry* 56, no. 1 (February 1993): 66; for actual experimental results, see Rebecca N. H. de Leeuw et al., "The Impact of Prosocial Television News on Children's Prosocial

Behavior: An Experimental Study in the Netherlands," *Journal of Children and Media* 9, no. 4 (2015): 419–34.

22. See David Gauntlett, *Moving Experiences: Media Effects and Beyond* (Eastleigh, UK: John Libbey; Bloomington, IN: Distributed in North America by Indiana University Press, 2005), or online at http://www.theory.org.uk/tenthings.htm (accessed January 8, 2016).

23. See Annette Hill, *Shocking Entertainment: Viewer Response to Violent Movies* (London: John Libby Media, 2005).

24. Reported in Wayne Wilson and Randy Hunter, "Movie-Inspired Violence," *Psychological Reports* 53 (1983): 435–41.

25. For an excellent rendition of the Left's attack on the corporatization of the media, see Robert Waterman McChesney, *Rich Media, Poor Democracy: Communication Politics in Dubious Times*, 2nd ed. (New York: New Press, 2015).

26. Internet Movie Database, "Business Data for Fahrenheit 9/11," http://www.imdb.com/title/tt0361596/business (accessed January 8, 2016).

27. An excellent book on this topic of the ecological fallacy of traditional psychology is Edward S. Reed, *Encountering the World: Toward an Ecological Psychology* (New York: Oxford University Press, 1996), particularly 18–19.

5

Film Criticism: What Is a Bad Movie?

Most people go to the movies for one specific reason—to be entertained. But beyond that, the moviegoing experience is a personal one. Most professional film critics evaluate movies according to a rather specific set of criteria—mostly the qualities of filmmaking as a craft. Production qualities, plot development, and acting are the primary standards by which most film critics measure the quality of a film. But those form only one set of standards for evaluating a film, which is certainly the case when considering the fact that some of the greatest box office successes have been critical failures—and the other way around. The two *Ride Along* (2014 and 2016) movies come to mind. Apparently, there is a large audience for these films even when film critics warn viewers that they are going to the theater to see bad movies. Nevertheless, audiences are entertained.

And entertainment value seems to be an important standard by which to measure the quality of a movie. Apparently, there is something entertaining about a car-chase formula that hasn't escaped Hollywood executives. And even though critics find most car chases after the defining sequences in *Bullitt* (1968) and *The French Connection* (1971) hackneyed and boring, the public can't seem to get enough. Audience members find it entertaining, and, truth be told, it is.

When there is a car wreck on the freeway during rush hour, traffic can be backed up for miles. Before the wreck is cleared and the bodies are carted off, drivers can't help but slow down just to take a look. Rubbernecking is a human trait. A morbid curiosity is not an indication that we are monsters or moral degenerates just because we take an interest in the macabre, the gruesome, or the antisocial. Even social moralists probably slow down just to take a look. In fact, as suggested in previous chapters, much of the criti-

117

cism of the modern media's parading themselves as being concerned for the moral and cultural sensibilities of the masses is, in reality, a thinly veiled contempt for the tastes of the average movie patron. Much of the junk science that purports to prove that media messages lead to societywide misbehavior is simply part of a larger political agenda of one group or another.

Mobster films, horror films, and slasher films have been the commercial staple of Hollywood since the beginning. By the standard of simple entertainment, these types of films are like roller-coaster rides: they take us out of our everyday humdrum existence and give us a window into something that we never witness in person—a mob hit, a face melt, a barroom brawl, or a car chase (in which no one gets hurt). And the popularity of those genres probably means little more than that—a little metaphorical rubbernecking.

Professional film critics are possibly rubberneckers of a sort as well. But when they go to the movies, car wrecks or natural disasters do not entertain them. They are looking for something different and are thus measuring a film by a different standard. What they are looking for is something they haven't seen before—and what a tough audience they must be. After watching five or six films a week for years, professional film critics must have seen just about everything at least once. Therefore, what probably thrills professional critics is originality. They are quick to praise the small independent production, the foreign import, or the directorial efforts of a promising newcomer (witness the critics' over-the-top reaction to Sofia Coppola's *Lost in Translation*). This is not to say that these films are not noteworthy—for the film scholar, they are probably the raison d'etre—but the critic's seal of approval isn't always a ticket to enjoyment.

By contrast, what a "bad" film is to a professional critic is the sequel, the remake, the big-budget production that must recoup its investment by appealing to the lowest common denominator, and the niche film designed to appeal to a specific segment of the public—car-racing buffs, for example.

It now becomes clear that there are several standards by which to measure the quality of a film.[1] The first thing to consider is the artistic/aesthetic standard. As noted, commercial films are mostly product, not art. Nevertheless, some filmmakers, whether because of their skills or their clout, are able to make films that are more art than product. John Ford, because of his clout, was able to make films such as *The Searchers* (1956) that were stories against the grain. But he also operated for most of his career under the studio system, or what I call the second monopoly of Hollywood, when block booking and vertical ownership of the industry made it possible for studios to make vanity projects.

But making commercial films as art is probably more the exception to the rule. Film scholars make a distinction between two types of directors: technicians and auteurs.[2] For the technician, scripts are a kind of architectural plan for a film; the film is constructed from the script. And while the films of the technician may be competently constructed or even elegantly crafted, they hardly represent an independent vision that reflects the aesthetics of the director. Auteurs, on the other hand, create a distinct vision; they have a distinct style regardless of the script. That the auteur allows his or her personal vision to dominate the film, irrespective of the demands of the market, makes the film of the auteur an art form.[3]

It is hard to know how many auteurs fail in the market—probably more than we would think—simply because their films never achieve enough commercial success to be widely screened. But in some exceptional circumstances, the public takes a shine to the work of an auteur and gets to experience creative magic in the local Cineplex. Some of the noted auteurs of the American film industry are Alfred Hitchcock, Orson Welles, Sam Fuller, Nicholas Ray, Fritz Lang, John Ford, Stanley Kubrick, David Mamet, and Woody Allen. Each one of these directors produce films that have a notable style, a feel, and even signature conventions, such as Hitchcock's habit of appearing once on screen in all his films.

As dominant as the American film industry has been, there have probably been as many or more foreign filmmakers who could be considered auteurs, including David Lean (British), Sergei Eisenstein (Soviet Russian), Jean-Luc Godard (French), Werner Herzog (German), Federico Fellini (Italian), Pedro Almodóvar (Spanish), and Ingmar Bergman (Swedish), just to name a few. Perhaps the reason that so many foreign directors are auteurs is that they are often relatively free from the demands of the market. Many, if not most, of these foreign filmmakers were subsidized in one way or another by their respective governments. Furthermore, there is greater respect in the law for filmmakers as artists. Under European Union Law, a film's director is considered the "author" of the film.

So it seems that by taking the market, if even partially, out of the filmmaking equation, there may be a greater likelihood that the films produced are more likely to be art than product. Even fascist totalitarian regimes, which have utterly and completely controlled their film industries, have nurtured some brilliant filmmaking, such as Leni Riefenstahl's *Triumph of the Will* (1934) or Eisenstein's *Battleship Potemkin* (1925). By the same token, during Hollywood's golden age of cinema, or what is termed in previous chapters the second monopoly of American cinema, many fine films were produced simply because the moguls wanted them produced as a kind of homage to their vanity. But even so, auteur filmmakers such as Charlie Chaplin and Orson Welles were either harassed or driven out of town by the Hollywood power structure of the golden era.

Today in the rough-and-tumble market of filmmaking corporatization, film auteurs still exist, but their films are produced for relatively limited release. Modern American film auteurs include the Coen brothers (Joel and

Ethan), Woody Allen, David Mamet, and Robert Altman, among others. Any film they make is worth a look—if you can find it. But most art films don't make it out of the larger markets, and even when they do, they are generally shown on a limited number of screens for a limited period of time. Fortunately, most of these films will also become available on DVD or streaming video.

Another standard by which to measure the quality of a film is by its technical merit, or how well the moviemakers employed their craft. This category of criticism encompasses everything from acting to direction, special effects, and script continuity. Script continuity is the degree to which a film maintains its internal consistency. It may not make sense in the real world for dinosaurs to be wandering an island off the coast of Costa Rica, as they do in *Jurassic Park* (1993), but within the context of that film, it makes perfect sense. But even the finest films often lack the detail of plot continuity.

Spoiler Alert!!! Don't read the next two paragraphs if you haven't seen *Blade Runner*.[4]

For example, there are a number of different cuts of the science fiction classic *Blade Runner* (1982). When I first saw the film, the impression given at the end of the film is that Harrison Ford, the hunter, or "Blade Runner," elopes with his prey, the "replicant" Rachael. The movie has an ambiguous ending because Rachael, as a replicant, has a severely limited life span. So even though the happy couple drives off into the sunset, it may be a bittersweet ending, as Rachael is soon to die.

However, in a version of the film labeled the "theatrical cut" screened recently in a local theater in my town, there was a fifteen-second dream sequence I'd never seen before that completely changed the meaning of the film. In that dream sequence, we are given evidence to the effect that the Blade Runner is actually, himself, a replicant, and he doesn't even know it. If that is the case, then all of the interactions the character has with other principals in the film are given an entirely different context . . . and all of this from the inclusion of a fifteen-second clip.

I liked the film, as confusing as it was when I saw it for the first time, mainly because Ridley Scott creates an enthralling vision of a dystopian Los Angeles in the not-so-distant future (2019!!!). The characters in the film are compelling and interesting, if not completely comprehensible. But the film is so much better with the dream sequence included. Now I can understand what is going on in the plotline and can appreciate the film for its story as well as its aesthetics.

The fact is that, in terms of craft, American films produced for general release are probably the most technically proficient films in the world. Even the worst American commercial film rarely falls below the threshold of at least being technically competent. And when it's really done well, modern filmmaking is a marvel.

What is less likely to be competent is the thought that is put into a film. This is probably the case for five reasons. First, while filmmakers are well trained in the craft of making movies, they may have neglected the obligatory liberal arts education—courses in philosophy, literature, and politics—that would help their films make better sense.

Second, because of the trend toward outsourcing the production of a film, there is no single intelligence guiding its production. Financiers may want the film to do and say one thing; writers something else; directors another thing; and editors may envision yet another message entirely. The outsourcing of film production has led to the release of many a commercial film that is a visually stunning and magnificently acted but in which the story line is an unmitigated mess.

One of the more prominent recent examples in this regard is Joss Whedon's *Avengers* (2012). This film is incomprehensible from beginning to end. In fact, the plot is such a mess that about halfway through the film the screenplay calls for a scene in which the principal characters actually get together and explain to each other (and presumably to the audience) what exactly they are doing and why. Other than that, the film is more like a series of tableaus held together by a variety of grunting, thumping, and grinding noises. The acting is as good as it can be, given that there is no plot. But one thing that can't be faulted about this film is that it is visually stunning. The script, however, appears to have been passed around like a Thanksgiving turkey.

Third is the problem of plagiarism, which includes copies, remakes, and sequels. For example, *La Femme Nikita* (1991), an excellent French action film, was remade in the United States as *Point of No Return* (1993). There is nothing wrong with rehashing an old idea. After all, there is always a terrible shortage of really good plotlines. Besides, great literature usually revolves around some of the enduring questions of life, love, hate, sacrifice, and so on, that need to be rehashed. However, the American version of *La Femme Nikita* was an exact copy of the French movie, but in English. Why not just dub the film in English? There was nothing original about this film.

Fourth is the problem of script gimmicks. In that respect, the recently released *Gravity* (2013) is one of the worst films ever made. I'm no physicist, but one object—say, a debris field—can't travel in the same orbit at twice the speed of another object—say, a space capsule. And it is all downhill from there. So that the film heroine can save herself, she is visited by a ghost astronaut who helps her negotiate the instructions in an abandoned Russian and then Chinese escape pod. I haven't been to China in a while, but when I was there, without a phonetic transcription of the Chinese language I had trouble finding a men's room, much less operating one of their spaceships.

Finally, there is the siren song of special effects. Many a film has been dashed against the shoal of special effects. What technicians can do these days on film is remarkable. All one needs to do is to take a look at Stanley Kubrick's *2001: A Space Odyssey* (1968) and compare it to *Blade Runner* (1982) and then to *The Matrix Reloaded* (2003) and finally to *Mission Impossible: Rogue Nation* (2015) to see how far we have come in the production of special effects. But these special effects do not come without a price.

Special effects cost money, to be sure, but at some point they cost the story as well. Regardless of their purpose in service of the film, special effects—although downright distracting—cost so much that they can't be cut from the final print. Imagine if, in the final edit of a film, the director were to suggest that a million-dollar special effect be deleted. What would be the producer's reaction? A million-dollar investment is just too valuable to sacrifice for a mere story line. The result is a product such as the *Avengers: Age of Ultron* (2015), *The Transformers* series (2004–2017), or the "reboot" of *The Planet of the Apes* series (2011–2017), which are visually stunning, technologically advanced, and pretty much impossible to understand. At least when David Lynch makes an incomprehensible film, such as *Mulholland Drive* (2001), he does so intentionally.

But these problems listed above are really literary problems related to a script. Since most of us don't live in the film world and are not professional film buffs, the standards listed here are of some value but aren't particularly useful to the average filmgoer. Most of us go for the story. Assuming that most commercial filmmaking is at least technically competent, the determinant of an excellent as opposed to a mediocre or substandard film lies in the script. Therefore, shooting a coherent movie with a tight script is probably of more than just passing interest to an aspiring filmmaker. It is the difference between fast food and caviar.

A lot of mediocre films are financial successes because they give the public something that it wants—thrills, awesome special effects, car chases, steamy love scenes, the right stars, and so on. Entertainment is certainly important, and we shouldn't give that standard short shrift, but whether films are entertaining is really not the subject of this book. It may be that in providing entertainment the industry may be subtly degrading society. That is certainly the argument made by ideologues on both ends of the political spectrum. Even if the audience does not realize it, films contain plotlines and messages that may be historically inaccurate, morally questionable, or downright subversive. Since, as we have seen, many people get their information about the world from the entertainment media (talk radio, for instance), the hidden meanings of films may be reinforcing ideas or behaviors that do have a public policy impact. Certainly, Arnold Schwarzenegger's election to the governorship of California was related in some way to the fantasy persona that he cultivated in his film roles.

Take, for instance, the film *Batman* (and, to a lesser extent, the sequels). The first modern remake of *Batman* (1989) is in many ways a work of art. The world created by director Tim Burton, a master of this sort of aesthetic sensibility, is meticulously designed to connote Gotham City's ominous sense of malevolence. The cast is great—any film with Jack Nicholson is worth taking a look at—and the story is fine. This is all true except for the fact that the *Batman* story has a somewhat questionable provenance.[5]

When the *Batman* comic strip was first introduced in the 1930s (at about the same time as the aptly named *Superman* strip), the United States was enduring a depression. The world was dominated by totalitarian regimes. It was not entirely clear that democracy would, or should, survive. After all, if the Great Depression demonstrated anything, it was that democratic governments appeared powerless to take care of their citizens. In the time before World War II, fascism began to gain a limited appeal in the United States and other industrialized democracies. Some of this flirtation with fascism manifested itself in the popular culture of the day. For example, in 1933 publisher William Randolph Hearst financed and cowrote a modestly successful film titled *Gabriel over the White House* (1933). The plot of the film, which involves the replacement of a democratically elected president with a more "suitable" leader, is unmistakably fascist.[6]

The *Batman* comic strip is born of the same ilk. In the *Batman* story, the democratically elected government of Gotham City is supine. The government is unable to exert control and is corrupt to the core in any event. Consequently, the city is being taken over by criminals. The citizens of Gotham are no longer able to move about independently for fear of falling victim to crime. Indeed, the wealthy orphan Bruce Wayne lost his parents to just this kind of street violence. He decides to avenge himself against "the criminals" (i.e., their class) who have taken his parents and his city. So he dons strange body armor and a mask, develops all sorts of technical crime-fighting aids, and adopts the symbol of the bat. He then goes to town in his spare time and arrests, and often punishes, "bad" people. Fortunately, he never makes a mistake and never punishes the wrong guy—hence no need for constitutional rights or the niceties of law. Once he cleans the city of its bad people, he returns to his mansion. Of course, the city can always call on him again in its time of need (which is apparently pretty often) by projecting the symbol of the bat onto the clouds.

This is a flat-out fascist solution for the problems that ail democratic society. It is probably not the case, however, that by screening this film we are going to turn out a generation of Hitler youth. After all, at least in the West, fascism still appears to be an ideological museum piece. Democracy is now ascendant. And so whatever messages of the *Batman* series may have resonated in the psyche of the 1930s are merely entertainment today. But that doesn't mean that we don't have our own present demons that need to be exorcised through popular entertainment.

Let's take, for instance, the *Dirty Harry* (1971) series. In the 1970s there was a substantial rise in the crime rate. Public concern over that increase was reflected in the entertainment media of the time through higher body counts and rates of victimization in dramatic television series and the movies. The *Dirty Harry* movies were enormously popular in their day because they provided a kind of cathartic release for moviegoers who had a fear of crime but also believed that the government's response was inadequate. The problem is that the *Dirty Harry* solution for crime, while satisfying to the audience, is hardly the way to run a society governed by the rule of law.

In the film, Clint Eastwood, playing Detective Harry Callahan, is judge, jury, and executioner. It is not to besmirch the fine career of Eastwood to say that his portrayal of Inspector Callahan is subversive—subversive in the sense that his portrayal may undermine support for the rule of law. It is not his fault. When he had an opportunity to make his own film, *The Unforgiven* (1992), Eastwood depicted violence, the consequences thereof, and the role of the law marvelously—well deserving of the Academy Award that the film and director received. But as Dirty Harry, Clint Eastwood plays fast and loose with the US Constitution, which makes this in some sense a bad film. In *Dirty Harry*, Callahan makes no secret of his contempt for the law and for the bureaucrats and the courts that enforce it. At least Inspector Callahan is upfront about his beliefs.

A much more dangerous and subtle play to the darker side of the public's appetite for vengeance occurs in the enormously popular film *The Untouchables* (1987). In what is otherwise a gripping and exciting film (with a screenplay written by one of the great playwrights of our time, David Mamet) occurs one of the oddest and most contradictory moments in American film history. Kevin Costner, playing the prototypical G-man and straight shooter Eliot Ness, murders a suspect in custody. It is an act that is so out of character, such a cheap sop to the visceral emotions of the audience, such an easy way out for the filmmakers, that it virtually ruins the film. The suspect who is killed, Frank Nitti, is no doubt a bad guy and deserves what he gets, but that is not the point. If the point of the film is the age-old struggle between good and evil, law and lawlessness, then the murder of a suspect already subdued, no matter what he is accused of doing, muddies the waters. Eliot Ness is no longer as straight as he seems. While he is better than the man he kills, he is not much better. He's just a hit man for the government. Who will stand up for justice if not Eliot Ness?[7]

And this isn't an issue that has gone away. In the wake of 9/11 and in a substantial reduction of the crime rate, the bad guy mantle has been passed on to the "terrorist." In the enormously controversial film *Zero Dark Thirty* (2012), the hunt for Osama bin Laden is facilitated by the torture of terrorist suspects in American custody. To be fair, this sort of thing isn't presented as a sop to the audience but as a kind of unpleasant necessity and, to a certain extent, even the main protagonist, a CIA agent played by Jessica Chastain, seems to be a bit conflicted. Nevertheless, it goes on, and I think that's a pretty accurate reflection of the current attitude in the United States toward the torture of terrorist suspects, an unpleasant if, strictly speaking, illegal necessity.

But it's not just in the crime genre that muddled movie thinking is going on. In the 1980s the women's liberation movement became a prominent part of America's social scene. In trying to cash in on this political movement, filmmakers attempted to create film plots and roles more sensitive to the plight of women. One such film was *Working Girl* (1988), starring Melanie Griffith, Sigourney Weaver, and Harrison Ford. It is sometimes the case that filmmakers try to do the right thing but get it wrong. *Working Girl* is such a film.

In it, Tess, a secretary from a working-class neighborhood on Staten Island (played by Griffith), tries to break into the ranks of the junior executive in her Wall Street brokerage house. However, her way is blocked by sexist men and a particularly predatory female boss (played by Weaver). The film is supposed to be about how, through hard work and pluck, this woman manages to gain the first rung on the ladder leading to the top. This is a modern Horatio Alger tale with a twist. In this story, the protagonist is a woman, giving the film the veneer of a contemporary story about a woman's liberation.

Why is this a bad film? The production values and acting are first class, but the problems start with the main plot and encompass the entire outline of the film. While hard work and pluck are supposed to be rewarded in our capitalist system, in this film they are nothing of the sort. In the beginning of the story we find that, no matter how hard she tries or how many night school classes she attends, Griffith, viewed by her co-workers as merely a voluptuous secretary, is never taken seriously. Her multiple attempts to move to the level of management trainee are constantly rebuffed by the personnel office. Finally, in desperation, while her boss is out of town, she assumes the role of her supervisor and manages through this subterfuge to work out a big deal and bed a handsome dealmaker from another firm (played by Harrison Ford). The problem with all of this is that it has nothing to do with capitalism or women's liberation. Tess gets ahead through cheating the system and the judicious use of her lovely body. If anything, this film is an advertisement for socialism because, stripped to its core, the message of the film is that the only way for Tess to get ahead is to cheat and sleep her way to the top.

And what a "top" it is. In the last scene of the movie, Tess succeeds in getting her own office as a junior executive. This accomplishment seems dubious. One gets the sense that being a junior executive in this firm is just like being a glorified secretary. As if to reinforce that point, as the credits role and the music swells (a lovely, inspirational tune sung by Carly Simon), the camera pulls back from the building in which Tess's office, put in perspective, resembles a cell in a beehive. This last scene delivers a punch like a knockout blow. This is what she fought for—so that she could have her own secretary and have someone else get the coffee? In a magnanimous gesture, Tess makes it clear to her new secretary that she'll get her own coffee. This probably means that Tess will be a "good" boss—sort of like a good slave master. Nevertheless, the reality is that the secretary is still in the "pool." But then again, so is Tess herself.

If there were a sequel to this movie, my guess would be that Tess, after having spent the best years of her life slaving away for the company, will be laid off in a cost-saving measure before her pension vests. After all, her supervisors will reason, she was promoted because she slept with and married the character played by Ford, which brings us to the ludicrous and insulting way in which women (and working-class people in general) are treated in this film.

When the evil witch (Weaver) is vanquished, in a parting shot she is told to get her "bony ass" out of the building, as if the character played by Weaver really cares what some CEO thinks of her ass. Can't women just be evil in their own right? Do they have to be demeaned as well? Look at it from another perspective: Would John Wayne shoot a bad guy and then comment on the size of his penis?

As for the working people, the way this film treats them is an abomination. Joan Cusack and Alec Baldwin, cast in roles as Tess's best friend and boyfriend, play their roles as drunken louts from Staten Island, incapable of expressing or even having an intelligent thought. I suppose this is a plot device necessary to convince the denser of us that what Tess is doing to achieve a higher level of dronedom is worth it. The alternative to a luxury apartment on the Upper East Side is a life of drinking, whoring, and wearing bad clothing. This in fact may be the way that producers see the world, but it is patently untrue and insulting to working men and women, most of whom have lives worth living.

Far from being a paean to women's liberation and capitalistic justice, this film would resonate well in the former Soviet Union. *Working Girl* could be interpreted to mean that if the only way that working people can get ahead in a capitalist system is to cheat, steal, and lie (in more ways than one) their way to the top, then maybe the capitalist system should be overthrown once and for all. Other films of this "liberationist" ilk include *Pretty Woman* (1990), where the protagonist solves her problems by marrying money;

Thelma and Louise (1991), where the heroes of this female buddy flick solve their problems by killing themselves; and *Striptease* (1996), the only film in history inspired by a cosmetic surgical procedure, Demi Moore's breast enhancement.

Since the turn of the twentieth century, women's films have changed. Emblematic of that change is Kenneth Branagh's recent remake of *Cinderella* (2015). In the original Cinderella story, the poor relation of a minor aristocratic family is forced into servitude when her father dies. The only way that she can get out of her fix is to call upon her fairy godmother to produce some magic that allows Cinderella to charm and bag the local prince. In the 2015 remake, the structure of the story is basically the same, but in the end we are given the impression that Cinderella has a lot more options (what we like to call "agency" in the academy). Basically, she can take or leave marriage to the prince, and he'll be lucky to have her, too. Theirs will be a marriage of equals, and he and she shall rule wisely and with justice.

Even the bad girl in this film, played in a marvelous turn by Cate Blanchett, is given a lot of context, and we can get a lot of insight into how this woman became such a bitch. The point here is that women's roles have changed, reflecting a different perspective of the times. It is rarely now the case that women in films are portrayed as helpless as they were in the 1990s. Other recent films of this ilk include *Maleficent* (2014), *Lucy* (2014), *Her* (2013), *Under the Skin* (2013), and many more. Maybe these films don't accurately portray women, either. The film industry is still dominated by men. So these may be portrayals of strong women from a man's perspective. What will be the next iteration of this evolution will be interesting to see. What would a strong woman character look like from the perspective of a filmmaker who is really working in a gender-equal environment?[8]

In the discussion of judging a film, we can apply another standard by which to measure the quality of a film aside from its entertainment value or technical quality. The films examined in this chapter are viewed from the sociopolitical perspective. Up to now, we have mainly outlined the standards used by professional film critics to measure the quality of a film, but it is also the case that film reviewers and the public can view a film from an ideological perspective. To capture the spectrum of opinions on the quality of films from the ideological perspective, it is essential that we understand the broad outlines of American political thought.

POLITICAL IDEOLOGY AND AMERICAN FILM

It may come as a surprise to some that American political ideology is generally regarded as being relatively homogeneous. In comparison to the range of political thought in other countries—such as France, Germany, Italy, or practically any other Western democracy—the range of American political thought is relatively narrow. In the United States, we have no large-scale fascist or socialist movements. There are no political groups in support of a return to monarchy or dictatorial control. In the United States, most of us share three core beliefs: a belief in political democracy, a belief in free market economics, and a belief that all individuals, by virtue of being human, are deserving of basic human rights.

Given the spirited and sometimes nasty tone of American politics, it is hard to believe that there is less political difference between Mitt Romney and Barack Obama than among the party leaders on the ends of the political spectrum in almost any other country. However, when Republicans and Democrats debate industrial regulation, tax cuts, or health care reform, they discuss "how much and for whom" rather than what fundamental changes need to be made in the political process or how we should construct our economic system. This is not to say that one side can't charge the other with being socialist or authoritarian; after all, it is the job of politicians to highlight their differences from their opponents, but in an unfavorable light for the latter. But beneath the veneer of spirited political competition in the United States, there is a core of consensus. Again, this is not to discredit the substantial differences between the parties and candidates in the United States. However, these differences for the most part take place within a common consensus.[9]

In what is to follow, I identify six ideological types that exist within the American consensus. Then, for the purposes of comparative contrast, I outline two ideological perspectives that are outside the American consensus. But even a description of the socialist and the fascist views will give us some idea of reactions to American film abroad.[10]

Finally, I choose a fairly recent controversial film, *American Sniper* (2014), and display critiques of it from each of the American ideological perspectives. As the reader, identify your own point of view, or portions of your point of view, from the list.

First, however, we need to discuss the American consensus in a little more detail.

It is quite remarkable that, as culturally diverse as our population is, we are so politically homogeneous. The reason is that most Americans have in their family background the shared experience of flight, or, as I described it in chapter 1, the immigrant experience. This experience has at the same time both a leveling effect and the effect of producing a nation of individualists. Save for Native Americans, no American has any more of a claim to being an American than anyone else. Furthermore, the immigrant experience has the effect of inculcating us with a healthy fear of government. After all, most immigrants have fled oppressive governments or social regimes.

Thus, Americans are basically egalitarians and largely individualists, and most would therefore agree that *the government that governs best governs least.* There are times, however, when we need a government. In times of war, for example, a government organizes an army for defense. Most of us would also agree that the court system, the police, and other basic functions of government, such as the building of roads and other infrastructure improvements, are essential. But the devil is in the details. How much should government do, and how should we pay for it? What are the legitimate rights of individuals, and what kinds of behaviors should be restrained? These are the baselines of debate in American politics. To settle or at least adjudicate these debates, we rely on a representative democracy. Democratic rule makes the most sense for our individualist state because through democracy the restrictions that the government imposes are basically restrictions that we place on ourselves. Consequently, there is a consensual agreement in the United States concerning the legitimacy of democratic governance. Furthermore, because we are individualists or life entrepreneurs, we tend to believe in free market economics, where each individual can make or break himself or herself in the rough-and-tumble of the market. Thus, an outline of the American consensus. But as I have said, the devil is in the details. The following are some of the more prominent divisions of American politics.

Six Ideological Types within the American Consensus

Libertarian

Libertarians believe that the government that governs best governs least—period. Libertarians promote the minimal state with the only absolute guiding principle being the absolute respect for property rights. Libertarians define property rights rather broadly to include not just a person's right to obtain and possess property but also the property rights that one has in one's own body. Thus, libertarians oppose the expropriation of property in all forms. To the extent that government exists, it does so to protect the property rights of the individual. In terms of public policy, libertarians oppose most forms of taxation, zoning restrictions, firearm bans, drug laws, and government activities beyond the police function and national defense.[11]

While most Americans are libertarians to some extent, they reject in one way or another the absolutism of the libertarian. Thus, while most Americans believe that the government that governs best governs least, they do so with a few provisos.

Welfare Liberals

Welfare liberals also believe that the government that governs best governs least. However, it is often the case that individuals find themselves in circumstances in which the government should help them out.[12] Children, the disabled, the sick, the aged, and the infirm are generally at a disadvantage through no fault of their own. Children, for instance, can't choose their parents. Sickness and particularly the ill effects of aging are unavoidable. Consequently, welfare liberals support government programs to provide for public schools, public hospitals, aid to the indigent, public health, and other components of a social safety net. These liberals are generally tolerant of social differences, behaviors, and other religious practices. However, they do not tolerate unfair discrimination, defined as that made on the basis of race, gender, or political conviction.

Of course, the problem with welfare liberalism is in deciding who are genuinely at a disadvantage through no fault of their own. Is the smoker to blame for his heart disease, the overeater for her diabetes? At what age should children be responsible for themselves? These are questions that dog the welfare liberal ideology and are often raised by those in our society called *conservatives*.[13]

Secular Conservatives

Secular conservatives also believe that the government that governs best governs least. However, there are times that government ought to intervene in order to facilitate the market or preserve the existing order of society.[14] The government can often help the market be more efficient by providing an adequate infrastructure. Consequently, conservatives, along with liberals, support public education, public health, road building, some forms of trade regulation, and a strong national defense.

Where they disagree with liberals is on the issues of *why* and *how much*. Conservatives support social programs as an investment and therefore hold those programs to an investment standard. When policies such as public education begin to show a diminished return, conservatives tend to lose interest and begin to promote privatization. Because conservatives hold these programs to an efficiency standard rather than a rights standard, as liberals do, conservatives are less willing to be expansive in public spending to cover all possible needs. Therefore, secular conservatives disagree with welfare liberals on the size and scope of the welfare state.

Unlike libertarians, however, conservatives do not believe that anything goes in terms of behavior. Certain standards and traditions need to be upheld, if only to protect the smooth, working order of society. For example, conservatives support harsh antidrug penalties because, from their position, drug abuse leads to crime and wasted lives. Conservatives have in the past generally opposed gay marriage and civil unions because of the perceived threat that such relationships pose to traditional notions of child rearing, the nuclear family, and the allocation of public benefits. However, in recent times, much of that opposition has drifted away, as it appears that the gay lifestyle has no effect on the efficiency standard.

The problem with the secular conservative position is that if social programs are held to an efficiency standard, many individuals in need fall through the cracks. One policy popular among conservatives, school vouchers, may help a middle-class child move into a private school, but as school vouchers are generally proposed, they won't be enough to get a poor child into a private school. Thus, the efficiency standard tends to be class biased. A decline in funding for facilities such as public housing, transportation, hospitals, and schools tends to weigh most heavily on the poor. The question liberals (in opposition to conservatives) then pose is: Are housing, health, nutrition, and basic education rights or privileges?

Religious Conservatives

Like the others, religious conservatives believe that the government that governs best governs least. However, if the government acts in a way that contradicts religious doctrine, or if the government doesn't act at all when the moral order of society is threatened, they want the government to intervene. Religious conservatives agree in many ways with both liberals and conservatives. They agree with secular conservatives on most social and economic issues. And in general, they agree with liberals on the importance of social programs to provide for children, the sick, and the indigent. However, the Bible, the Koran, and the Torah guide their beliefs in the promotion of government action.[15] Because these books are literally the word of God, religious conservatives cannot compromise on issues on which the secular government and the religious texts contradict. Consequently, religious conservatives reject the notion that there should be in government a separation of church and state. Furthermore, they believe that government should subsidize religious organizations as being the primary suppliers of social benefits. Therefore, religious conservatives don't disagree with liberals on the need for alms for the poor; they disagree on how those services should be delivered.

While religious conservatives generally support a free market economy, they would do so with some provisos. The problem for religious conservatives is that the market is neither moral nor immoral—it is amoral. So, when there is a market for abortion on demand, pornography, liquor, and gambling, religious conservatives support government intervention to close these markets. Religious conservatives do not measure programs by an efficiency standard, as do secular conservatives; they do not measure programs by a rights standard, as do liberals; they measure programs by a biblical standard. Programs that do not meet that standard are by definition a violation of the word of God and must be opposed.

Of course, secular conservatives object to the religious conservatives' rejection of the efficiency standard. Furthermore, secular conservatives may have a problem with religious conservatives who oppose teaching science in school or who impose arcane restrictions on gambling and alcohol. Liberals, for their part, don't believe that religious organizations have the resources to adequately supply social services on their own. Furthermore, liberals believe that religious organizations are discriminatory and thus not the way that government funds should be distributed in a democracy.

Religious Liberals

It should be noted, however, that not all religious people are conservatives. A significant segment of the religious community is liberal. Its members believe in the secularization of politics and that the holy books can be read to mean that a much more activist government is in order.

Religious liberals are more likely to support the separation of church and state, as they are more tolerant of diverse lifestyles and practices. They tend to side with welfare liberals when it comes to providing for the welfare state. They believe, as do welfare liberals, that health care, schooling, food, and housing are rights, not privileges. They arrive at this conclusion in their reading of the Bible.

Two Ideological Perspectives Outside the American Political Spectrum

Socialism

One of the most common smears in American political discourse is to label an opponent a socialist (the fact that *socialist* in our country is a smear is remarkable in and of itself). Yet there are few true socialists in the United States, and no real socialist movement. Socialist movements, however, are strong and alive abroad. Therefore, we should consider their reaction to American culture, if only to understand the attitudes of many abroad.

True socialists also believe that the government that governs best governs least. The ultimate goal for the socialist is the withering away of the state. In that socialist utopia, there would be no need for government because states would have no need to go to war against one another, and for individuals it would be "from each according to his ability, to each according to his needs." In the meantime, however, socialists believe that the source of many of the world's problems is a function of the capitalist system. Capitalism, according to the socialist, is inherently exploitative. To maintain this exploitative system—that is, workers being exploited by the owners of the means of production—capitalist states are forced to subdue other states and, at the same time, to subdue their own workers. Capitalists control their workers in a number of ways. Because they own the media, they use propaganda to maintain their control and cover up their crimes. By and large, socialists reject religion as "the opiate of the masses." According to socialists, capitalists use religion to pacify exploited workers. And finally, if worse comes to worse, capitalists use force.[16]

This is not part of the American debate. No leading candidate for political office in the United States proposes state ownership of the means of production (although there have been some calls for nationalized health care in the style of the Canadian system, but Canada is hardly a socialist state). The problem with socialism is that it may be wildly inefficient. Capitalists cannot see how centralized planners can outperform the market in the distribution of goods. Furthermore, individualists cannot see why they should sacrifice their own ambitions for the good of society or for the good of people at large. Thus, socialism has not found, and is unlikely to find, much of a following in the United States. *Socialist*, however, is not the only smear used in the rhetoric of American politics. Another label bandied about in the United States is *fascist*.

Fascism

Fascism did not die with Adolf Hitler. It is alive and well all over the world, but it hasn't had much of a presence in the United States since before World War II. Fascists believe that there is a natural hierarchy in society, that in society there are the strong and there are the weak. According to the fascist, it is the role and indeed the obligation of the strong to rule and even prey upon the weak. Of course, the problem with this prescriptive order is determining who are the "strong" and who are the weak. The fascist invariably self-identifies as the strong and identifies the "other" as the weak.[17] Liberals and conservatives reject fascism, among other reasons, because fascism rejects democracy; religious conservatives and liberals reject fascism, among other reasons, because of its total and complete rejection of individual rights. In a fascist regime, the individual is obligated to sacrifice everything for the good of the state. There are no significant fascist movements in the United States except for some scattered white power groups and vestiges of the Klu Klux Klan.

Political Polarization

No discussion of the current state of American politics can be complete without a discussion of a recent political phenomenon—the polarization of American politics. Up until the turn of the twenty-first century, American political parties tended to be an admixture of relatively bland and often overlapping policy preferences that reflected the relative narrowness and overlap of the American ideological range. Then, for a variety of reasons beyond the scope of this book, both parties began to drift toward their ideological extremes, with the Republicans moving to the right and the Democrats to the left. While the contours of American ideology remain pretty much the same, the parties became more representative of the extremes. This is now so much the case that political candidates from one party or the other have trouble deviating from their party lines without risking the loss of party support. Public opinion surveys show that while the polarization of the general public lagged the parties, the public is now catching up. Thus, the general range of American political ideology has not so much changed as we now as a people have divided into camps, what one author refers to as the process of "the Big Sort."[18]

No political debate in this country, including that over the content of film, is free from the influence of political polarization. And what has changed beyond the ideological distinction is the maneuver for political advantage. It is not enough to make one's case on the substance, the debate becomes nastier as debate points hinge on proving the other side not just wrong but also stupid, willfully ignorant, and even disloyal.

Polarization plays itself out in the current political environment on issues ranging from economic policy, to social issues, to even foreign policy. During the Cold War it was said that "politics stopped at the water's edge." But in the absence of a monolithic threat embodied in the Soviet Union, the goals of foreign policy have become much more diffuse and the tactics much more in dispute. Everyone wants to fight the "terrorists," but nobody is entirely sure who these terrorists are and how they are to be opposed. That debate plays itself out in Congress, in the press, and even in the popular arts. I've already hinted at the controversy surrounding the film *Zero Dark Thirty*, where suspects held in American custody are tortured for information (essential, it is made to seem, to the assassination of Osama bin Laden). In the case below, I will discuss the critical response to what was the top *domestic* grossing film of 2015, *American Sniper* (2014).

DOMESTIC POLITICS AND *AMERICAN SNIPER*

This is a movie about the military service of Chris Kyle, a US Navy SEAL who served as a sniper in Iraq in the aftermath of the invasion there in 2006. Kyle is credited with more than 160 confirmed kills, although the military claims that it doesn't actually tally that information. Much of the film is based on Kyle's autobiography, *American Sniper: The Autobiography of the Most Lethal Sniper in U.S. Military History.* Clint Eastwood, the director of the film, shoots the movie "without comment," meaning that, unlike many of his other films, Eastwood doesn't present the story with much of an angle. There is certainly a subplot concerning Kyle's personal life and his troubled marriage, which could be presumably blamed on the damage done to him in his service in the war. But as far as the action that lies at the heart of the film, Eastwood presents the war story in a very straightforward way. This incident happens, then the next incident happens, and so on.

The problem is, and this is beyond Eastwood's control, that in his choice to stay away from judging the activities of Kyle in the war, Eastwood has made an editorial statement in and of itself. There are any number of ambiguities associated with the war in Iraq, and even Kyle's role in it. This is not to say that Kyle is responsible for the situation he was in; he was, after all, just following orders. But in this war the role of the troops is different from, say, the role of soldiers in World War II or even Korea or maybe even Vietnam.

Here is a partial list of the ambiguities presented by but not commented on in this movie:

1. The Iraqi war was a war of choice pursued on the basis of false evidence that had something to do with Saddam Hussein's supposed development of weapons of mass destruction. Most of this turned out not to be true and, therefore, after an expenditure of $2 trillion, the loss of hundreds of thousands of lives, and the fact that the region is now in flames and is largely under the influence of our mortal enemy Iran, by almost any measure this war turns out to be one of the worst foreign policy blunders in American history.

    There is absolutely no comment about this in the film. Chris Kyle's primary motivation is to protect his fellow soldiers, which is a noble pursuit and probably what most soldiers are thinking about in the heat of battle. But is pretty clear, at least as his character is presented in the film, that Kyle and his fellow soldiers care little about the people they are supposed to be liberating. There is not even a tip of the hat here to the supposed mission of the US occupying force to establish democracy and restore justice in Iraq.

2. Saddam Hussein was a bad guy and deserved what he got. However, as it turns out, Iraq is really not a country at all but a collection of warring parts, and in order to hold what he occupied together, Hussein deployed the brutal techniques of an occupying force. With Hussein gone, the United States was cast in the role of an occupying force. Because the United States was unwilling to do what Hussein had done to hold the country together, under US occupation, Iraq has now fallen apart. US soldiers of the occupying force were thrown into this

impossible role by their feckless leaders, who had no interest in trying for even a basic understanding of Middle Eastern politics. (I suspect at some point they understood—it is not that hard to fathom—but by the time they realized what a mess they were in, they were in too deep to do anything about it—without sacrificing their political careers, that is.)

The unexplored irony of this film is that, were their positions reversed, were Iraqi troops occupying, say, Texas, Chris Kyle would be a "terrorist." He would probably be shooting at the occupying force and, I would say, good for him. However, as jarring as the word *terrorist* is as used in the previous sentence, the term is used unquestioningly in this film to apply to Kyle's targets who pose no actual danger to the United States and would be alive today were the invasion of Iraq never to have happened.

3. Finally, there is something about what Chris Kyle is doing over there that is vaguely troubling. It is not as if he is storming a beach or charging a machine gun nest. Kyle's job is to hide behind the front line and kill terrorists who threaten American troops. While what he does requires courage and skill, he is basically hunting bad guys and gals and their children. Blowing away bad guys and gals from a distance is an important job, but it is particularly difficult in an environment where nobody is identifiably the enemy. In fact, according to his book, Kyle's first kill in Iraq was a woman carrying an infant and a hand grenade as she approached American marines.

Also, apparently, Kyle liked his work. One of the dramatic moments in the film comes when Kyle's wife begs him not to volunteer to go back. However, Kyle demurs and returns to the war.

All of this is sort of troubling. Kyle is a hero who killed something on the order of 160 men, women, and children, most of whom were technically civilians and who were by any standard no immediate threat to the United States. In fact, had the United States not invaded Iraq, those who Kyle killed would probably be alive today, maybe without a grudge against the United States at all. This is not a critique of Kyle. As I have said, he was just following orders.

After he returns to the States for the final time, Kyle does some wonderful work with Gold Star Families (those who have lost a family member in the Iraqi or Afghan wars). Not so great, in my opinion (and, as it turns out, for Kyle) was his decision to invite troubled vets out to the firing range to get tips on and practice shooting with the most prolific sniper in American history. On one of those trips, a mentally disturbed veteran turned a gun on Kyle and killed him. Thus, Kyle becomes in some sense another casualty of the Iraqi war.

As I've said, Clint Eastwood presents this story without comment. And predictably enough, the film provoked a tremendous amount of controversy. In fact, the debate over the film became a cipher for the spectrum of the American political debate.

Before we examine this film from the perspective of the aforementioned ideologies, let's first consider the standard movie review. Glenn Kenny, film reviewer for *Vanity Fair* and various other publications, comments:

> Eastwood's handling of various battle scenarios, including those in which Kyle is compelled to take down women and children, is typically anti-elaborate for the director. Grim, purposeful, compelling. Violence and its relation to both American history and the American character is one of Eastwood's great themes as both a filmmaker and a film actor. But he is not a director of an overly analytical or intellectualizing bent, and this turns out to be one of this movie's great strengths. It has nothing to say about whether the war in Iraq was a good or bad idea. It simply IS, and Kyle is an actor in it, and he's also a devoted husband and father. But Kyle is more than just an actor in the war: he's a true believer in what he's doing, and his intensity in this respect bleeds into his relationships back at home in ways that can't help but be unsettling.[19]

Kenny applauds the artistry and the passion of the filmmakers without passing judgment on the film's content.[20] This is one standard of evaluation, to be sure, but it can also be used as a standard to praise *The Triumph of the Will* (1934), Leni Riefenstahl's celebration of the Nazi Party. Do film reviewers owe us more? Do we want them getting out of their expertise—the film business—to comment on something that they probably know little more about than we do?

Typical of a critique from the Left is Amy Nicholson's review in *LA Weekly*:

> It's clear in his book that Kyle had become numb to death. On killing two Iraqis on a moped with one bullet, he joked, "It was like a scene from *Dumb and Dumber*." (Naturally, Eastwood also omits that.) Eastwood can't carve a morally complicated movie when his main character—in life and onscreen—defined people in black and white: There's bad guys and good guys and anyone else is a pussy. The film hints, whisper-soft, that perhaps Kyle was afraid to think too hard about the life-and-death decisions his country asked him to make—a fear Kyle himself would have phooeyed. He was a hero doing and saying the things a hero should, and Eastwood is too tongue-tied to prevent this unexamined jingoism from echoing through the multiplex.[21]

Nicholson focuses not on the artistry of the film but on the destructive consequences of the war in Iraq. Her standard for criticizing this film is the effect that *American Sniper* may have on those who watch it and those for whom this film is made.

A typical, mainstream response to this film is from David Corliss, writing for *Time* magazine:

> In *American Sniper*, now playing in a few theaters before opening wide on Jan. 16, director Clint Eastwood and star Bradley Cooper depict Kyle as the guardian angel of American soldiers in Fallujah and Ramadi, and the exterminating angel of those who would kill them. It's a gritty, confident portrait of a man whose life may have been somewhat messier than this Hollywood version.[22]

To say that the real version of Kyle's life was "somewhat messier" than his Hollywood portrait is an understatement of jarring proportions. Among the other claims Kyle made was his statement that he had been hired to act as a sniper in New Orleans after Katrina. He claimed two kills (of which there is no record). He also claimed to have foiled a carjacking and to have killed both of the perps (again no record). In addition, he claimed in a televised interview to have punched out former Minnesota governor Jesse Ventura in a barroom brawl. Ventura sued Kyle for defamation, arguing the incident never happened. The court awarded Ventura $1.8 million in damages.

From the secular conservative perspective, a column in the neocon magazine *The Weekly Standard* is illustrative. Fearing a "triggering" response (whatever that is) to a viewing of *American Sniper* at the University of Michigan, Ann Arbor, administrators decided to substitute a screening of the film *Paddington* (2014) (about a Peruvian teddy bear lost in London's Paddington station). UM head football coach Jim Harbaugh then tweeted, "Michigan Football will watch 'American Sniper'! Proud of Chris Kyle and Proud to be an American and if that offends anybody then so be it!" The screening of the film was subsequently reinstated. There is so much going on here in terms of the nature of American campus and national politics that it would take another chapter to discuss. But, failing that, *The Weekly Standard* opined:

> As if to conclusively illustrate what an infantilizing atmosphere America's universities are cultivating, the scheduled showing of *American Sniper* was replaced by a screening of *Paddington*. That movie, based on the popular children's book series about a family that adopts a stuffed bear found abandoned in a train station, presumably required no trigger warnings. However, according to *Tablet* magazine, *Paddington* author Michael Bond was inspired to create the character because of the "Jewish evacuee children he remembered seeing in the train stations of London during the Kindertransport of the late 1930s." Contemplating a generation of children whose parents were killed in the Holocaust could prove pretty damn triggering, to say nothing of the necessary and righteous violence dealt out by an earlier generation of Chris Kyles that put an end to the horror. Bond further says of his beloved creation, "Paddington stands up

for things, he's not afraid of going to the top and giving them a hard stare." In that respect, at least, it turns out *Paddington* and *American Sniper* are not wholly dissimilar.[23]

In this one paragraph is a snide comment on the political correctness of American university campuses and a sly comparison of the Holocaust in World War II to the holocaust the Iraqis would suffer in the absence of the American military intervention. There is also the suggestion that topics related to the Holocaust are okay on campus, but not the war in Iraq. Finally, *The Weekly Standard* staff equates the war in Iraq with World War II, suggesting that opposition to the war in Iraq is tantamount to protesting the war against the Nazis and the Chrysanthemum Throne.

Religious conservatives are in a more difficult position in regard to this film. The Bible is pretty clear about the wrongfulness of killing. However, under certain circumstances, turning the other cheek doesn't seem to cut it. Movieguide.org, which bills itself as "The Family Guide to Movies and Entertainment," is highly conflicted on this film:

> Based on a true story, AMERICAN SNIPER is full of strong Christian faith, self-sacrifice and patriotism. The movie is endlessly captivating and full of jeopardy, and Clint Eastwood does a magnificent job directing. That said, after countless killings, even the audience may become war weary. Also, a couple characters lose faith and courage. Finally, AMERICAN SNIPER contains many "f" words, extreme violence and some lewd content. AMERICAN SNIPER is a powerful but difficult movie for patriotic people of faith and values.[24]

Accordingly, the weakness in this film appears to be in the "143 obscenities and eight profanities" uttered on screen, not to mention "a factual portrayal of false religion where Muslim characters, including the villains, profess their faith." If only soldiers didn't cuss and other people didn't pray to Allah, this film would be okay.

But then there is the tricky question of how to interpret all of this killing. Some religious people might be scandalized by more than the use of the "f word" in the midst of all this carnage. From another religious perspective, *Commonweal* magazine comments:

> *American Sniper* takes an ambiguous position in this evolution. One can view the film as a PTSD chronicle, since it explores the trauma and the stress that disorder a soldier upon his return from war. But what Eastwood is really up to, finally, is romanticizing the code of the warrior, a task he performs with powerful sentimentality and symbolism. The real Chris Kyle survived his four tours and returned to the United States only to be killed by a troubled vet he set out to counsel, and Eastwood closes his film with footage of Kyle's actual funeral: a motorcade, followed by a ceremony in the Dallas Cowboys stadium.

In the end, whatever doubts the film may have raised about the merits of the Iraq war melt away into the American pageantry of the funeral—flags, flowers, football—and the prospect of grieving Navy Seals pounding gleaming gold trident pins into the wooden casket in a ritual of brotherhood.

> This solemn pageantry is very much a piece of who we have become in the post-9/11 era. Kyle and Taya's decision to marry, made immediately after watching the World Trade Center attacks, places their relationship in the tradition of wartime romance, where the pressure of impending battle both sharpens and hastens the commitment of marriage. But more significantly, it also sacralizes the attacks; the scene in which the couple console each other while watching the towers fall emanates a holy quality, its dire implications blending weirdly with the sacrament of marriage and configuring military service as a sacred responsibility.[25]

The reviewer, Rand Richards Cooper, laments the tendency to conflate the sacred with the secular, as the biblical admonition to "render unto Caesar" has no meaning when Caesar (the State) is regarded as a god. Surely not every action, every decision, every intervention by the State, even a state as democratic and well meaning as the United States, stands up to a biblical test.

Finally, what is the view of this film from abroad? One would think a film about American troops occupying another country and shooting a bunch of civilians wouldn't get much of a reception abroad. Indeed, while *American Sniper* was the top-grossing domestic film for 2015, 64 percent of its $547 million in sales was domestic. And while $547 million (on a $58 million budget) is a lot of money, it was only thirteenth in worldwide rankings basically because the film wasn't marketed at all outside North America, Europe, and Australia.

In the *Frankfurter Allgemeine Zeitung*, reviewer Peter Körte compares *American Sniper* to *Dirty Harry* and asks (to paraphrase in translation): Is Chris Kyle a trigger-happy killer in uniform or a patriot and hero who has selflessly served his country? He stays away from an answer.[26]

Julia Beyer in *Le Figaro* recounts the making of the film (directors David O. Russell and Stephen Spielberg were recruited to direct *American Sniper*, but both rejected the project before Clint Eastwood was hired), and suggests (to paraphrase in translation) that "there was entirely too much kindness to Chris Kyle" and that Eastwood was intimidated into soft selling his approach to the film by the right-wing blogosphere.[27]

According to Stephen Bede Scharper in the *Toronto Star*, "*Sniper* creates an eerie vibe that the best soldiers are virtually robotic. The true heroes, it suggests, are those who ignore their conscience or the larger ethical concerns of their actions."[28] Scharper fears that the film glosses over the ethical and moral dilemmas associated with this war.

No wonder this film did not sell well abroad.

This and most art is framed by the ideological perspective of the viewer. Even in making a film without comment, Clint Eastwood has opened the door to controversy. While this film is technically very well done and the story is interesting and compelling, the question remains: Is this a bad film?

From my perspective, this is an exceptionally bad film. The fact that it is so popular is perhaps more troubling still. I enjoy war movies as much as any genre and know that killing is a necessary part of war. But unless there is a consensus on the justice of a particular war—for example, World War II—a war movie cannot be shot without comment. A better approach would be Francis Ford Coppola's *Apocalypse Now* (1979). Coppola captures the ambiguity and scope of the Vietnam War. Spielberg, however, doesn't have to comment on the moral rightness of World War II in *Saving Private Ryan* (1998).

Thus, here again, the quality of a film is in the eye of the beholder. If I watch a film from a particular political or cultural perspective, I'm likely to arrive at a judgment on the quality of that film based on my preexisting beliefs. I can appreciate the technical talent that it takes to make a film like *American Sniper*, and I can understand why Clint Eastwood decided to present the story "without comment," but I'm more than a little troubled by the result because it perpetuates our inability to be reflective about some of our recent decisions to go to war. And as that famous essayist and philosopher George Santayana once said, "Those who cannot remember the past are condemned to repeat it."

Feature Film: *Up in the Air*

As we have seen, even films that are on the surface devoid of political content can promote, ignore, or distort certain political beliefs. In a bit of a departure from the standard movie review, I have chosen to analyze one particular film, Up in the Air, *from several different ideological perspectives.*

Up in the Air was a reasonably successful ($166 million gross on a $25 million budget) film that features George Clooney playing Ryan Bingham, a road warrior whose job is to travel around the country firing people. His company does contract "wet work" for corporate executives who are too timid to do their own firing. Bingham likes his job and is really good at it. He gently eases employees out of their jobs, and often their careers, with a very light touch. And among all of the attributes that make him well suited for his work seems to be the fact that firing people all day doesn't seem to bother him. And, oh, does he love the road. He has an apartment back in Omaha, where his corporation has its headquarters, but nothing makes him happier than a drink from the minibar in his upgraded room at the Airport Marriott.

Up in the Air, **Paramount Pictures/Photofest, 2009**

Bingham also moonlights as a motivational speaker whose main recommendation is to clear one's life of all personal attachments. Why anyone would listen to that kind of tripe, much less pay for it, is hard to
fathom, but his motivational speech is made necessary, I suppose, by the
desire of the scriptwriter to establish that Bingham is basically a soulless
person. Speaking personally, I don't think that necessary given Bingham's
pleasure in his lifestyle and work.

But all of this dissociative bliss is rocked by two women who enter
Bingham's life—one another road warrior who becomes his lover, and
the other a young woman who becomes his mentee.

What happens after that establishes that Bingham basically has a good
heart, brought out by his relationship with these two women. The problem is that his metamorphosis is crushed by the betrayal of his girlfriend,
who, in a reversal of roles, turns out to be using him as a sexual object as
she, unbeknownst to him, enjoys a home and hearth. Thus, the picture
ends on a rather downbeat note as Bingham goes back on the road, sad-
der but wiser and, more to the point, totally disconnected.

There is a subplot in this movie about the damage that Bingham does
when, like the Grim Reaper, he flies into town to let people go. As the
titles roll, we see the interviews of what are presumably real people who
are laid off from their jobs. In that case, the vibe is rather upbeat as the
unemployed are anywhere from philosophical to hopeful as they look to
their future as a new adventure full of opportunities. This, I suppose, is a
sop to the resiliency of our fellow citizens and the opportunities provided
by our free market economics.

Let's now examine it from various political perspectives.

Libertarian

There are really two editorial criticisms taking place in this film. One has something to do with the soullessness of Bingham's life and the other with the soullessness of the capitalist system. Of course, we have no business criticizing either. Bingham's life is his own. If he chooses to sit on a metaphorical mountaintop contemplating his navel, it is no business of ours. We, of course, have every right to comment on it, but it is really not our business how someone else leads their life. When people are allowed to make their own choices, they tend to make the choices that are best for themselves.

Furthermore, there is nothing wrong with what Bingham does for a living. Firing people contributes to the creative destruction that is the essence of a free market economy. He obviously feels okay about it, and so should we.

Welfare Liberal

Like the libertarians, we have no comment on how Bingham lives his life. However, insofar as it appears that Bingham has no more to offer his "firees" than a packet of papers and some bromides, welfare liberals would be concerned about the fate of those who are fired, particularly as a result of some structural change in the economy (we are not that concerned about those who are fired "for cause"). Thank goodness we have a provision for unemployment compensation and other programs for the poor and elderly, such as food stamps, Medicaid, Section 8 housing, Medicare, and Social Security. Depending on how you look at it, these programs may be inadequate. But at least the long-term unemployed have something.

Secular Conservative

Unlike the libertarians, we do have an issue with the way that Bingham lives his life. Where would we be in this society without the nuclear family? If Bingham's advice to jettison all social connections is to be taken seriously, how are children to be raised? It is precisely because he has no family outside of his professional life that he has no scruples. It is no wonder that the woman he sleeps with, who describes herself as Bingham "with a vagina," turns out to be a monster. In order to ensure proper order in society, we should incentivize the family by providing subsidies in the form of tax breaks for home ownership and child rearing.

As far as his job is concerned, we have no comment. However, we would hope that the unemployed he creates get back on their feet, and if they don't, we would incentivize charitable giving (in the form of tax breaks for charitable contributions and tax exemptions for nonprofit aid organizations) for the purpose of aiding the poor. The government, however, should probably stay out of helping the poor. Finally, it would be appropriate for the government to provide the infrastructure necessary for American corporations to compete. Then maybe it wouldn't be necessary for companies to lay off so many workers in the first place.

Religious Conservative

Not only do we have an issue with the way that Bingham lives his life, drinking and fornicating across the fifty states, but we also have an issue with the entire movie, which depicts a society devoid of the presence of God. It is a gross misrepresentation of the United States to suggest that a person can live his life without ever coming in contact with a religious person or institution. Nor is religious faith ever presented as an option for the afflicted in this film. Of course, this is Hollywood's vision of America, a giant anthill devoid of faith. Were Bingham to accept God and his commandments, he would live a life of joy. So perhaps there is some truth in the conclusion of the film as Bingham flies high above the society and the God he has rejected straight into the jaws of Hell.

As to his work, it is no wonder that Bingham is so cynical and unmoved by the havoc he creates. It is necessary sometimes that people be let go from their jobs, but there is no excuse for the act of firing to be done with a smirk and sarcasm. We know, however, that those who have faith are never alone and that those who are troubled will find their solace in the Lord.

Religious Liberal

We differ little from the analysis above. We just arrive at some different conclusions. We would hope that society be guided more by the compassion in God's love than the fear of a fiery hereafter. Perhaps, then, more people would be attracted to the church and Bingham would more likely see the error of his ways. The foreboding of the conservative church alienates the young and drives them away from God. Perhaps Bingham doesn't see God as an option because he has no knowledge of the loving God. And perhaps the same can be said for those with whom he works and those he is assigned to fire.

But people who haven't yet seen the light don't deserve to suffer, and faith in God cannot shelter and feed the afflicted alone. Furthermore, because private charity has never been enough to help the poor, we see nothing wrong and, in fact, encourage government assistance to the poor.

Socialist

This film is a persuasive argument for the destruction of capitalism. Ryan Bingham is basically doing the dirty work for business owners (hereinafter referred to as the bourgeoisie) who don't have the guts to face their employees and fire them personally. In a capitalist system, workers are treated like inanimate objects. Once they have exhausted their usefulness, they are disposed of like the rest of the trash that is thrown into the dumpster. Note that older workers, mothers with children, and the sick and disabled are particularly vulnerable to this sort of thing. The government tells us that there is assistance available for the unemployed and that there are laws against age discrimination. But the fact that trying an age discrimination case is so expensive and so unlikely to prevail means that the law is more veneer than substance.

Aid to the poor is virtually nonexistent in the United States, and what paltry assistance that exists is constantly being reduced. But this is all part of the plan—workers who are no longer useful should be left to their own devices. The faster they die, the fewer resources they consume.

The workers that are left are so frightened by layoffs that they are willing to grant concessions to their employers that ensure that they are never paid anywhere close to the true value of their work. If they were to organize, to stand up against the owners as one, the organizers will be fired, put in jail, and, if necessary, killed. The press would then praise the authorities for taking care of the troublemakers.

There is a special place in hell reserved for Ryan Bingham, who betrays his class interests and seems to enjoy it in the bargain. The irony is that about halfway through the film it appears that Bingham himself may get the ax, but through some mysterious contrivance on the part of the filmmakers, capitalist propagandists themselves, Bingham keeps his job and gets to go on acting as a traitor to the masses.

This system is rotten to the core. There is no way it can be saved. The solution to this problem is the destruction of capitalism.

Fascist

In society like in nature, there are the strong and there are the weak; there are lions and there are antelopes. Lions eat antelopes. When a lion eats an antelope, we don't say, "Bad lion!!! Don't eat that antelope!!!" Eating antelopes is what lions do. Eating antelopes is good for lions, but it is good for antelopes too. Lions cull the herd of the sick and the lame.

Ryan Bingham is a lion. It is his job to cull the herd, and he is good at his job. The result is a workforce that remains strong. What Bingham does is not only good but also right. It would be morally wrong to burden society with the sick and lame. Eventually, if we listen to the priesthood, scam artists who make their living producing nothing, who tell us to love the other as ourselves, all we do is weaken America. And then America will eventually fall.

This film implies that Ryan Bingham is doing something wrong and that we should feel sorry for him. Maybe if that is our reaction to this film, we should feel sorry for ourselves.

Don't agree? What do you think?

EXERCISE

Interpret a current top-grossing film from five different political perspectives: libertarian, welfare liberal, secular conservative, religious conservative, and religious liberal.

SUGGESTED READINGS

Braudy, Leo, and Marshall Cohen. *Film Theory and Criticism: Introductory Readings.* New York: Oxford University Press, 2009.

Kipen, David. *The Schreiber Theory: A Radical Rewrite of American Film History (Melville Manifestos).* Brooklyn, NY: Melville House Books, 2006.

Monaco, James. *How to Read A Film: Movies, Media, and Beyond: Art, Technology, Language, History, Theory.* Oxford; New York: Oxford University Press, 2009.

Ryan, Michael. *An Introduction to Criticism: Literature, Film, Culture.* Chichester, West Sussex; Malden, MA: Wiley-Blackwell, 2012.

Schreiber, Michele. *American Postfeminist Cinema: Women, Romance and Contemporary Culture (Traditions in American Cinema EUP).* Edinburgh: University of Edinburgh Press, 2015.

Thomson, David. *How to Watch a Movie.* New York: Knopf, 2015.

NOTES

1. For a good discussion of film criticism, see Warren Buckland, *Film Studies* (New York: Hachette Book Group, 2015), particularly chapter 6.

2. For a comprehensive discussion of auteur theory, see Barry Keith Grant, *Auteurs and Authorship: A Film Reader* (Malden, MA; Oxford: Blackwell, 2008).

3. See Andrew Tudor, *Theories of Film* (New York: Viking, 1974), 121–24, for a discussion of the director as auteur.

4. And if you haven't seen it, get yourself to a "smart" TV and order the film immediately.

5. For an excellent discussion of the sociological meaning of the comics, see Arthur Asa Berger, *The Comic-Stripped American: What Dick Tracy, Blondie, Daddy Warbucks and Charlie Brown Tell Us about Ourselves* (New York: Walker, 1973); on Batman in particular, see 160–71. See also Marc DiPaolo, *War, Politics and Superheroes: Ethics and Propaganda in Comics and Film* (Jefferson, NC: McFarland, 2011).

6. See Deborah Carmichael, "*Gabriel over the White House* (1933): William Randolph Hearst's Fascist Solution for the Great Depression," in John E. O'Connor and Phillip C. Rollins, eds., *Hollywood's White House: The American Presidency in Film and History* (Lexington: University of Kentucky Press, 2010), 159–79.

7. For an examination of vigilantism in comparative perspective, see H. Jon Rosenbaum and Peter C. Sederberg, "Vigilantism: An Analysis of Establishment Violence," *Comparative Politics* 6, no. 4 (July 1974): 541–70.

8. For a good discussion of this issue, see Michele Schreiber, *American Postfeminist Cinema: Women, Romance and Contemporary Culture (Traditions in American Cinema EUP)* (Edinburgh: University of Edinburgh Press, 2015). Also see Suzanne Ferriss and Mallory Young, *Chick Flicks: Contemporary Women at the Movies* (New York: Routledge, 2008).

9. The classic exposition of this point is made by Samuel Huntington in *American Politics: The Promise of Disharmony* (Cambridge, MA: Belknap, 1981), 230–31, or Louis Hartz in *The Liberal Tradition in America: An Interpretation of American Political Thought since the Revolution* (New York: Vintage, 1955). For a further discussion and partial refutation of this point, see Rogers M. Smith, "The 'American Creed' and American Identity: The Limits of Liberal Citizenship in the United States," *Western Political Quarterly* 41, no. 2 (June 1988): 225–51.

10. For a textbook discussion of these ideologies, see Terence Ball, Richard Dagger, and Daniel J. O'Neill, *Political Ideologies and the Democratic Ideal*, 9th ed. (New York: Routledge, 2013).

11. For a classic exposition of the libertarian ethic, see Robert Nozick, *Anarchy, State, and Utopia* (New York: Basic, 1974), especially chapter 7.

12. For an important justification of the welfare state, see John Rawls, *A Theory of Justice* (Cambridge, MA: Harvard University Press, 1971).

13. For a discussion of the unique form of American conservatism, see George H. Nash, *Reappraising the Right: The Past & Future of American Conservatism* (Wilmington, DE: ISI Books, 2009).

14. For a good outline of this argument, see Irving Kristol, *The Neoconservative Persuasion: Selected Essays, 1942–2009* (New York: Basic Books, 2011).

15. Clyde Wilcox and Carin Robinson, *Onward Christian Soldiers? The Religious Right in American Politics* (Boulder, CO: Westview Press, 2011).

16. There are many versions of socialist thought; the description here is drawn mainly from Karl Marx, *The Communist Manifesto*, in *The Marx-Engels Reader*, ed. Robert C. Tucker, 2nd ed. (New York: Norton, 1978): 469–500.

17. For more on this concept, see Kevin Passmore, *Fascism: A Very Short Introduction* (Oxford: Oxford University Press, 2002).

18. Bill Bishop, *The Big Sort: Why The Clustering of Like-Minded America Is Tearing Us Apart* (Boston: Houghton Mifflin, 2008); for a more academic treatment, see Alan Abramowitz, *The Disappearing Center: Engaged Citizens, Polarization, and American Democracy* (New Haven, CT: Yale University Press, 2010).

19. Glenn Kenny, *American Sniper*, http://www.rogerebert.com/reviews/american-sniper-2014 (accessed January 12, 2016).

20. He can't even bring himself to say that Kyle "killed" women and children. Instead, he uses the term *take down*, which sanitizes the act and makes the act of killing seem more like a rugby scrum.

21. Amy Nicholson, "*American Sniper* Is a Rah-Rah War-on-Terror Fantasy," *LA Weekly*, December 22, 2014, http://www.laweekly.com/film/american-sniper-is-a-rah-rah-war-on-terror-fantasy-5304457 (accessed January 12, 2016).

22. Richard Corliss, "Review: In *American Sniper*, Clint Eastwood and Bradley Cooper Are Right on Target," *Time Online*, December 31, 2014, http://time.com/3649364/american-sniper-movie-review/ (accessed January 12, 2016).

23. *The Weekly Standard*, "Hair Trigger," http://www.weeklystandard.com/hair -trigger/article/914619 (accessed January 12, 2016).

24. *Movieguide: The Family Guide to Movies and Entertainment*, "*American Sniper*: Defending the Sheep," https://www.movieguide.org/reviews/american-sniper.html (accessed January 12, 2016).

25. Rand Richards Cooper, "*American Sniper*: Staking out a Political Position," *Commonweal*, https://www.commonwealmagazine.org/american-sniper (accessed January 12, 2016).

26. Peter Körte, "*American Sniper*: Das Böse muss man nehmen, wie es kommt," *Frankfurter Allgemeine*, http://www.faz.net/aktuell/feuilleton/kino/video-filmkriti ken/clint-eastwoods-film-american-sniper-ueber-chris-kyle-13442196.html (accessed January 12, 2016).

27. Julia Beyer, "*American Sniper*: Retour sur la polémique," *Le Figaro*, http://www.lefigaro.fr/cinema/2015/02/16/03002-20150216ARTFIG00251--american -sniper-retour-sur-la-polemique.php (accessed January 12, 2016).

28. Stephen Bede Scharper, "The Trouble with *American Sniper*: Scharper," *Toronto Star*, http://www.thestar.com/opinion/commentary/2015/03/02/the-trou ble-with-american-sniper-scharper.html (accessed January 12, 2016).

6

Why They Don't Make Them Like They Used To

Why are films so different today from those of the past? There are really three main areas of development in the evolution of commercial film that have had a profound effect on the content of film: technological developments, changes in the market, and the evolution of American political culture. Each of the changes has had a varying impact on the sociopolitical content of film. Let us consider each of these developments in turn and their potential for future change.

TECHNOLOGY

Until now, three major technological developments have driven the evolution of the American film industry. As discussed in chapter 1, first is the development of a mechanical pull-down device that allowed for the conversion of still photography to motion pictures. Second is the invention of capabilities to record sound right onto the film stock itself, allowing for the efficient and improved synchronization of sound and motion in motion pictures. Surprisingly, those two technological advances, introduced at the turn of the twentieth century and in the 1920s, respectively, have been, up to recently, the most important developments in film technology in the last one hundred years. Until quite recently, most films were still shot on photographic film stock, with cameras that were in many ways mechanically similar to the cameras used by D. W. Griffith in shooting *The Birth of a Nation* (1915). Third is the introduction of computer-generated special effects. But even before the advent of the computer, Hollywood had been able to produce some remarkable special effects—in the fantasy film *Jason and the Argonauts* (1963), for example. Nowadays, however, special effects are even more spectacular, cheaper, and easier to produce because of the advent of computer technology. Finally, probably the most important technological development since sound is the advent of streaming video technology, which is the function of several technological advances: improvement in storage capacity, bandwidth efficiency, and home computing technology.

Of course, the question is, how important really are these technological developments to the content of commercial films? This question really has two answers. On the one hand, technological developments have probably less effect on the nature of films than what one would think. In film, to paraphrase Shakespeare, the play is still the thing. At another level, however, technological developments present and future can change the content of film because they change the economics of film. Digital photography and computer-generated special effects will have an increasing effect on who can make movies, how those films will be distributed, and what decisions filmmakers will make in the production of film.

For many of those who are middle-aged, one of the fondest memories of youth is that of gathering around the television set to see the annual screening of *The Wizard of Oz* (1939). Even never having viewed *The Wizard of Oz* in a movie theater, I still find the experience of seeing the film transporting. Nevertheless, most commercial films don't translate well to television, and it is not just because of commercial interruptions on "broadcast" television, the censorship euphemistically called "editing for content," and the fact that wide-angle photography will not fit onto most television screens (resulting in the development of "letterbox" presentation of films, which may be necessary but is still distracting).

We now have a chance to view movies on the Turner Movie Channel, subscription streaming services, or DVDs without commercial interruptions; yet sometimes something gets lost in the translation. It turns out that the film industry did not have to worry all that much about the advent of television. Up to now, either television doesn't compete with film or it actually provides another outlet for Hollywood films or, even more recently, original content. In fact, some of the most creative work in the film industry, maybe the most creative work, is being done in the streaming video market—content that will never be seen in the theater.

As noted in a previous chapter, the advent of on-demand, streaming video services such as Netflix and Amazon Prime has not only made it possible to create a true television serial—serial in the sense that one episode can build upon another—but also changed the audience for its product. Stay-at-home parents, invalids, senior citizens, and even the poor (streaming videos are relatively cheap on a per-view basis) can now watch creative, original programming from the comfort of their living rooms. That means that the audience for television, if not the movies, is older and more sophisticated than the audience for Hollywood blockbuster films.

Thus there is some really excellent television programming that is available as an alternative to the dreck of commercial television. There has been a veritable gold rush of content production. Netflix, the original streaming video company, started out carrying whatever content it could find. And the novelty of programming on demand (plus some sly billing practices) attracted a huge customer (and investor) base. But because the giant production companies were unwilling to share their original content and the core of their movie libraries, and because another giant, Amazon (plus other, smaller companies), entered the field, Netflix's growth began to flatten out.

Netflix then hit a home run. They produced their own show. It turns out that there is a tremendous pool of production talent out there available for hire. Up to this point, the traditional studios had a stranglehold on production because it was believed that, like producing cars, film production was a very specialized and very difficult task to start from scratch.[1] HBO had been producing its own content for years, much of which had been excellent, but for a captive audience paying a higher rate. When Netflix got into the production business, many experts in the investment community questioned the wisdom of that decision. However, when *Orange Is the New Black* became a huge hit, the floodgates opened. Companies such as Amazon or Xbox that were never thought of as production companies found that it was profitable to produce their own content. HBO and the other more traditional production companies also expanded their product lines and began to sell to other content providers after an exclusive release and an appropriate waiting period.

It turns out that streaming video, view on demand is uniquely suited to television serials. One need not watch an episode or a particular show at a particular time, but shows can be watched from first episode to last, at the convenience of the customer. This phenomenon even spawned the new concept of binge watching, or watching many episodes of a serial in one sitting.

The consequence has been a proliferation of outstanding shows that are too numerous to list here. In fact, the problem may now be that there is actually too much content and not enough time to watch it. However, the great thing about streaming video is that it can be warehoused and brought out on demand, increasing the shelf life and viability of shows beyond what Hollywood ever dreamed possible.

This gold rush in streaming video has had an effect on the demand for traditional films. US ticket sales for the industry are essentially flat, but revenues have experienced a significant leap since 2009, roughly corresponding to the time at which the film industry went digital. There are significant cost savings associated with the digitalization of movie production. First, a professional-grade digital camera is smaller, lighter, and cheaper than a camera designed to shoot movies on film. Filming on location is faster and easier and, therefore, cheaper. Second, postproduction is much quicker and easier. The editing process for film used to involve painstaking manual labor, cutting and splicing edits on physical film stock. Editing a digital film is more in the nature of editing a document in a word processing program. Finally, distribution is much more efficient using a movie-theater version of streaming technology. Commercial theaters receive films in the form of a disc storage cube, which is inserted into the projection system and records (for the purpose of royalty payments) the number of times a film is shown. That information is then transmitted to the distributor. In the predigital age, the transport of films and accounting, which required on-site monitoring, was an administrative nightmare. Now those problems are more a thing of the past.

The pirating of film is still a major problem, but it is no worse now than it was when illegal copies were made of a VHS. Furthermore, China, which is now a major market for American films and also used to be a hotbed of intellectual property rights violations, has "grown up" in the industrial sense. They have become more dependent on foreign trade, and they, too, have intellectual property that they want to protect. The US government has made a federal case out of the pirating issue and communicated the same to the Chinese government. Therefore, the Chinese government is now doing a better job of cracking down on copyright thieves.

ECONOMICS

As discussed in previous chapters, part of the reason that movies are so different today is that the movie industry has gone through three eras of monopoly: the short-lived Edison trust, the golden age of Hollywood cinema, and now the corporatization of American film. Monopolies have a profound effect on film content because decisions made about the content of film in a monopoly are in large part a reflection of the eccentricities of the trust holders.

It should be noted, however, that even monopolies come under pressure to change and to alter their products. The best way to understand the evolution of a monopoly, and most institutions for that matter, is to reference the work of noted historian Arnold J. Toynbee. In his massive multivolume *A Study of History*, Toynbee came to the conclusion that the history of humankind advanced in a pattern that was both predictable and idiosyncratic. He termed that pattern *challenge and response*. As he describes it,

The effect of a cause is inevitable, invariable, and predictable. But the initiative that is taken by one or other of the live parties to an encounter is not a cause; it is a challenge. Its consequence is not an effect; it is a response. Challenge-and-response resembles cause-and-effect only in standing for a sequence of events. The character of the sequence is not the same. Unlike the effect of a cause, the response to a challenge is not predetermined, it is not necessarily uniform in all cases, and is therefore intrinsically unpredictable.[2]

According to Toynbee, excessive scientism in the social sciences has mislead us to believe that we can reliably predict the outcome of human history. However, because of the eccentricity of the actors' decisions and because of the decisions of others, according to Toynbee, it is impossible to predict in describing behavior whether an individual makes the right or wrong decision. Furthermore, even decisions that appeared to be right at the time have in the end proven disastrous. The example that Toynbee uses is the decision that the emperors of Rome made in building a system of roads, with the result being that "all roads lead to Rome." What was intended to be a public works project for the benefit of trade and defense eventually became a barbarian-invasion route that led to the sacking and collapse of Rome.

Toynbee makes an important point in positing challenge and response as his vision of the pattern of history. Therefore, in examining the evolution of the film industry, we reference Toynbee when we recognize that the decisions made by the studio heads, writers, directors, and corporate CEOs are not the only decisions possible and that the effects of those decisions, even if they seem right at the time, can in the end prove to be mistaken.

Let's take, for instance, the rise and fall of the Edison trust. No one could ever accuse Thomas Edison of being a man with a lack of vision. And yet, when it came to motion pictures, he appeared to have a blind spot. He never recognized the true potential of their mass exhibition. It appears that his judgment was clouded by his experience with one of his earlier inventions, the phonograph. The phonograph and its progeny was, and still is, used as a personal medium. For the most part, records, tapes, discs, and now music downloads are essentially produced for private consumption. But films, as it turns out, are much better viewed in a theater. Edison never saw the difference, and his refusal to recognize the exhibition potential of films led him to eschew its development as a mass medium. Instead, he decided to build a monopoly in filmmaking based on the collusion of the film technology producers. This decision turned out to be a serious mistake for two reasons. First, others recognized the potential of film, and they acted to subvert and elude the monopoly. Furthermore, Edison made his decision to form a monopoly in an era of reform when the government was actively trying to break up trusts.

Edison's miscalculation led to the transfer of filmmaking into the hands of a rather small, ethnically homogenous group of European Jewish immigrants who just so happened to be the marketers of the Edison trust product. It is merely an accident of history that the Jews invested so heavily in the arcade and theater business at the turn of the century. In another era, another group, with their own eccentricities, would have likely come to dominate the film industry. But as it was, first-generation Eastern European Jews came to dominate the industry, and they brought with them their own set of values.

Having been in the minority in both the Old World and the New World, and, in fact, throughout most of their history, Jews were particularly conscious of their conspicuous outsider status. As a result and in order to produce a marketable product, the Jews of Hollywood attempted to "out-American the Americans." The films of the golden era of Hollywood cinema rarely strayed from the established dogma of American culture. It is ironic that the films of the golden era that are now praised by some for their wholesomeness were more often than not produced by men with an accent and with a set of religious practices foreign to most Americans. And as if to remind Jews of their outsider status, Hollywood Jews had to clear their product through the self-appointed, Christian-dominated production board that oversaw the content of their films throughout almost all of the golden era.

Therefore, the content of the Hollywood-era films should be seen in part as the Hollywood moguls' response to the challenge of making films for the majority culture that were not only artful and entertaining but also acceptable and inoffensive. In their response, the moguls were a remarkable success. But they eventually faced a set of challenges for which they were not prepared and made a series of decisions that led to the end of the monopoly of the golden era. Just as Edison had failed to see the potential of mass-marketed, full-length dramatic feature films, the moguls failed to adapt to the threat of television. In addition, they had to react to the revival of the European film industry after the war, but in a way that would conform to the production code. Their reaction in the 1950s to these challenges were the release of big-budget biblical epics, Cinerama spectaculars,[3] bedroom farces, along with the introduction of a new and more edgy genre known as film noir, which managed to slip below the radar screen of the censors. But in the end, it wasn't enough. Losing audiences and hemorrhaging money, the moguls' movie empires collapsed, to be bought up piecemeal by industrial conglomerates and corporate raiders.

The movie business was then rebuilt to conform to the business model of a modern, publicly held corporation. The studios both expanded and contracted their business. They expanded their business into amusement parks, television production, music, and, in regard to cinema, the financing and distribution of films. But at the same time, for the most part, studios got out of the production of films. Instead, they outsourced production, as would any other modern manufacturing corporation. This has been the structure of the movie industry more or less to this day.

Their product is technically competent, more often than not pedestrian, but in the main profitable. In many cases, films these days, even big-budget ones, can be excellent. Furthermore, a whole product line of specialty films known as *indies* has sprung up in the industry to cater to niche audiences; though, in fact, indies are generally financed and/or distributed by the majors. The majors have designated production companies such as Searchlight Films (Fox), Castle Rock (Time Warner), Miramax (Walt Disney), and Sony Pictures Classics (SONY) to produce movies with an "arthouse" feel. These films are often daring and sometimes excellent. Finally, the industry has adapted in fits and starts to new technologies that allow for the viewing of films and now television serials in private, on demand. Nevertheless, there is always going to be the problem of film piracy, which, as bad as it is in the United States, is worse abroad. Indeed, after 1995, when President Bill Clinton precipitated a confrontation with the People's Republic of China over intellectual property rights, there has been an ongoing struggle over the piracy of American music and films.

What are going to be the new challenges to the American film industry, and how will it respond? Probably the most notable challenge to the film industry establishment began with the remarkable success of Mel Gibson's *The Passion of the Christ*. This film, which personally netted Gibson as much as $500 to $600 million, was privately financed, targeted at an audience that was thought to be unprofitable, and promoted in a most unusual way. By keeping the production as secret as possible leading up to its release and by refusing to show the film in prerelease screenings to anyone but a sympathetic audience, *The Passion* generated a firestorm of controversy that helped promote its release in no other comparable way. Whether intentional or not, this innovation could not have failed to attract the notice of the corporate Hollywood moguls. Their conclusion was that there was an untapped market in the religious community, and there is. But it is always going to be a limited market. Religious people are limited in time and resources to their church activities. And after trying out some imitation films, big-time Hollywood gave up on the religious community. There are not many more blockbusters there.

But what corporate Hollywood may have missed in this incident is the fact that there are plenty of untapped markets for film. And more important, it is possible for movie production to take place outside the traditional studio system. As noted above, a number of companies not traditionally associated with the film industry have gotten into the production of "content," including Amazon (books), MTV (music videos), Pixar (animation), Playtone (a record label owned by Tom Hanks), Xbox (video games), Marvel Studios (comic books), and many others. And the audience for this content has changed and, thus, the content itself. Television serials are aimed at an audience that in the past because of cost, childcare, and mobility issues were less likely to go to the movie theater. The result has been a rush of intelligent, cutting-edge, intelligent entertainment produced with a mature, mainly domestic, audience in mind. And because of the digitalization of the industry, which speeds up the product cycle, more and more of this new product is relevant in terms of current politics and current events.

Of particular interest to those of us who study the politics of film are the films and serials based on historical events. There is a danger in recreating historical events that writers and directors will exercise a certain degree of poetic license to produce a "clean" or entertaining plotline or even a story that fits a particular agenda. The problem is that for most of the viewing audience, the movie they are watching may be the only interpretation of a historical event that they will ever see. The result may be that for large numbers of people, there will be a fundamental misunderstanding of what actually happened in the recent past. That is a form of propaganda, plain and simple, and the excuse that some producers have made that, after all, "it's just a movie" isn't good enough. Some real damage can be done. And "tit for tat" isn't a good enough excuse, either.

So, for example, in the movie *Mississippi Burning* (1988), the FBI is cast in a heroic role even as, in reality, it was trying to ruin the reputation of Martin Luther King and cast many in the civil rights movement as communists. That is wrong and should be adjudged so. But it does not justify the treatment of President Lyndon Johnson in *Selma* as a reluctant partner in the civil rights movement, dragged along by the tide of political necessity. Furthermore, there is no evidence to suggest that Lyndon Johnson was in cahoots with the FBI in what the film suggests in an orchestrated attempt to insinuate that Martin Luther King was cheating on his wife.[4]

One gets the sense that the agenda of the filmmaker is to diminish the contribution to the civil rights movement of whites in general. That would then counter a history of the depiction of the civil rights movement in film as mainly a top-down phenomenon, a depiction that tends to diminish the role of the African American community in its own cause. That, of course, is untrue as well. But tilting too far in the other direction creates an imbalance and diminishes the quality of the film. A more balanced approach to the story would have been more accurate and would have probably helped at the box office as well.

Of course, sometimes the truth must be told. No one would accuse the producers of the film *12 Years a Slave* (2014) of sanitizing the issue of slavery. The movie was an important film for what it taught. But more to the point, at least in regard to this section of the chapter, the film did better at the box office. The unvarnished truth can sell.

But what is clear is that with the digitalization of Hollywood film, the audience for film is both broader and narrower. The studios can still go for blockbuster hits, pictures with lots of bangs and crashes, little substance of meaning, and a scarcity of dialogue. There is still a market for films that please at the same time a sixteen-year-old boy in the suburbs of Cincinnati and a Chinese worker in Guangzhou. But there is also smaller (and yet profitable) market that has come to exist in only the last few years. The advent of the serial drama and the "little" film have expanded the market for "film" to the living room and an older, more sophisticated audience. And the product is sometimes stunning. *Boardwalk Empire, The Wire, Orange Is the New Black, House of Cards*, and many others are extremely fine shows. To someone who likes film, it's like being a kid in a candy store.

THE CULTURAL/HISTORICAL CONTEXT

When David Easton, a prominent political scientist, wrote about political systems, he discussed the context in which a political system operates. Rather than determine what kind of public policy a system will produce, context—historical, geographical, and cultural—delimits the response.[5] Certain ideas, concepts, and conventions fall outside the boundaries of a society's context. Regardless of the technological opportunities or limitations of films and despite the corporate structure of the film industry, certain stories are either appropriate or inappropriate given the time and place in which a film is produced. Nevertheless, some verities, as discussed in previous chapters, are based in American political culture so that American films of the past, even when viewed today, still have a certain ring of truth. In the following section, I discuss the evolution of film content. The list and discussion are by no means exhaustive, but what is to follow are films representative of their time.

Way Down East

In *Way Down East*, directed by D. W. Griffith, Lillian Gish plays Anna, a young girl born of modest means. She is forced to live with the family of her wealthy cousins, where she meets the dashing ladies' man Lennox Sanderson (Lowell Sherman). Sanderson cons the innocent Anna into thinking that he wants to marry her, and he stages a fake wedding to get her into bed. Of course, as is always the case in these sorts of things, a pregnancy results. Sanderson rejects Anna and reveals the false pretenses under which he seduced her. To make things worse, Anna's mother dies, and the

***Way Down East*, United Artists/Photofest, 1920**

baby is born with an illness to which it eventually succumbs. Anna is now penniless and alone, scorned as a wanton woman. Anna begins to wander the roads and comes upon the house of the Bartlett family. The Bartletts show compassion toward her and take her in, where she draws the attention of the Bartletts' son David (Richard Barthelmess). But as fate would have it, the Bartletts are neighbors of the Sandersons, the family of the man who seduced Anna. Eventually, the truth comes out that Anna was involved with another man, and David's father feels compelled to throw Anna out of his house. In despair, Anna tries to commit suicide by jumping onto an ice floe in a river in the dead of winter. David comes to the rescue and proclaims his love for Anna, and they get married and live happily ever after.

When the movie business started, many of the earliest feature-length films were adapted from stage plays. *Way Down East* had been an enormously popular stage play in the late nineteenth century, so it was an obvious choice for film adaptation. Thus, the film is both familiar to modern sensibilities and foreign. First, the plot has an obvious religious allegory. Anna is a martyr to society's cruelty. But through the proper application of religious doctrine, forgiveness, and generosity, she is redeemed to find a fulfilling life. The film is Victorian rather than Edwardian in its mores, meaning that the act of sex outside of marriage is considered taboo, so that for some who view the film today, the customs of the film may seem remarkably strict and arcane.

However, are we really so different today? While there isn't the same social stigma associated with illegitimacy, don't we still condemn women who have children outside of wedlock—despite the fact that most teenage mothers are seduced by men much older than themselves? There is at least one major difference. In theory, we try to get the fathers to pay for their sins. However, the effort is less than fulsome: it is almost exclusively a civil matter, and the father still probably assumes less of a stigma for siring an "illegitimate" child than the mother. The economic consequence for the mother is substantially worse as well. In other words, despite the fact that *Way Down East* is a silent film and the characters dress and act a little different, how much have we really changed as a society? The major difference is that without the divine intervention of David Bartlett, many young women today are condemned to ride the ice floe over the falls.

All Quiet on the Western Front

This is probably the greatest antiwar film of all time. Based on a novel of the same name, written by Erich Maria Remarque (who had himself been a German soldier in World War I), the film was well received both critically (winning the Academy Award for Best Picture) and financially. On a personal note, when I first saw this film in the 1960s, it blew me away. I was raised on John Wayne and James Bond, and I had never seen or read anything about war that did not focus on glory. *All Quiet on the Western Front* has an entirely different take on war, one I had never seen before.

In the film, Paul Baumer, a young German high school student (played by Lew Ayers), is persuaded by his respected professor to join the army and go to war. In the army he finds friendship and camaraderie, but also the waste and horror of war. The film is filled with heartbreaking scenes as the audience begins to grasp the pointlessness of World War I. The fact that Baumer is German is important, as in many films the Germans are cast as homicidal maniacs, whereas in this film, Baumer is just another young man. One of the most moving scenes of all is the one in which Paul has to spend the night in a foxhole with a French soldier he has just stabbed. As the man dies before him, Paul comes to realize the dreadfulness of what he has just done. The French soldier, he finds, has a family; he feels pain; he is another young man who just happens, by accident of birth, to speak another language; and Paul has killed him. It is important not to reveal the

All Quiet on the Western Front, **Universal Pictures/Photofest, 1930**

end of the film. If you haven't seen it, you should; after you do, you can in good conscience consider yourself a student of politics and film.

This film will appear to modern sensibilities as being quite unusual. Besides the production values of the time, the film is about a theme—the pointlessness of war—that is rarely explored today. There was a brief period in the aftermath of the Vietnam War when filmmakers took a shot at anti-war themes—*Apocalypse Now* and *Platoon* are two notable examples. But one gets the sense that those two films and others don't go as far in condemning war as did *All Quiet*. The battle scenes in *Apocalypse Now* and *Platoon* are thrilling and cathartic, as if they solve some problem. And the main critique of war in these films reflects the debate of the time over the Vietnam War, which questioned the leadership that led us into war and the conduct of the war but never really the use of war as a way to solve problems.

That is what makes *All Quiet on the Western Front* unique. In the aftermath of World War I and the apparent failure of that war to change the international system, it appeared to Americans that all that bloodshed had been pointless, except to line the pockets of the manufacturers of arms (the so-called merchants of death) and to protect the colonial holdings of the victorious European powers. *All Quiet on the Western Front* even goes so far as to question the usefulness of nationalism—in this case German nationalism, but nationalism nonetheless. And as such, the film provides us with a unique window into its time, the isolationist period that led up to World War II. Perhaps, then, *All Quiet on the Western Front* is the most daring and original film discussed in this section. It really has very little to do with our modern sensibilities, especially in considering the recent popularity of *American Sniper*, but it is nevertheless a window into an unusual, albeit brief, period of our past.

Sergeant York

This film is a different take on World War I, but it isn't really about World War I at all. *Sergeant York* is metaphor for what at the time was a menacing threat, the rise of fascism in Europe and in Asia, while overcoming the lingering distaste for the Great War. The film was an enormous success with both the audience and critics, winning two Academy Awards (including Best Actor for Gary Cooper), and being nominated for nine others. The film ended up being one of the one hundred top-grossing films of all time.

Alvin C. York (Cooper) is a backwoods Tennessee farmer who has been raised by the "good book" to believe that the killing of another man is wrong. He leads a simple life, only aspiring to get a good piece of bottomland. To that end, he scraps and scuffles and even tries to use his marvelous skill at shooting to win the money that he needs in order to buy the land. All of this setup is unusually long and detailed, and it is intended to provide us with context as the main act begins. When the United States enters World War I, York is drafted. As a conscientious objector, York appeals his induction into the army, but to no avail.

At the basic training camp, York is a good soldier, liked and respected by his fellows but distrusted by his superiors, who see in his record that he tried to claim conscientious objector status. But there is one thing about York that everyone admires: his remarkable marksmanship. Because of his skill as a shooter and his natural talent as a leader, the captain of his company proposes promoting York to corporal. But the captain is concerned about York's reluctance to kill, even an enemy in battle. In what is one of the most surreal scenes in the movie, York and his captain debate the morality of killing. York relies on the Bible. "Thou shall not kill" is pretty unambiguous. The captain can't argue with that. So, instead, the captain gives York a book on American history to read—presumably to demonstrate that the United States, which is a good thing, was actually founded by violence, which in pursuit of a good thing is acceptable. He then sends York on leave to consider a response.

York goes back to the Tennessee hills and reads the book. In the end, he comes to the conclusion that killing in the pursuit of the good is acceptable. This is a strange transformation for someone who is quite obviously a fund-

Sergeant York, **Warner Bros./Photofest, 1940**

amentalist who believes in the literalism of the Bible. But as a plotline convention, it is the only way to justify what follows.

Cut away to France and the battlefield. York's company is assigned to assault a hilltop controlled by several German machine-gun nests. The casualties are appalling, and York is thrust into a position of command. On his own initiative, York, circling around the Germans, wipes out an entire

German machine-gun nest and captures almost one hundred prisoners. The producers even use some comic relief in the battle scene when York makes a noise like a turkey, causing the Germans to pop up and be shot in turn. As the Americans march the Germans off to captivity, a German officer pulls out a pistol and shoots one of York's friends. The German is then shot in turn. This incident is an obvious sop to German perfidy.

In the aftermath of the battle, York's captain asks York how he overcame his aversion to killing. York replies that he has come to the realization that you have to take lives to save lives, ironically a justification later to be used to defend the nuclear destruction of Hiroshima and Nagasaki. York is then awarded a lot of medals and gets the bottomland he always wanted.

Sergeant York reflects one side of a spirited debate in 1940 to 1941 over the advisability of getting involved in the war, which had just broken out in Europe the year before. Pacifism of the kind reflected in *All Quiet on the Western Front* was still quite widespread in the United States, along with a strain of isolationism that was making it difficult for Franklin Roosevelt to assist the British and their allies in the war against the Germans. It may seem strange in the modern context to realize that until the attack on Pearl Harbor and before the German atrocities of World War II became widely known, there was both popular support for the German cause, even the fascist style of government, and widespread opposition to the war. *Sergeant York* is an answer to most of these objections. The film takes the pacifist message head-on, and even the Germans as the projected enemy are portrayed as evil.

While the names have changed, the subjects of modern films are not so different. After the war, the Russian and Chinese communists were the enemy, then the "terrorists" after that.[6] In order to keep current, Hollywood is always trying to capitalize on the enemy du jour. Sometimes the enemy is treated in metaphor. In *Star Wars* (1977), Darth Vader, wearing an exaggerated German helmet, represents an evil empire intent on ruling the universe on behalf of "the dark side." The reference to the Cold War is unmistakable, with a random Nazi artifact thrown in. Even President Ronald Reagan referred to the Soviet Union as the evil empire.

What makes *Sergeant York* unusual is that rather than being a film that reinforces existing beliefs or provides a cathartic release in seeing our enemies vanquished, the film is an advocate, a part of the political debate of its time. In general, the moguls stayed away from anything but the most superficial treatment of political controversies (see, for example, *Gentleman's Agreement*, 1947); when they did enter the political fray, it was through themes related to political slam dunks, such as prison reform in the South (*I Was a Fugitive from a Chain Gang*, 1932). In the case of *Sergeant York*, however, the war in Europe was important enough in 1940 for the moguls—specifically, those of Warner Bros.—to take a chance on a film that advocated what at the time was a controversial point of view.

The Bridge on the River Kwai

The top-grossing films from the 1950s in order of box office receipts (controlled for inflation) are *The Ten Commandments* (1956), *Ben Hur* (1959), *Sleeping Beauty* (1959), *The Robe* (1953), *Around the World in 80 Days* (1956), *The Greatest Show on Earth* (1952), *Lady and the Tramp* (1955), *The Bridge on the River Kwai* (1957), *House of Wax* (1953), *Peter Pan* (1953), and *The Caine Mutiny* (1954). With the exception of the Disney animation, this is a pretty forgettable lineup. In the 1950s, Hollywood operated under pressure from three sources: television, the revival of the European film industry, and the production code. To meet the challenge of the avant-garde, the tiny screen, and the code, Hollywood was forced to rely on technological gimmicks and biblical epics. *House of Wax* (1953), for example, was shot in 3D, requiring patrons to wear plastic glasses.[7] A number of terrific films were made in the 1950s, such as *The African Queen* (1951), *On the Waterfront* (1954), and *North by Northwest* (1959), but they did little to forestall the collapse of the studio system. But probably the most memorable movie statement of the decade was *The Bridge on the River Kwai*.

The Bridge on the River Kwai, Columbia Pictures, 1957

Of its eight Academy Award nominations, *The Bridge on the River Kwai* won seven, including Best Picture. It is also one of the top-grossing films of all time. In it, British Colonel Nicholson (Alec Guinness, who won the Oscar for Best Actor) matches wits with Japanese prisoner-of-war camp commander Colonel Saito (Sessue Hayakawa).

This is a film about a clash of cultures; it is also about duty and the obligation of soldiers in time of war. Colonel Nicholson is a by-the-book commander who, prisoner or not, is very much in command of his troops. Colonel Saito is a classic Japanese warrior. He cannot understand the lack of shame and the obstinacy, even in the face of death, of his nemesis Colonel Nicholson. Nicholson, for his part, reflecting the British colonial tradition, has simply no interest in Colonel Saito's Japanese point of view. To Nicholson, there is the British army way of doing things and the wrong way of doing things. In the end, it is he who breaks Colonel Saito and not the other way around.

This film has a number of unusual plotlines, unusual in the sense that they deviate from the typical war film of the 1940s. For one thing, in a departure from typical Japanese stereotyping, Colonel Saito is treated as a rather sympathetic character. There is also the question of whether, in the exercise of his sense of duty, Colonel Nicholson is actually collaborating with the enemy.

One of the most remarkable characters in this film is Commander Shears (William Holden). For his time, Shears is quite unlike the usual movie war hero and is in fact more of an antihero (presaging the characters portrayed in *Hud* [1963] or *MASH* [1970], classic 1960s-era counterculture films). Shears is a common seaman who, when his ship is torpedoed off the coast of Thailand, assumes the identity of an officer in the hope of getting better treatment as a prisoner of war. He escapes the camp where he is held (with Colonel Nicholson) and maintains the fiction of his rank even after the British rescue him. When asked by the British to help guide them back into the jungle to blow up a bridge that Colonel Nicholson and his men are building, Shears demurs. Only when he is confronted with the fact that the British have discovered his ruse is he forced to "volunteer" to return to the River Kwai. But Shears is acting against type. He is not a coward, he is not a pacifist—for lack of a better word, he is a survivor. As Shears puts it, in addressing one of the gung-ho British commandos,

> You make me sick with your heroics. There's a stench of death about you. You carry it in your pack like the plague. Explosives and [suicide] pills—they go well together, don't they? And with you it's just one thing or the other: destroy a bridge or destroy yourself. This is just a game, this war! You and Colonel Nicholson, you're two of a kind, crazy with courage. For what? How to die like a gentleman . . . how to die by the rules . . . when the only important thing is how to live like a human being.[8]

After two world wars and Korea, maybe Americans had had enough. Maybe they were ready to accept this type of character. And in the end, when the bridge on the river Kwai lies in ruins and Colonel Nicholson, Colonel Saito, and Shears all are dead, the last words of the film, uttered by a cynical British doctor observing the scene, are "madness, sheer madness." *The Bridge on the River Kwai* is not your typical war film. In it we can see the stirrings of the 1960s.

Lonely Are the Brave

Unlike the other films discussed in this section, *Lonely Are the Brave* did not do well at the box office. The studio limited the release of the film, and while the film did well in Europe, it didn't have much success in the United States. This relatively modest film, shot in black and white, is now considered a classic. And if you can ignore period costumes and props, the film holds up well because it is based on a theme that was and still is basic to American political culture.

The back story to this film is that it was written by Dalton Trumbo, who had been blacklisted by the Hollywood studios in the early 1950s for refus-

Lonely Are the Brave, **Paramount Pictures, 1962**

ing to inform on fellow movie-industry employees who were suspected of being communists. From that point onward, Trumbo was not permitted to submit scripts under his own name. So, at great financial cost to himself, he was forced to hire a "front," a person who submitted scripts written by Trumbo under another name.[9]

Trumbo—who was a friend of Kirk Douglas, star of the film—was not even allowed to set foot on the grounds of a Hollywood studio during the latter half of the 1950s. However, by the early 1960s Douglas and the producers of the film decided that the time had passed for the blacklist and that Trumbo deserved to have his name on the credits of the films he wrote. His first public attributions after the blacklist were for the enormously successful films *Spartacus* (1960) and *Exodus* (1960). Threatened boycotts of these films failed. Nevertheless, two years later the studios inexplicably limited the release of *Lonely Are the Brave*. Dalton Trumbo by this point was probably absolved, but the theme of the film is a downer and maybe, unlike *Spartacus*, a little too close to home.

Lonely Are the Brave opens with a cowboy camp, a smoking campfire, a horse, and a wide-open prairie. At first we get the impression that this is a typical western set in the late nineteenth century, but then a jet flies overhead. Jack Burns is a cowboy from the old school. He doesn't have a driver's license, a Social Security card, a home, a car, or any of the accoutrements of modern life. He is constantly at odds with the modern world. When he runs into a barbed wire fence, he cuts it. When he runs into a highway, he crosses it on his horse, a dangerous proposition to all involved. He follows his own rules, which are not without morality, just not the rules followed by the rest of the world, so that when he finds out that a friend has been thrown in jail for transporting illegal immigrants, Jack thinks nothing of getting into a barroom brawl to get himself into jail to visit with and help his friend. That being done, he then decides to break the two of them out of jail and make a run for Mexico.

His friend Paul won't go. Paul has a family, he has responsibilities, and he can't live his life on the run. This is the central conflict of the film. On the one hand, we want the freedom enjoyed by Jack Burns to go where we want and do what we want. On the other hand, we have responsibilities of living in a community that have their own compensations. Thus, there is a constant tension in the United States between our freedom and our responsibilities. Everything from the debate over taxes to the clash over the environmental movement to the debate over gun ownership is symptomatic of the peculiarly American conflict between the rights of the individual and the health of the community. Nowhere is this conflict more affecting than in the American West, where the disappearance of wilderness has destroyed a way of life. In that respect, *Lonely Are the Brave* is an achingly poignant film that should resonate at some level with most Americans.

National Lampoon's Animal House

Without exaggeration, it is possible to say that this film shaped a generation. It shaped a generation of films; it shaped a generation of comic actors; and to some extent, it shaped the youth generation of the 1980s. Let me say from the start that this film is funny—very funny. And on this point, I am not alone. *Animal House* is one of the fifty top-grossing films of all time, with box office receipts of almost $300 million (in 1998 dollars). It is also politically incorrect in practically every way imaginable. It is misogynistic, racist, antiestablishment, anti-intellectual, and about every other *anti* you can think of, but at the same time it's just a lot of fun.

For those of you who haven't seen it, the film centers on the Delta House, a fraternity at mythical Faber College. The Delta House is the filthiest, raunchiest, most slovenly fraternity house on campus, and Dean Wormer means to close it down. Bluto (John Belushi), Otter (Tim Matheson), Boon (Peter Riegert), and Pinto (Tom Hulce) lead the Delta House through a series of hijinks that became for a time the rites of passage for many students in college, including a toga party, a road trip (spawning a movie of the same name), seducing the dean's wife (well, that doesn't quite qualify as a rite of passage), a food fight in the cafeteria, stealing a midterm exam, and a number of other lighthearted and, fortunately, relatively nonconsequential adventures.[10] The picture ends in a paroxysm of cheerful destruction as the

National Lampoon's Animal House, **Universal Pictures/Photofest, 1978**

Delta House lays waste to the local town in retaliation for being placed on "double-secret probation" by the dean. As the credits role, we are informed that the misfits of the Delta House are the leaders of tomorrow, and in some sense that is true. The future is now.

Animal House is distinctive in its complete disregard for convention. In laying waste to the niceties of gender, ethnic, and other social relations, the movie not only makes it fun to flout conventional niceties but also makes it cool. A whole generation of moviegoers evolved through this movie and other influences with a contempt for civility, often sneered at as political correctness. They are, after all, free to do whatever they want. In that sense, there is a connection between *Animal House* and *Lonely Are the Brave*. Jack Burns and the boys at the Delta House have something in common when they flout authority. But the difference is that Burns flouts authority on principle; the boys at the Delta House flout authority because it feels good. In that sense, the philosophy of the Delta House is nihilism.[11] Their only motivation to act is to feel good, so that when thinking and feeling become indistinguishable, as individuals they are little more than the sum of their appetites. In that sense, using the term *animal house* to describe the Delta House is probably right on the mark.

This sort of coarse humor has now become the discourse of American media entertainment. It is not just in the movies that this sort of *Animal House*–like, politically incorrect humor is on display. It is on television, too. For example, see the cartoon series *South Park*. In books, see the writings of P. J. O'Rourke. It has even entered our political realm as talk radio, which is mostly dominated by mainly secular conservative commentators and that owes much of its style to the kind of politically incorrect comedy rolled out in *Animal House*. In appropriating the humor of the Delta House, conservatives have made the ideology of Nixon, Reagan, and George W. Bush, and now Donald Trump, cool.

Raiders of the Lost Ark

In some ways, the 1980s resemble the 1950s in the sense that there is a disconnect between films that achieved financial success and films that achieved critical success. For the audience of the 1980s, political commentary was out and escapism was in. Contrast the films of the era that achieved critical success with those that achieved financial success. On the critical side, Academy Award winners include *Ordinary People* (1980), *Chariots of Fire* (1981), *Gandhi* (1982), *Terms of Endearment* (1983), *Amadeus* (1984), *Out of Africa* (1985), *Platoon* (1986), *The Last Emperor* (1988), and *Driving Miss Daisy* (1989). These are some terrific films, but they are generally downers. In all but a couple of these films, the main character dies in the end. That's not the kind of entertainment that excites when, as President

***Raiders of the Lost Ark*, Paramount Pictures, 1981**

Reagan put it, "It's morning in America." On the other hand, the top-grossing films of the era were *E.T.* (1982), *The Empire Strikes Back* (1980), *Return of the Jedi* (1983), *Raiders of the Lost Ark* (1981), *Beverly Hills Cop* (1984), *Ghostbusters* (1984), *Batman* (1989), *Back to the Future* (1985), and *Tootsie* (1982). These are some pretty good films too, but with the exception of *Tootsie*, they are all in one way or another cartoons.

In *Raiders of the Lost Ark*, mild-mannered archeology professor Indiana Jones (Harrison Ford) dons his signature hat, grabs his bullwhip, and heads off to collect (steal) the artifacts of ancient civilizations. Nowadays, no self-respecting archeologist would despoil the site of an ancient civilization by removing its artifacts. But in the era that the film is set, leading up to World War II, Jones is in the business of collecting for his university's museum in the United States.

The film opens with Jones hacking his way through a South American jungle to retrieve a golden idol. What follows is about twenty minutes of death-defying, nonstop action and special effects that have become the signature of many a Steven Spielberg film. In the end, however, Jones is frustrated by his archrival Belloq, an evil French archeologist who steals the idol from him. Jones barely escapes with his life.

Jones is then enlisted by the US government to search for the fabled Ark of the Covenant, which apparently bestows on those who possess it the power of God. US intelligence services fear that the Nazis are close to finding the Ark. The problem is that if they possess the Ark, they will have the power to conquer the world. Indiana Jones accepts the mission and sets off on his quest. Along the way he meets up with Marion (played by Karen Allen), an old flame; a sadistic Gestapo agent; an old Egyptian friend; various evildoers, including a monkey who turns out to be a Nazi spy; and, finally, his old nemesis Belloq. In the end, through a series of hair-raising adventures, Jones retrieves the ark; God smites the Nazis; and in the last scene, the ark, now stored in a crate, is carted off to a corner of a vast, government warehouse to be lost for another millennium.

This movie is a lot of fun, but it isn't Shakespeare. It has marvelous special effects, handsome characters, and lots of action, including some terrific "happy killing"[12] and the best "face melt" in motion picture history. In that sense, the film is analogous to its era, as the United States faced down the evil empire of the Soviet Union, a feat led by a handsome, swashbuckling president (himself a former actor) engaged in a variety of adventures, including the full-scale invasion of a small tropical island, Grenada.

President Reagan was a master of the art of the political spectacle. A spectacle is a staged event designed to elicit an emotional rather than an intellectual response.[13] In that sense, as pure entertainment, most movies are spectacle. So it is not too much of a stretch to suggest that, because of his skill in inducing an emotional response, former actor Ronald Reagan became our first movie president, one who in his days as an actor could have played Indiana Jones. The problem is that in the movies, inducing an emotional response is entertaining; in a political system, inducing an emotional response (fear, anger, and greed) is antidemocratic. After all, in a democracy, voters should have to think to vote. Therefore, in the sense that it was the ultimate spectacle, *Raiders of the Lost Ark* was a movie for its times.

Malcolm X

The remarkable thing about this picture is that it was made at all. To suggest in a previous era that a mainstream Hollywood film depicting the life of a Muslim African American activist who called for resistance "by any means necessary"[14] would get made and make money would be preposterous. Civil rights issues had been treated in the past, but mostly from the white political perspective or in a sort of idealized way from the black perspective that soft-sold the effects of discrimination.

One can in some sense track the progression of civil rights through its movies—those of its era and those that predate it. First there was the minstrel show as depicted in *Show Boat* (1936, remade in 1951), where the music is lovely and the dancing is great (another example of this is *The Littlest Rebel*, from 1935), but where stereotypes abound. Then there was the

Malcolm X, **Warner Brothers, 1992**

"they are just like us" school of films, represented by *The Defiant Ones* (1958), a film in which a black convict and a white convict are chained together and have to learn to get along. Then, in the earliest days of the civil rights era, Hollywood took on more controversial issues, such as mixed-race marriages, as in *Guess Who's Coming to Dinner* (1967). Hollywood later wrote its own history of the civil rights movement in *Mississippi Burning* (1988), a film in which blacks and civil rights activists in general have remarkably little to do with the success of the civil rights movement. In fact, the protagonists in the film are two FBI agents who presumably were taking time off from spying on Dr. Martin Luther King (on the orders of J. Edgar Hoover, director of the FBI) to finally enforce the law.[15] In *Driving Miss Daisy* (1989), the theme is that blacks have been discriminated against, but so have many of us. The film is well done but walks a fine line of recalling the depiction of African Americans from an earlier era.

In *Malcolm X*, director Spike Lee confronts civil rights conventions head-on. In the opening scene, when he features the police beating of Rodney King, he implies that the issues of discrimination and racism in America are still very much a part of our nation's culture. He then proceeds to deliver a sympathetic (some would say idolizing) biography of one of the most polarizing figures in the middle part of the twentieth century. While there are mistakes of emphasis and of fact, Lee's movie is not just a good film but also an important film.[16] Probably not many whites have read Malcolm X's autobiography. In viewing this film, they may get the only information they ever receive about Malcolm X and a major part of the civil rights movement. Our leaders are anxious to tout the nonviolent approach advocated by Dr. King, but in Malcolm's more strident politics, we get a sense of the rage in the black community that sometimes and in some segments exists right below the surface. In that sense, this movie is important because it somewhat accurately documents and much more accurately engenders the ethos of the civil rights era from the black perspective.

Parenthetically, Denzel Washington was marvelous in the role of Malcolm X. He didn't get the Academy Award for Best Actor, but he should have. Instead, he received the award for his work in the film *Training Day* (2001), which represents the latest stage in the evolution of black-white relations on screen. In it, Washington portrays a crooked cop who plays villain to Ethan Hawke's hero. The fact that Washington happens to be black is of little significance to the plot. In that sense, *Training Day* is color-blind, and while we still struggle with issues of race in this country, that ethnicity is unremarkable in this film and others is an advance in and of itself.

The Hunger Games: Mockingjay Part 1

After the financial collapse of the great recession in 2008, Americans are reeling from one of worst failures of capitalism in the last fifty years. While we want to recover and prevent a relapse, nobody knows exactly what to do. Republicans make policy proposals that are simply absurd, and Democrats want to kick the can down the road. This ambiguity is reflected in our entertainment. Nobody knows exactly what to do when capitalism fails and democratic politics can't find the solution. This is the question that *The Hunger Games: Mockingjay Part 1* and other films like *The Wolf of Wall Street* try to answer.

This is the third in what has become the tiresome Hunger Games "franchise." The first film in the series, *The Hunger Games* (2012), was a mildly interesting story of revolution against oppression and, more important, teenage love and unrequited love. There was also a lot of action and some really good special effects. The plotline, for those of you who haven't seen at least one in the series, is that an imperial, decadent center led by President Snow is holding sway over the outer provinces by a combination of military power and bread and circuses. Somehow the center has managed to force the provinces (or "districts") to sacrifice on an annual basis two of their youth (drawn by lot). These teenagers then compete in a fight to the death for the prize of a lifetime of luxury.

There is a lot that is pretty improbable about all this, but what holds the film together are the teenage love stories, an excellent cast, and a lot of

The Hunger Games: Mockingjay Part 1, Lionsgate, 2014

really good killing. In the end, in a modern show of girl power, Katniss Everdeen, played by the ever radiant Jennifer Lawrence, wins the day and saves her (sort of) boyfriend in the bargain.

The first film made a lot of money, and, as these things are wont to do, it spawned a sequel that is basically a very thinly veiled reprise of the story and action of the first film. But, as they say, the plot thickens . . .

At the end of the second film, we find that Katniss Everdeen's success and demeanor has inspired a nascent revolutionary movement. *Mockingjay Part 1* is the first of a two-part story of the revolution galvanized by Katniss's success. Part 2, which as of this writing is just about to be released, will presumably depict the success of the revolution. And then, I hope, that will be the end of it. And given the decline in receipts for the third film, things are looking up in that regard.

Part 1 is the story of a very risky enterprise, and I'm not talking about the revolution. The producers have decided to double their money by shooting one movie and splitting it into two. Quentin Tarantino did this with *Kill Bill: Volumes One and Two*, so why not *Hunger Games*? After all, there are always enough outtakes to fill a half hour, and if you extend a scene by a minute or two and there are forty to sixty scenes in a typical movie, you've got an extra hour. Part 1 reeks of this sort of thing.

And now let's get to the plotline. We know that the center and President Snow are bad. That is clear enough. But what are the revolutionaries planning to replace it with? The revolution in this film reminds me of the recently failed Occupy Wall Street movement—rebels without a cause. I suspect for the purposes of the viewing (and even not viewing) audience that the rebels can't be socialists, but there's no avoiding the reality that, at the end of all this, there is going to be some serious redistribution of holdings, and for their part in the Hunger Games and other atrocities, some extensive war crimes trials, ending, I presume, with some executions. Hey, but, after all, this is the movies, and what I suspect will happen is that they all will live happily ever after. (Except for the bad guys who will be killed in the most humiliating way.)

Postscript: Mockingjay Part 2 *isn't bad at all. I think if you want the gist of this and the two best films in the series, you can get away with watching the first and last installment.*

CONCLUSION

Without the motivating force of the Nazi or Soviet threat, and even in the aftermath of September 11, we lost some of the shared feeling of community that comes with the pursuit of a common cause. Thus, while the end of the Cold War and the economic boom of the 1990s are by any standard wonderful things, they come at a price—the loss of community. Consequently, movie plots based on a premise of self-sacrifice for the community—for someone other than our immediate families—seem a little silly in the modern context.

Now that we have gone through another round of wars and another economic collapse, one would think that films would come to reflect a concern with economic inequality and/or the threat of our new enemies. However, the new political phenomenon that tends to dominate our discourse is partisan polarization. So it probably pays in public discourse to stay out of politics because no matter what the story line, the narrative is likely to annoy one side or the other or, in the worst-case scenario, both.

So, for example, in the recent film *Our Brand Is Crisis* (2015), two cynical political consultants compete in a presidential race *in Bolivia*. Nobody can be offended by that. Except, it seems, the critics, who don't think the film is hard-hitting enough. In a polarized political environment, in trying to hit the center, the filmmakers have hit nothing. Fairly typical of the criticism of the film comes from Rafer Guzman of the generally conservative *Daily News*:

Our Brand Is Crisis can't decide if it's a jaundiced spoof like *Thank You for Smoking* or an early episode of *The West Wing*. Shady tactics abound—phony leaflets, whisper campaigns, a dead llama—but they feel like movie-plot stuff. The discussion of polls, strategy and Sun Tzu's *The Art of War* never feels like it comes from within a real campaign bunker.[17]

Or from the generally liberal *New York Times*:

Like most American movies about politics, *Our Brand Is Crisis* plays it straight down the noncommittal middle. In place of an obvious party line, it has good intentions and personalities along with a faith in both American democracy and the kind of happy endings that made Mr. Smith's trip to Washington such a success. It casts a skeptical eye at the gospel of globalization that's preached by Jane's team, but its outrage is more directed at cynicism than at any specific system.[18]

There is not enough "red meat" in this film to satisfy political junkies from either side. And because there is no killing or elaborate special effects, it is fairly safe to predict that this film is going to be a terrible flop.[19]

So why don't they make 'em like they used to? The answer is quite simple. They don't make 'em like they used to because they can't. In part this is true because the economy of the film industry is not what it was in its golden era—a monopoly. The studios didn't have to respond to a captive market in the past in the same way that they respond to a free market now. A cynical public would not sit through a 1930s version of *Mr. Smith Goes to Washington*. What now passes for a realistic depiction of American politics is just as cynical and exaggerated as the original *Mr. Smith Goes to Washington* is in its own over-the-top patriotic way.

Critics today would probably pan Frank Capra's *Mr. Smith Goes to Washington* just as they have praised two of the most cynical movies ever produced about American politics: *Bulworth* (1998) and *Wag the Dog* (1997), and, more recently, the television series *House of Cards*. For better and for worse, the public has a dynamic sense of what is real. Thus, the films of today reflect modern sensibilities both good and bad—as will the films of tomorrow.

Most films produced for general release are not great art. They reflect the simple reality that in order to recoup the enormous cost of an elaborate production, film studios must cater/pander to a low common denominator. This is not to mention the fact that since the lion's share of an American film's profits is derived in foreign release, modern high-budget filmmakers must be conscious of how their films will translate into Urdu, Hindi, Arabic, Chinese, or French. Such an economic imperative dictates that films in need of a large foreign gross contain more physical action, less dialogue, and scripts that are much less reflective of core—and sometimes, from the world's perspective, eccentric—American values.

But what is particularly exciting about the current market is that every once in a while, a low-budget film makes a breakthrough or is at least modestly successful, and that fact encourages the production of ever more ambitious films by independent production companies. Furthermore, there has developed a hybrid film art, the on-demand, pay-per-view, streaming video environment that has produced some remarkably successful, top-quality serials. And the great thing about these shows is that special effects are by and large too expensive, so the creative effort of the show has to be invested in the story and the acting. Although many of these shows are not all that good, they are at least reflective of a dynamic, creative environment that will eventually produce products just as good as *Citizen Kane*. Therefore, we should be relatively optimistic about the future quality of American film.

Finally, it is quite remarkable how little modern technology has changed the character of film. A bad story is still a bad story no matter how many computer-generated graphics, long shots from a helicopter, car chases, face melts, high school cheerleaders in short skirts, or graphic sex acts it employs. Film is still, after all, a two-dimensional medium. Special effects can never compete with the Technicolor of the imagination. Nevertheless, there appears to be a niche for special effects–based films. *The Avengers* (2012), a film without a plot that basically stars some special effects, ranks twenty-eighth among the top-grossing films of all time (adjusted for inflation).[20] That ranking probably means that we will have to endure ever more elaborate and mindless films of the same ilk. But then again, we don't have to go see them.

What this ultimately means is that they don't make 'em like they used to, and that is a good news–bad news story. The good news is that in the wide-ranging and dynamic market for films, there are many good, creative, and uplifting products to be consumed. Unfortunately, many of the good films are not very popular, and many of the bad ones are. But such is the nature of a free market. Should we aspire to control the market, say, by censoring or restricting the production of films, we won't just return to the days of the golden era; we will also be returning to the days when a vast assortment of topics of social import and historical significance were off limits to film. Nevertheless, there are those who attempt to censor films. The next chapter explores the general issue of film censorship. Each form of censorship brings with it a set of good, bad, and unintended effects. Thus, as an alternative to the free market, censorship probably isn't worth the effort and may in fact be downright dangerous.

Feature Film: *Mr. Smith Goes to Washington*

Mr. Smith Goes to Washington, **Columbia Pictures/Photofest, 2016**

Both the good and the bad in our society are reflected in the content of our dramas—thus, the reason why they don't make 'em like they used to. The rights and wrongs of society have changed dramatically across time—and it's not just that we tolerate more violence and explicit sexual behavior in our films. Beyond simply graphic depictions, our modern dramas contain subtle (and not so subtle) distinctions that make it difficult to remake for popular consumption the great films of the past. To illustrate my point, for my feature film, I have rewritten *Mr. Smith Goes to Washington* from a twenty-first-century perspective.

FX Channel, in cooperation with GE films and Amazon Prime with the cooperation of Bridgestone Tires and General Brands, presents *Mr. Smith Goes to Washington.*

Episode One—Senator Wilson Lee dies in office. The governor of the state, in consultation with his largest campaign contributor, B. Langston Parker, decides to appoint the dimwitted Jefferson Smith to fill the rest of Senator Lee's term. Smith is appointed because he is a "nonpolitician" with no political experience, which puts him in good stead with the "know nothing" wing of the governor's party. Smith is supposed to play a caretaker role and, more important, play no role in blocking Parker's plan to carve out a tax break for Parker Industries in pending tax legislation.

Episode Two—Smith goes to Washington and takes in the sights. Senior senator from the state, Missy Haines, who happens to also be in the pocket of Langston Parker, is assigned the responsibility of distracting Smith, just in case he gets any ideas into his head about actually acting as a senator. Haines tries to seduce Smith, but he's not interested— turns out he is gay.

Episode Three—Smith's chief of staff Alderon Jones, a veteran of Capitol Hill, takes Smith under his wing and shows him the ropes of the Senate. Smith wants to sponsor a bill that makes it illegal to wear certain types of clothing. Plaid pants, bellbottoms, leisure suits, all polyester, and wearing white after Labor Day are all to be strictly forbidden. Smith falls for Jones, and they have passionate sex on Smith's red leather sofa.

Episode Four—Jones urges Smith to "come out," but Smith demurs. He believes that if his father finds out that his son is gay, given his heart condition, it will kill him. Jones gets mad and tries to out Smith, and the senator retaliates by firing him. Jones files a harassment suit against Smith in federal court. Smith is outed in the press. He comes out and is the first openly gay senator in US history. (His father is fine; he knew all the time.)

Episode Five—Three other senators come out, including a prominent conservative from North Carolina. The gay agenda gets a boost, and Smith's bill gains a clear pathway to passage in the Senate. In the meantime, Smith finds out about the Parker Industries tax break. Parker Industries, which has a terrible record on gay rights issues, becomes the target of the newly formed Gay Caucus in the Senate. There is a bipartisan move to get rid of the tax break for Parker Industries in the new tax bill.

Episode Six—Parker calls in his favors and a story is leaked to the press to the effect that Smith has been having sex with underage boys as young as seven years old. Smith is arrested, and the Senate moves to consider his expulsion. Smith takes the floor of the Senate and begins to filibuster.

. . .

Episode Twelve—In the last episode of the season, Senator Smith has moved into a brownstone in Georgetown and is now wholly invested in Parker Industries. Maybe it's time for our first gay president?

Okay, this sounds a bit silly, but the cynicism about politics in American film is so pervasive now that *Mr. Smith Goes to Washington* in its traditional form in the current environment could never get made. Not only are Americans naturally predisposed to be cynical about politics, but in the current historical context, with Congress getting a positive rating in the teens, Americans are also downright mad. The problem is that at some point they might just give up on our government. Then what?

EXERCISE

Pick a major feature film from the relatively distant past (before 1980) and rewrite the plot according to the politics and cultural sensibilities of the modern era.

SUGGESTED READINGS

Berger, Arthur Asa. *Media Analysis Techniques*. Los Angeles: Sage, 2013.

Chaudhuri, Shohini. *Cinema of the Dark Side: Atrocity and the Ethics of Film Spectatorship*. Edinburgh: Edinburgh University Press, 2014.

Hayward, Susan. *Cinema Studies: The Key Concepts*. Abingdon: Routledge, 2013.

Howells, Richard, and Joaquim Negreiros. *Visual Culture*, 2nd ed. Cambridge: Polity, 2012.

Kauffmann, Stanley. *Regarding Film: Criticism and Comment*. Baltimore: Johns Hopkins University Press, 2001.

Silverblatt, Art, et al. *Media Literacy: Keys to Interpreting Media Messages*. Santa Barbara, CA: ABC-CLIO, 2014.

Turner, Graeme. *Film as Social Practice*. Abingdon: Routledge, 2006.

NOTES

1. The irony is that Elon Musk and Tesla (unlike DeLorean) disproved the whole car production monopoly myth as well.

2. Arnold Toynbee, *A Study of History* (London: Oxford University Press, 1972), 97.

3. Cinerama was a film-display technique that attempted to recreate the full range of human vision. The technique involved the use of a giant, concave viewing screen with three projection screens shot by three cameras. Cinerama debuted in 1952 in the travelogue *This Is Cinerama*, which ran for only thirteen weeks in one theater in New York City and was nonetheless the top-grossing film for the year. See Greg Kimble, "This Is Cinerama," *Cinema Technology*, December 2002, www.cinerama adventure.com/kimblearticle.htm (accessed January 15, 2016).

4. See "Bill Moyers on LBJ and 'Selma,'" *Bill Moyers and Company*, January 15, 2015, http://billmoyers.com/2015/01/15/bill-moyers-selma-lbj/ (accessed January 15, 2016). According to Moyers:

As for how the film portrays Lyndon B. Johnson: There's one egregious and outrageous portrayal that is the worst kind of creative license because it suggests the very opposite of the truth, in this case, that the president was behind J. Edgar Hoover's sending the "sex tape" to Coretta King. Some of our most scrupulous historians have denounced that one. And even if you want to think of Lyndon B. Johnson as vile enough to want to do that, he was way too smart to hand Hoover the means of blackmailing him.

Amy Davidson, "Why 'Selma' Is More Than Fair to L.B.J.," *New Yorker*, January 22, 2015, http://www.newyorker.com/news/amy-davidson/selma-fair-l-b-j.

5. David Easton, *A Systems Analysis of Political Life* (New York: Wiley, 1967), particularly chapter 7.

6. See Jack Shaheen, *Reel Bad Arabs: How Hollywood Vilifies a People* (New York: Interlink, 2001). This is apparently an enduring theme, as evidenced by the current Republican presidential debates and by the publication of a second edition of this book, *Reel Bad Arabs: How Hollywood Vilifies a People*, 2nd ed. (Northampton, MA: Interlink, 2014). There is also a 2006 documentary of the same name.

7. This gimmick is in revival and much more successful than in its 1950s iteration. I still get the sense that directors don't quite know how to incorporate 3D into films. But they are getting better. Martin Scorsese makes particularly good use of this technique in his 2011 film, *Hugo*.

8. Internet Movie Database, "Memorable Quotes from *The Bridge on the River Kwai*," http://www.imdb.com/search/text?field=quotes&q=War%20Is%20Over&realm=title&start=51 (accessed January 15, 2016).

9. One of the screenplays that Trumbo wrote under a pseudonym actually won an Oscar for *The Brave One* (1956). Woody Allen starred in a film on just this subject, titled *The Front* (1976). The critically acclaimed film *Trumbo* (2015) is also directly on point (but doesn't mention *Lonely Are the Brave*, focusing more on *Spartacus*).

10. Although, given the sensitivity to the "rape culture" on modern college campuses, in the modern context this film may have gone too far.

11. "Nihilism is the belief that all values are baseless and that nothing can be known or communicated. It is often associated with extreme pessimism and a radical skepticism that condemns existence. A true nihilist would believe in nothing, have no loyalties, and no purpose other than, perhaps, an impulse to destroy." Alan Pratt, "Nihilism," *Internet Encyclopedia of Philosophy*, http://www.iep.utm.edu/nihilism/ (accessed January 15, 2016).

12. *Happy killing* is a term that can be used to describe cartoon killing or killing without consequence.

13. For a complete discussion of the idea of a presidential spectacle, see Bruce Miroff, "The Presidency and the Public: Leadership as Spectacle," in *The Presidency and the Political System*, ed. Michael Nelson, 10th ed. (Washington, DC: CQ Press, 2013), 231–57, or Bruce Miroff, *Icons of Democracy: American Leaders as Heroes, Aristocrats, Dissenters, and Democrats* (New York: Basic Books, 1993).

14. See Malcolm X's speech "The Ballot or the Bullet," April 3, 1964, http://www.edchange.org/multicultural/speeches/malcolm_x_ballot.html (accessed January 15, 2016).

15. For a good discussion of the historical inaccuracies of both fact and emphasis

in this film, see William H. Chafe, "Mississippi Burning," in *Past Imperfect: History According to the Movies*, ed. Mark C. Carnes (New York: Henry Holt, 1996), 274–77. There is some irony in the fact that J. Edgar Hoover himself takes it on the chin in the recent film *J. Edgar* (2011). In that big-budget, mainstream film, Hoover is portrayed as a neurotic, cross-dressing homosexual, a portrayal that probably has the former FBI director turning in his grave.

16. On the inaccuracies of the film, see Clayborn Carson, "Malcolm X," in Carnes, *Past Imperfect*, 278–83.

17. Rafer Guzman, "*Our Brand Is Crisis* Review: Politics, Breezy but Uneven," *Newsday*, November 29, 2015, http://www.newsday.com/entertainment/movies/our-brand-is-crisis-review-politics-breezy-but-uneven-1.11021032 (accessed January 15, 2016).

18. Manohla Dargis, "Review: In *Our Brand Is Crisis*, the War Room Goes to Bolivia," *New York Times*, October 29, 2015, http://www.nytimes.com/2015/10/30/movies/review-in-our-brand-is-crisis-the-war-room-goes-to-bolivia.html?_r = 0 (accessed January 15, 2016).

19. It has 32 percent out of 100 on the "Tomatometer" and ranked eighth in its first weekend at the box office (looking pretty bad). Update: Three months after its release, *Our Brand* has grossed $7 million on a $28 million budget.

20. In the middle of the film, I went out for popcorn and found the longest line possible at the concession stand.

7

Movies, Censorship, and the Law

Make no mistake about it, American films are censored now and always have been. When we talk about the advisability of film censorship, it is not a discussion of whether or not but how and how much. Films are censored in one of three ways: by the market, by the industry, or by the government. The real question in the debate over film censorship is what form of censorship should take place and under what circumstances. In this chapter, I examine the pros and cons, as well as the reality, of each form of censorship.

CENSORSHIP IN THE MARKET: BIAS AND BOYCOTTS

The market censors film in two ways: through the decisions that consumers make and through those that producers make. A vigorous debate centers on which influence is more important. Specifically, is marketing an art or a science? In the main, as discussed in previous chapters, and in the absence of market distortions, consumers ultimately choose what products to consume.[1] Thus, for the most part, consumers drive film content. To assume otherwise is to assume (1) that filmmakers have some hidden agenda that they will pursue at the expense of their profits and in disregard of the bottom line of their now publicly held companies or (2) that there is some kind of outside, third influence, such as the government, that is an active player in the regulation of film content.

As discussed in previous chapters, the first assumption is difficult to support. It is remarkable that the critics of the film industry's moral and political character are capitalists (Marxist critics excluded) who forget all that they know about economics when it comes to analyzing the film industry.

Granted that Hollywood filmmakers tend to be liberals, there still doesn't seem to be much evidence to suggest that any kind of conspiracy centered in Southern California is intent on corrupting the morals of our youth. This is especially true in the current competitive market for films. A movie executive with an agenda beyond making money is cruising for a financial loss and a dismissal.

There are, of course, subtle exceptions to this rule. Don't cross Hollywood and expect to get away with it! In the 1990s, when the Chinese government looked the other way while Hollywood films, CDs, and other entertainment products were being pirated for a billion Chinese consumers, the result was a literal anti-Chinese film festival that included *Seven Years in Tibet* (1997), *Kundun* (1997), and *Red Corner* (1997). And yes, it is probably the case that the religious Right takes it on the chin as well when people like Jerry Falwell are depicted in an uncomplimentary manner in films such as *The People vs. Larry Flynt* (1996), a film that celebrates, of all things, *Penthouse* publisher Larry Flynt's role as a defender of civil liberties. But Falwell and his crowd don't go to the movies (to repurpose a famous line from the film *Apocalypse Now*, "Charlie don't surf"). Why should Hollywood care what he thought?

But this brings to mind a more subtle form of censorship produced by the market. If certain groups don't have economic clout or visibility, or if they are not an audience for film, their depictions in film can be uncomplimentary or nonexistent. The role of religion in film is an instructive example. Critics of the depiction of religion from the Left argue that the communitarian, cooperative, pacifist tendencies in religion are given short shrift in Hollywood films. For example, in the otherwise excellent film *Witness* (1985), the protagonist police detective John Book, played by Harrison Ford, is forced to hide from some bad guys by living among the Amish. But when the time comes to confront the bad guys, Book and apparently the screenwriters have learned nothing from the Amish. What we get in the end is the traditional gunfight and a terrific kill scene in which one of the villains is literally drowned in a silo of grain. While that outcome is cathartic, it is not very thoughtful and is in fact a perversion of the story heretofore seen. But when morals are treated in American film, they tend to emphasize the paternalistic, hierarchical Old Testament versus New Testament values of religion.[2]

By the same token, conservative critics often argue that organized religion is treated with contempt by Hollywood, with its priests depicted as charlatans (or worse) and its adherents as morons. For example, in his book *Hollywood Worldviews: Watching Films with Wisdom and Discernment*, author Brian Godawa analyzes films from a conservative Christian perspective.[3] It is his contention that the existential, postmodern worldview of Hollywood filmmaking depicts a meaningless life in which the characters in film do not act; they simply are.[4] For example, according to Godawa, in the film *Forrest Gump* (1994), the protagonist lives a life that has little or no significance or meaning because he is not motivated by any sort of higher calling. In that sense, the story of *Forrest Gump* is a metaphor for life without God: things happen, wealth is obtained—but for what purpose?

In response to this sometimes shoddy treatment, religious groups have threatened economic retaliation against the entertainment production industry. In the 1920s, groups associated with the Catholic Church helped found the production code and the Hays Committee. They backed their calls for censorship with a threatened boycott, a threat made effective by the fact that the market for films at the time, in large part, consisted of working-class and immigrant groups who belonged to the Catholic Church. In the 1980s and 1990s, groups from the evangelical religious Right, who don't tend to go to the movies, organized stock ownership programs and economic boycotts in order to pressure entertainment companies into altering the content of their product.

For example, in January 1985, Republican senator Jesse Helms (North Carolina), through an organization called Fairness in Media, promoted a stock purchase program of CBS by religious conservatives. The purpose of this move was to pressure the management of CBS into correcting what Fairness in Media took to be CBS's liberal bias. Fairness in Media sent out a million letters under Senator Helms's signature urging each recipient to purchase twenty shares of CBS stock at a cost of about $1,500 (CBS was trading at about $75 a share at the time). Considering that there were about thirty million shares of CBS stock outstanding, Helms would have had to realize about a 75 percent response rate to gain control of the company. The attempt failed. CBS had a market capitalization of $2.4 billion, too much for an ideologically driven crusade.

Boycotts have been no more successful. In 1996, the 15.6 million members of the Southern Baptist Convention voted to boycott the Disney Corporation. They and other conservatives, including a group called the American Family Foundation, objected to the content of some of the films produced and distributed by Miramax Films (a subsidiary of Disney) and to the fact that Disney accommodated gays who sponsored events at Disney-operated amusement parks. Furthermore, in 1998 the American Family Foundation of Texas managed to pressure the Texas State Board of Education to sell its 1.2 million shares of Disney stock. Disney resisted the boycott, perhaps recognizing that the boycott of Miramax's *Pulp Fiction* made by religious conservatives was a nonstarter (the film grossed over $200 million on an $8 million budget) and that most Americans would ignore a boycott against one of the nation's top tourist destinations anyway. The reward for Disney was one of the great successes of the stock market and of corporate performance in the 1990s: Disney stock grew about 500 percent (split adjusted from 1990 to 2000).

In the current streaming video environment, where theater attendance has stalled and/or films are largely made for foreign consumption, boycotts are even more difficult to arrange. When films (and television serials) are viewed in the privacy of the living room, boycotts are more difficult to pull off. In fact, one of the side effects of the digitalization, streaming video era is to open up film production to all genres and all levels of violence and nudity. The only limit is not what the public can tolerate, but what it will purchase.

The market determines the content of films in two other ways. First, films will be only as good as the skills of the people who make them. On the demand side, there is such a large market for entertainment that even substantially flawed products can enjoy financial success. As such, a couple of recent blockbusters and financially successful films, besides being technical marvels, haven't been half bad in the plot department. *Titanic* (1997) and *Spectre* (2015) both had stories to go along with their special effects. Nevertheless, the brain-dead *Marvel's The Avengers* (2012) also did well ($1.5 billion!!!), becoming, as of this writing, the fourth top-grossing film of all time. That being the case, we probably haven't seen the last of the *Avengers* movies (including *Avengers: Age of Ultron*, currently on release).

Another way in which the market censors films is by excluding or ignoring unpopular ideas. Many filmmakers may be liberals, but they sure aren't socialists. Thus, they would respond to the market wherever it takes them. In the 1960s there were produced many socially conscious (and often tendentious) films about the plight of farmers, the dangers of nuclear power, prison reform, the civil rights movement, the labor movement, and the environment. Those films don't seem to get made these days, at least for wide release.

This is a chicken-and-egg problem. Are film corporations suppressing "subversive" messages that they oppose, or are they responding to the lack of demand? And if there were a demand for anticapitalistic messages, would corporations engage in the ultimate irony of sponsoring films critical of themselves?

Particularly in the aftermath of the financial meltdown of 2008, Hollywood has gotten more critical of corporate America, albeit haltingly so. *Avatar* (2009) is basically the story of a mining corporation on an alien planet, backed up by the Earthen military exploiting minerals at the expense of the native population (who worship an "earth god" and bear a remarkable resemblance, except for their blue hue, to Native Americans). The real irony of this movie is that was being distributed by Twenty-First Century Fox, whose CEO Rupert Murdoch is also responsible for the conservative Fox News. Another big-release film critical of the corporate culture is *The Wolf of Wall Street* (2013), and a number of smaller films besides. The "great recession" produced a narrative that Hollywood simply could not ignore.[5]

These problems aside, on balance the range and quality of American motion pictures are the envy of the world. There is still very limited foreign competition for this particular American product (Bollywood, the Indian film industry, produces more films and sells twice the tickets of Hollywood but garners only about 30 percent of the revenues).[6] This is still true in the modern era, even after the demise of the Hollywood studio trust, the advent of television, the corporatization of American media, and the digitalization of film. That is why it is possible to say that the real golden era of the American film industry is now. The range and quality of Hollywood's best films are unsurpassed and getting better, and the caliber of that product is attributable to the general marketization of the industry. Those who wish to return to the film industry's past, even if those days could be reproduced, are really arguing for a form of censorship different from the one imposed by the market—that is, for one imposed by the industry or through the government. Those forms of censorship, however, would likely produce an inferior product with biases every bit as bad and worse than the occasional brain-dead, corporate-centered, bottom-line filmmaking that is all too common in the blockbuster film. At least in the current environment, creative, thoughtful, and even subversive films can get made. Could the same be said for certain periods in the past?

INDUSTRY SELF-CENSORSHIP

When in the past the film industry was under pressure from social critics, it often attempted some form of self-censorship. This was generally more than a publicity ploy. Throughout most of the 1930s, Hollywood operated under a strict production code that imposed severe limitations on film depictions and content. The code was imposed by the movie studios on themselves and was made enforceable by the vertical integration of the industry. Since the studios controlled the distribution and exhibition of films, it was virtually impossible for a film to be exhibited that had not been cleared by the production code censors.

In a sense, the production code came about as a by-product of governmental pressure. From the beginning of the film industry, when nickelodeons were midway attractions at carnivals, the government has attempted to censor film content. One of the first film censorship ordinances in the United States was adopted in 1907 in Chicago, resulting in the establishment of a local film censorship board. A number of other communities and states followed suit.

For film distributors, this patchwork of censorship made distribution difficult not only because it limited the product but also because local censorship made the task of film distribution all the more expensive. Each film print had to be tailored to demands of a different community. In the process, prints were recut so often that they were destroyed, and given the expense and shortage of film stock in the early days of the industry, local film censorship became such a burden that distributors were willing to fight. In 1914 a Detroit film distributor, the Mutual Film Corporation, challenged in federal court an Ohio law that established a state film censorship board. The board was charged with the responsibility of clearing for exhibition "only such films as are . . . of a moral, educational, or amusing and harmless character." The plaintiff, Mutual Film, argued that in addition to violating constitutional protections of freedom of speech and the press, the Ohio law, as a restraint of trade, was in violation of the interstate commerce clause of the US Constitution.[7]

The case was appealed all the way to the Supreme Court, where Justice Joseph McKenna, in writing for the majority of the Court, dismissed the plaintiff's argument that the Ohio Censorship Board was a violation of the Interstate Commerce Clause. After all, the censorship board's decisions applied only to films screened in Ohio. Furthermore, as to the matter of First Amendment freedom of speech, McKenna wrote,

> It cannot be put out of view that the exhibition of moving pictures is a business, pure and simple, originated and conducted for profit, like other spectacles, not to be regarded, nor intended to be regarded by the Ohio Constitution we think, as part of the press of the country, or as organs of public opinion. They are mere representations of events, of ideas and sentiments published and known; vivid, useful, and entertaining, no doubt, but, as we have said, capable of evil, having power for it, the greater because of their attractiveness and manner of exhibition.[8]

In other words, in this decision, the Court ruled that motion pictures were *product, not art nor a form of journalism.* Therefore, the State of Ohio could treat commercial motion pictures as it did any other product and impose requirements on their marketing and use.

This decision has to be viewed in context. In 1914, prior to the Great Depression, the Court (and federal government) was reluctant to interfere with what was then known as states' rights. Within reasonable limits, states had the authority to regulate their own internal commerce. Thus, at the time, the Court was in no mood to intervene in the sort of action brought by Mutual Film. However, pursuant to the logic of states' rights, states often violated what we now understand to be basic constitutional rights in much more extreme and serious ways than simply censoring movies. For example,

Jim Crow laws, which mandated racial discrimination in the South, were justified in part by their supporters as exercises in states' rights.

The result of the Mutual Film decision was to open the floodgates for censorship of American film. Numerous localities in the United States created their own censorship boards. Throughout the 1920s, Hollywood fought to comply with the various sensibilities of different state (and sometimes foreign) governments. Censorship, however, was a manageable problem for Hollywood in the 1920s because of the era's general permissiveness and also because of the relative simplicity of editing silent film. Silent films were relatively easy to cut and tailor for local audiences. With the advent of sound, however, it became increasingly difficult to meet the demands of censorship boards in different states and localities. Sound films are technically, and from the perspective of plot development, more difficult to edit. Besides, editing a talking picture was more likely to ruin the print.

With the collapse of the stock market in 1929, the film industry began fearing for its business (money spent on movie admission, in theory, is the ultimate discretionary expenditure). In the late 1920s and early 1930s, the industry began to push against the limits of censorship in order to lure patrons to the theater through the production of more daring and violent films. For example, in concert with the publicity in the press received by real-life mobsters such as Al Capone, Hollywood spawned an entire genre of gangster films. For their time, these films were daring not only in their depiction of violence but also in their treatment of gangsters as glamorous antiheroes.

The film industry, in its quest for increased attendance in the late 1920s, ran headlong into an energized religious movement. In particular, the Catholic Church, through the auspices of its organization the Legion of Decency, began to pressure the film industry to adopt a well-defined production code. The church was especially effective in this role because of its centralized organization and because it "represented" such a large percentage of the movie-viewing audience. The general backlash against the permissiveness of the Roaring Twenties, especially as depicted in the movies, emerged from several underlying causes.

First, as an entertainment medium, the movies became increasingly pervasive throughout the 1920s. According to some estimates, by 1930 some forty million people were regular moviegoers in the United States, of a total population of 130 million.[9] And there were many more viewers abroad. In the 1920s, according to the *Saturday Evening Post*, "The sun never sets on the British Empire and American motion picture." In that sense, films were really the world's first mass medium. In the United States, much of the audience for these films included recent arrivals who lived in large cities and were disproportionately Jewish or Catholic. What had been a sideshow became a Main Street treat and, to some, a threat. Second, to the extent that the film industry was dominated by first-generation immigrants, often of Jewish descent, Christian Main Street felt a general uneasiness about the potential influence that a bunch of non-Christian "foreigners" had who were perceived to be vaguely in league with international communism and the general conspiracy that got the United States involved in World War I.[10]

With the crash of the stock market and the collapse of the banks, people often turned to religion (and xenophobia) for succor from and an explanation for hard times. In Europe, these economic hard times spawned the politics of fascism. In the United States, the Great Depression spawned the politics of populists such as Huey Long and Father Coughlin.[11] Even in more recent times—for example, during the McCarthy era—vestigial anti-Semitism toward Hollywood still existed even though film production and distribution was increasingly conducted by publicly held corporations (owned by almost anyone who held a mutual fund).

In the *Mutual Film* case, Hollywood became vulnerable to local censorship. And in reaction to the overt anti-Semitism that came at the end of World War I, the film moguls decided to "mainstream" the industry. In order to preempt the criticism that the industry was a subversive force, Hollywood formed a trade association, the Motion Picture Producers and Distributors of America (MPPDA), now known as the Motion Picture Association of America (MPAA). The MPPDA was commonly known as the Hays Office, named after William H. Hays.[12]

Hays was a former chair of the Republican National Committee from Indiana who served as Postmaster General in the Harding administration. That post is significant because in the cabinet government of the early twentieth century, the Postmaster General, who was in charge of most of the president's patronage appointments, was generally also the president's chief political operative. In 1922, Hays resigned as Postmaster General to front for Hollywood as head of the MPPDA. While the MPPDA is more generally known for its activities in the censorship of film through the production code, it was more importantly the agency that made it possible for Hollywood to set up its second monopoly. Everything from labor agreements within the industry to distribution agreements among the studios was coordinated through the MPPDA.[13] That monopoly made it possible for the industry to not only write a production code but actually enforce it.[14]

The introduction of the production code was probably not completely unwelcome in Hollywood. With the multitude of local codes, compliance for distributors was difficult and expensive. An industrywide set of standards would save money and provide cover for plotlines and themes that stretched the limit for what was acceptable on Main Street. Indeed, and somewhat ironically, in the earliest years of the production code, Hollywood produced some of its most daring films ever. For example, in the film

Red-Headed Woman (1932), a secretary played by Jean Harlow basically sleeps her way to the top and gets away with it. In another film from the same year, *Red Dust*, the lead, played by Clark Gable, has an enthusiastic and thoroughly requited love affair with the wife of one of his employees, but when he changes his mind and sends her back to her husband, he ends up with a prostitute who is hiding from the police, again lustily played by Harlow.

In 1927 the Hays Office published its first production code, to be administered by its own Studio Relations Committee. The code went largely unenforced until after the stock market crash of 1929. A combination of new, more titillating film content, the market crash, and the concomitant reinvigoration of religious movements in the United States forced the MPPDA to become more active in the advance clearance and censorship of film content. In 1930, the MPPDA published a set of general principles to be followed in the development of movie scripts:[15]

1. No picture shall be produced which will lower the moral standards of those who see it. Hence the sympathy of the audience shall never be thrown to the side of crime, wrong-doing, evil or sin.
2. Correct standards of life, subject only to the requirements of drama and entertainment, shall be presented.
3. Law, natural or human, shall not be ridiculed, nor shall sympathy be created for its violation.

In one form or another, the production code governed the production and content of movies for the next thirty-five years, after which, in 1966, it was replaced by an early version of the current rating system.

At first, the enforcement of the code was spotty at best. After all, the whole point of setting up the MPPDA was to head off regulation of the industry. And as noted above, some of the raciest commercial films in the golden era were made between 1930 and 1933. As in the case of the modern Disney boycott, filmmakers were willing to risk the ire of groups that they believed were not an audience for their films. But when it appeared that the government would get involved and force Hollywood to comply with the production code as a matter of law, the studio heads thought it would be the better part of valor to voluntarily comply with the code.

In 1933, at the height of the Depression, Congress passed the National Industrial Recovery Act (NIRA) that authorized heretofore unprecedented circumventions of a market economy, including a suspension of government antitrust efforts. In exchange for a formal recognition of the legality of certain industrial monopolies, the act required that industries adopt "voluntary" codes of conduct. NIRA was both good news and bad news for the movie industry. On the one hand, NIRA would now grant formal recognition to and acceptance of Hollywood's second monopoly. On the other hand, the industry would now have to adopt a voluntary code of behavior that, if ignored, might threaten the independence of the industry.

Seizing the opportunity to influence the film industry, a combination of religious groups (who objected to the content of Hollywood entertainment) and small-theater owners (who objected to the power that Hollywood had over distribution) lobbied in Washington to use the NIRA as a way to enforce the production code and to give theater owners more power in the film-distribution process.

Concurrently, the film industry saw the NIRA as a way to build the foundation for a cartel. The MPPDA coopted the Legion of Decency by establishing something called the Production Code Administration (PCA). The PCA was to be headed by Joe Breen, a strict Catholic moralist from Philadelphia. The PCA was given the authority to fine any theater owner $25,000 who displayed an unapproved picture. Note that this arrangement helped preserve the vertical monopoly by basically making it impossible for theater owners to screen independently produced films. As it turned out, the code was a small price to pay to build Hollywood's second monopoly.[16]

The threat of governmental regulation, periodic boycotts, and World War II compelled the PCA to be strict in its enforcement of the production code until well after the end of the war. In addition, to the extent that foreign sales became an important source of revenue for Hollywood in the 1920s, the MPPDA was in constant contact and consultation with foreign governments about the content of its films that were being screened abroad. In particular, the British government, which actively enforced its own production code, demanded that Hollywood export films that conformed to the British code. Furthermore, in its depiction of British colonialism, Hollywood would have to respect the authority of the Colonial Office in London. The Mexican, Chinese, and French governments were also regularly consulted about the content of exported films. But the end of the war brought pressure to bear on the enforcement of the code.

The first signs of the code's erosion came with the breakup of the vertical monopoly of the film industry. In 1948, the Supreme Court ordered in *United States v. Paramount Pictures, Inc.* that the studios divest themselves of the theater chains they owned.[17] The fact that independent theater owners could shop around for pictures to be screened would eventually create a competitive environment in the film industry that would forever change the nature of Hollywood films. Even so, as a practical matter, in the late 1940s and for most of the 1950s, the absence of independent and foreign productions and the de facto collusion of distributors didn't give the *Paramount* decision much force. Nevertheless, after the war, in order to attract an audience many Hollywood films became darker, more issue oriented, and critical of the veneer of proper society. But even those films were not free from the censor.

Sunset Boulevard, produced in 1950, is representative of the films of the postwar era. Not only does the film deal (albeit elliptically) with such subversive themes as the relationship between a gigolo and a faded movie star, but it also attacks Hollywood itself. One feature of the film was particularly disturbing to the censors of its day: the story of *Sunset Boulevard* is told from the perspective of a murder victim who begins and ends the film floating facedown in a swimming pool. So shocking was this artifice for its time that the film was often censored to exclude its eerie opening sequence. Even today, some prints of the film bear the censor's mark.

Also developing as a threat to the second monopoly was television. To compete with television, Hollywood began to probe the boundaries of the code in order to provide the moviegoer with a unique experience that could not be recreated on a black-and-white television set in the living room. In addition, and safe from the censors, were expanded technological innovations, such as widescreen Cinemascope, experiments with 3D movies, enhanced color, and improved sound technology, all of which were intended to counter the competition of television.

Ultimately, however, filmmakers began to press against the limits of censorship. In 1959, the comedy *Some Like it Hot* was actually brought to market without the PCA "bug" (seal of approval). In this Billy Wilder film, Jack Lemmon and Tony Curtis, playing a couple of itinerant musicians, witness a mobland massacre and go on the lam dressed up as women playing with an all-girl band. The last line of the film is one of the funniest in film history. Needless to say, cross-dressing and implied homosexuality was not up to code. The fact that the studios felt comfortable enough to bring the film to market without the bug and the fact that the film was a great success spelled the end of the production code.

In part, these explorations into the limits of film content were motivated by an influx of films from a reinvigorated postwar European film industry. With the notable exception of those made in Britain, European filmmakers were generally under no such code restrictions in their own countries. In the early 1960s, there developed a lucrative niche audience for foreign film as screened in independent theaters in large cities and close to college campuses. Besides the competition, this freeing up of the content of American film in the late 1950s and early 1960s was made possible by a series of court decisions that essentially reversed the 1915 *Mutual Films* Supreme Court decision. As we will see, the courts in the United States began to see the film industry as less of a business than a form of artistic expression to be protected under the First Amendment.

Despite the industry's efforts to maintain its audience, film attendance plummeted throughout the 1950s and into the 1960s. Desperate to find a solution to a declining box office, in 1968 Jack Valenti (a former official in the Lyndon Johnson administration), who had come to head MPPDA (now renamed the MPAA, the Motion Picture Association of America), scrapped the production code and replaced it with a rating system. The adoption of a rating system represented a significant change in the censorship of American film. No longer would films be filtered for content. Instead, under the new rating system, audiences were filtered for films. The rating system has gone through several iterations. The now familiar G, PG, PG-13, R, and NC-17 (formerly G, M, R, X) rating system was instituted with great success. The MPAA, through the Classification and Ratings Administration (CARA), has issued the following guidelines for rating films:

> *G-General audiences*: All ages admitted.
> *PG-Parental guidance suggested*: Some material may not be suitable for children (originally, "some material may not be suitable for preteenagers"; wording was changed when the PG-13 rating was introduced in 1984).
> *PG-13 Parents strongly cautioned*: Some material may be inappropriate for children under thirteen.
> *R-Restricted*: Under seventeen requires accompanying parent or adult guardian.
> *NC-17*: No one seventeen and under admitted.

If a film was never submitted for a rating, the NR (not rated) label would often appear in newspapers and so forth; however, NR is not an official MPAA classification.[18]

The onus is now on film producers to come up with a product that can get a rating that appeals to the largest target audience. Gone, too, were the days when the message of a film was subject to censorship. The Hays Office was notoriously capricious in its judgment of what themes were judged in violation of the production code. By contrast, the rating system is based on the number of and graphic nature of acts of violence and explicit sex as depicted in a film. The MPAA rating system is administered through the Association's Classification and Ratings Administration, which replaced the old Production Code Administration.

Because there were some fairly well-established guidelines to the assignment of ratings, filmmakers can now predict with a fair amount of certainty what their films' ratings will be. In addition, it is a fairly simple matter to edit a film to conform to a particular rating's requirements. For example, in the film *Eyes Wide Shut* (1999), some scenes of a sexual orgy were obscured (shot out of focus) in order for the film to receive an R rating instead of an NC-17. By the same token, the producers of the film *Sneakers* (1992) actually *added* obscenities to the dialogue in order to move the film from a G to a PG rating. For some audiences a G rating suggests a children's film.

To the extent that the film rating system connotes the character of a film, it also performs the function of an informal system of censorship. It is certainly true that many theaters will simply refuse to screen a movie with the rating NC-17. As a consequence, mainstream Hollywood releases are rarely rated as such. Other consequences for movie content may result from the rating system as well. As we have seen, G-rated films are often perceived as children's films and thus likely to be unpopular with the core, in theater, movie audience of teenagers. But, as conservatives often point out, G films, as rare as they are, tend to do well at the box office. Whether this fact is ignored by Hollywood because of its miscalculation of audience, because of its ideological predilections, or because G films are attended so well precisely because they are so rare is a matter of conjecture. But as long as the rating system is thought to influence the market for a film, it will act as an informal censor and an indicator of the principles that society holds.

The rating system is not beyond criticism. For example, films that depict graphic violence rarely receive more than an R rating, while films that depict graphic sexual activities often receive the dreaded NC-17. That order of priorities may tell us something about a society that would rather have its citizens see a screen depiction of a man killing his lover than having sex with her (or him, for that matter). Furthermore, it also says that we trust adults to make the decision whether children should see graphic violence, but we don't trust their judgment when it comes to allowing children to view sex. Nevertheless, disputed priorities aside, the rating system has the virtue of conforming to Supreme Court decisions, allowing filmmakers an opportunity to explore heretofore forbidden topics, while providing a modicum of protection for the young and an advanced warning for parents.

The rating system has undergone minor revisions (with more attention paid to film violence) but has remained essentially unchanged since 1968. As long as theaters are willing to enforce the system, ratings represent a grand compromise that is sensitive to the legitimate demands of a society concerned about its children and its First Amendment rights.

However, there is still the problem of enforcement. In a report to Congress in December 2001, the Federal Trade Commission studied the film industry's compliance with trade practices mandated by the industry and with its voluntary restrictions, such as the rating system. While the government found that the industry had done a commendable job in limiting the advertising of NC-17- and R-rated films to nontarget audiences, undercover investigators still revealed a high level of noncompliance in the areas of video rentals of R- and NC-17-rated films to minors and admissions of unaccompanied minors to R- and NC-17-rated films. While the advent of streaming video has probably accentuated the problem of underage viewing, a 2013 FTC probe revealed improved compliance with the rating system at the theater.[19]

The verities of the film business ensure that the censorship of film will always be a bone of contention because it is difficult for the industry to control itself. The irony of the forced dissolution of the vertical monopoly is that theater owners are independent and are thus under competitive pressure to violate the ratings system. The studios can no longer force compliance to the code and now the rating system. The collapse of the second monopoly and the rulings by the Supreme Court made production code enforcement impossible. In addition, it became clear that in the last twenty years of its existence the production code did not protect the industry from, and clearly may have contributed to, falling movie attendance. This conclusion did not escape the film industry's notice. It is unlikely, then, that the industry would or even could return to the era of the production code. Furthermore, as long as social conservatives are not perceived as an important audience for film, their boycotts will not be a credible threat. Consequently, the last resort for those who would censor movie content would be to appeal to the government. But government censorship of the movies in the United States seems unlikely as long as the American majority is aware of and protective of its constitutional rights and the courts are diligent in the same manner as well.

CENSORSHIP BY GOVERNMENT

On December 1, 1997, Michael Carneal walked into the lobby of Heath High School in Paducah, Kentucky, and shot several of his fellow students, killing three and wounding many others. The parents and estate administrators of Carneal's victims sued several video game, movie production, and Internet content-provider firms. According to their complaint, Carneal regularly played video games, watched movies, and viewed Internet sites produced by the defendant's firms. These activities, plaintiffs Joe James et al. argue, "desensitized" Carneal to violence and "caused" him to kill the students of Heath High School.[20] Consequently, the distribution of this material to impressionable youth like Carneal constituted a tort in the meaning of Kentucky law, entitling the plaintiffs to recover wrongful death damages from the distributing firms.[21]

Moreover, the plaintiffs argued that the defendant firms purveyed defective "products"—namely, the content of video games, movies, and Internet sites—triggering strict product liability under Kentucky law. A federal district court dismissed the plaintiffs' claim, and a federal appeals court upheld the dismissal. The court made a similar ruling in regard to the school shootings at Columbine High School in Littleton, Colorado. Finally, in 2011, the Supreme Court seemed to settle the issue once and for all by reaffirming the First Amendment protections that accrue to video games.[22] And if video games are protected, films must be as well.

Had the court found in favor of the plaintiffs, there could have been a massive chilling effect on the production of games, Internet content, and the movies. This attempt to censor films through civil action based on product liability laws is but one of many attempts since the invention of film to censor the industry. At one time or another, various communities across the country have attempted to impose community standards on the movies through a variety of direct and indirect means.

In this last section, I examine the continuing evolution of case and civil law in regard to government control over film content. This issue is particularly important (and evolving) now that pay per view, cable television, and subscription services have brought first-run unedited feature films and television serials to America's living room. Television and films were always treated to a certain extent differently, as the federal government had a "hook" into radio and television content through the broadcast station licensing process. The airwaves are publicly owned and thus allocated and regulated by the federal government. Books and movies, however, are treated differently. Up until recently, it could be fairly argued that if you didn't want to read an objectionable book or see an objectionable movie, you simply didn't have to buy the product. Nowadays, however, buying cable television or a subscription service also means buying a lot of programming that would, to some audiences, be considered obscene and, to other audiences (particularly children), even harmful.

The congressionally mandated V-Chip (for parents to censor what their children watch on television), streaming and cable service parental controls, and a voluntary rating system adopted by the television networks are just the latest reactions to the perception that viewers need some kind of information about television content. But are these measures enough? Or are they too much? As we shall see, there has been a dramatic evolution in case law in regard to the censorship of film. In fact, the courts have reversed themselves almost completely. From a position of tolerance for local film censorship, the courts are now fairly reluctant to give ground on censoring films regardless of their content. The same, however, cannot be said for television. Where streaming services fall into this matrix is still in play.

In theory, the courts should not make, but rather interpret, law. However, when the states or the Congress adopt laws that are unconstitutional or when an issue is so sensitive that politicians avoid it, the courts are often forced to intervene. As we have seen in the era prior to the Great Depression, the federal courts were loath to get involved in affairs at the state level or in private business. However, because states' rights (and, on occasion, claims to property rights) can sometimes conflict with the Bill of Rights, the federal courts have become substantially more active in overruling the actions of states since the Great Depression and with the advent of the civil rights movement in the last half century.

As we have seen, the *Mutual Films* decision of 1914 let stand, as an exercise of states' rights, the actions of a film censorship board in Ohio. That ruling legitimized the establishment of film censorship boards in states and localities across the country—that is, until 1952.

In 1950 a theater in New York City screened a film made in Italy titled *The Miracle* (which was part of a trilogy called *The Ways of Love*). A New York State film-licensing board had issued a license for the film's exhibition. Pursuant to the 1914 *Mutual Film* decision, states still were permitted to grant licenses to exhibit films. Subsequently, in response to public outrage about the content of the film, the board notified the theater owner that it planned to rescind the film's license based on the film's sacrilegious content. Eventually, the license was suspended, and the film's distributor was sued in state court. The state court upheld the board's decision to rescind the license, and the case was appealed to the federal courts.

Normally, as was the case in 1914, the federal courts at this time would be reluctant to intervene in state matters such as these. However, by 1952 things had begun to change. Beginning in the late 1920s, pursuant to the Fourteenth Amendment (the post–Civil War amendment that nationalized the Bill of Rights), the federal courts had begun to regularly hear cases involving the actions of states. So it was not entirely out of character for the U.S. Supreme Court to grant a hearing in the New York film licensing case (*Burstyn v. Wilson*, 1952). What makes this case so extraordinary is that the Court (as it rarely does) completely and explicitly reversed its earlier rulings when it took the critical step of ruling that commercial films were protected speech in the meaning of the First Amendment. Remember, in the *Mutual Film* case, the Court had ruled that films were merely product; in the *Burstyn* case, the Court unambiguously reversed the earlier *Mutual* decision when Justice Tom Clark wrote,

> It is urged [by the defendant New York State Licensing Board] that motion pictures do not fall within the First Amendment's aegis because their production, distribution, and exhibition is a large-scale business conducted for private profit. We cannot agree. That books, newspapers, and magazines are published and sold for profit does not prevent them from being a form of expression whose liberty is safeguarded by the First Amendment. We fail to see why operation for profit should have any different effect in the case of motion pictures.
>
> It is further urged that motion pictures possess a greater capacity for evil, particularly among the youth of a community, than other modes of expression. Even if one were to accept this hypothesis, it does not follow that motion pictures should be disqualified from First Amendment protection. If there be capacity for evil it may be relevant in determining the permissible scope of

community control, but it does not authorize substantially unbridled censorship such as we have here.

For the foregoing reasons, we conclude that expression by means of motion pictures is included within the free speech and free press guaranty of the First and Fourteenth Amendments. To the extent that language in the opinion in *Mutual Film Corp v. Industrial Commission* is out of harmony with the views here set forth, we no longer adhere to it.[23] (Italics added, this is going to be important later)

The Court made it clear that films are protected under the First Amendment. But the Court did leave the door open for some kind of "community control" that was something less than a total prohibition on film censorship. There are other exceptions to the First Amendment freedom of speech in regard to films. It was in defining what these exceptions are, those where the First Amendment does not apply, that the Court has expended the greatest amount of energy in delimiting film censorship in the last sixty years. On the one hand, the Court recognizes that there are certain types of speech that can be limited because they are a nuisance or are dangerous. For example, in *Chaplinsky v. State of New Hampshire* (1942) the Court ruled,

There are certain well-defined and narrowly limited classes of speech, the prevention and punishment of which has never been thought to raise any Constitutional problem. These include the lewd and obscene, the profane and libelous, and the insulting or "fighting" words—those which by their utterance inflict injury or tend to incite an immediate breach of the peace.[24]

This left open the door for the censorship of films that were a nuisance or lewd and obscene. But by what standard were those characteristics to be measured?

Sometimes the nuisance character of speech is obvious. For example, in *Kovacs v. Cooper* (1949), the court ruled that "when ordinances undertake censorship of speech or religious practices before permitting their exercise, the Constitution forbids their enforcement."[25] However, in this case the Court upheld the constitutionality of a city ordinance that forbid the use of sound trucks and other devices that made a lot of noise (even if they were broadcasting protected speech).

In addition, besides the potential for the public nuisance of sound, certain types of speech can be punished for being libelous. But libel laws in the United States are some of the most limited and narrowly defined in the world. According to what is known as the Sullivan test, a publication or statement can only be considered libelous if it can be proved that the statement was false and that it was published with "actual malice," which includes a reckless disregard for its truth.[26] These are exceedingly hard standards to meet in a court of law, and, as a result, very few people who are targets of smears even try.

But what more specifically has a potential for censoring film are obscenity laws, which for years local communities have tried to adopt and enforce. In general, in dealing with challenges to these laws, the courts seem to make a distinction between the merely insulting and the obscene. As long as a work of art—a book, a film, or a play—can be arguably said to have some kind of message, to make a point no matter how unpopular, it is to be considered a form of protected speech.

Probably one of the most important cases in regard to obscenity is *Roth v. the United States*, decided in 1957. That case still stands today as part of the foundation of constitutional law in regard to obscenity. The issue in the case was whether the constitutional rights of the defendant were violated when he was arrested for sending certain types of lewd, indecent, or obscene materials through the mails. In his opinion for the (6–3) majority, Justice William Brennan wrote,

> All ideas having even the slightest redeeming social importance—unorthodox ideas, controversial ideas, even ideas hateful to the prevailing climate of opinion—have the full protection [of the First Amendment]. . . . But explicit in the history of the First Amendment is the rejection of obscenity as utterly without redeeming social importance.[27]

Brennan defined obscenity as material that "deals with sex in a manner appealing to prurient interest . . . [defined as] to the average person, applying contemporary community standards, the dominant theme of the material, taken as a whole, appeals to prurient interest."

Finally, Brennan made it clear that the state was under no obligation to prove that a particular piece of obscene material had a direct, demonstrably negative effect on society. It was the lack of any socially redeeming character that defined obscenity for the purposes of censorship.

However, with every solution comes a new set of problems. For one thing, it was not clear that an entire work could be judged obscene merely because a particular passage or scene proved to be objectionable. Furthermore, to the extent that community standards seemed to determine what was obscene, the definition of obscenity was variable. That variability forced any number of obscenity cases into the courts to determine whether the work in question violated community standards. More to the point, judges found themselves having to watch a lot of dirty movies. If for no other reason, that burden forced the courts to come up with a more enforceable standard of obscenity.

Finally, in *Miller v. California* (1973), the Supreme Court refined Roth and laid out a three-part test for obscenity. A work was judged to be obscene:

(a) whether the average person, applying contemporary community standards would find that the work, taken as a whole, appeals to the prurient interest . . . (b) whether the work depicts or describes, in a patently offensive way, sexual conduct specifically defined by the applicable state law, and (c) whether the work, taken as a whole, lacks serious literary, artistic, political, or scientific value. If a state obscenity law is thus limited, First Amendment values are adequately protected by ultimate independent appellate review of constitutional claims when necessary.[28]

Thus, the standard for delineating obscenity became generalized and nationalized. In addition, the Court ruled that only the sale of "hardcore" sexual materials (as defined by the Court) could be subject to prosecution. Pornography is not protected under the First Amendment. Finally, the Court emphasized the importance of the jury system as a way of imposing community standards in finding the fact of obscenity.

Since the *Miller* decision, the courts have upheld a number of state and local ordinances that impose zoning and other restrictions on the licensing and sale of obscene materials. However, because major Hollywood distributors are rarely involved with the production and sale of obscene materials (hardcore pornography in the meaning of the Court's definition), these decisions have largely excluded government censorship of Hollywood film. Furthermore, because of the advent of pay-per-view streaming video, the application of the community standards test that works well with dirty bookstores and films in theaters has been rendered functionally meaningless. Thus, we are left with a largely unregulated marketplace in theatrical exhibition of major film productions.

Not many films are released exclusively for theatrical exhibition. Besides being released on DVD, films are also shown on premium cable channels and broadcast television. It has generally been the case that broadcast television has censored films pursuant to the licensing demands of the Federal Communications Commission. As discussed, because the FCC issues broadcast licenses to radio and television stations, it can rescind those licenses or regulate the recipients thereof in many ways. In regard to obscenity, the FCC has been guided by the "compelling interest" standard in broadcast regulation, meaning that the FCC will intervene in a programming matter only if the government has some kind of compelling interest in doing so (the *Sable* decision).[29] As a practical matter, this means that programming content is rarely regulated except when it comes to the protection of children (in the protection of whom the state has a compelling interest). This means that the FCC requires that broadcast stations restrict the airing of indecent materials to the hours of 10 p.m. to 6 a.m., when children are less likely to be in the audience.[30] Stations that defy the FCC can either be fined or have their broadcast licenses revoked.

There is now a relatively recent, new element added to the mix. Subscriber-based cable television can air unedited films or shows with pornographic content to home audiences. In 1996 Congress passed the Telecommunications Act, which, among other things, extended the child restrictive (so-called safe harbor) broadcasting hours of 10 p.m. to 6 a.m. to cable television programming. The Supreme Court, however, found this section of the law to be unconstitutional, as it went beyond the absolute minimum intrusion necessary to exercise the state's compelling interest as defined in the *Sable* decision.[31] In English that means that there were other, less restrictive ways to protect children. Specifically, in the same law, Congress required cable suppliers to provide subscribers with the option of purchasing a lockbox that could be used to block programming that might be objectionable to children. The Court interpreted that provision of the law as being adequate. After all, unlike broadcast television, which may require blanket restrictions, cable television, which is provided by subscription, can be controlled by the subscribers. Thus, especially when it comes to programming that can be voluntarily purchased, the courts have continued the legal tradition of allowing only the bare minimum of censorship of media content.

Finally, one other potential legal threat to the film industry comes from the area of product liability. I have argued here that commercial film is largely product, not art. That may be an important distinction in influencing the content of film, but, in the legal sense, the courts have ruled that it is irrelevant to First Amendment protections whether a film (or newspaper, for that matter) is produced for profit. Nevertheless, it is still possible that with the expansion of product liability law, filmmakers could be held liable for the content of their films. For example, it is increasingly the case that even though the smoking of cigarettes is a more or less voluntary act (they are addictive), juries have been awarding damages for the effects of smoking.[32]

Even though any reasonable adult capable of reading a warning label knows the danger of smoking cigarettes, the fact that there is evidence that tobacco companies knew about the dangers of smoking well before the public did and actually may have tried to enhance the addictive properties of their product points to some kind of legal culpability on their part.

The same might be said for Hollywood. Because the idea that film violence is associated with actual violence seems to be consensually held by most people, it might be possible to argue that a particular film is directly responsible for a particular act of violence. For example, as discussed in a previous chapter, John Hinckley viewed *Taxi Driver* as many as fifteen times before deciding to attempt to assassinate President Reagan in order to impress Jodie Foster. Would President Reagan or the other victims have had a cause of action against the producer of the film?

So far, the answer is probably not. Even though there is a fairly convincing (albeit flawed) case to be made by behavioral scientists that film violence begets actual violence, the question of product liability has to meet a higher standard. First there is the legal standard of what constitutes a "good" and a "bad" product. There can be such a thing as a good cigarette, at least in the legal sense. A good cigarette or gun or movie in the legal sense is one without manufacturing defects. Thus, if cigarette manufacturers purposely add something to their tobacco that makes their product more dangerous, they may be held liable. However, if they conform in the production of their legal product to a level of reasonable care, they can't be held liable for the consequences of what happens when someone smokes a cigarette. The same general principle holds true for gun manufacturers and, certainly, film producers. It is difficult to conceive of a bad movie in the legal sense—that is, a film with a manufacturing defect that causes harm.

Films are also protected speech in the meaning of the First Amendment. There have been attempts, for example, to hold gun manufacturers responsible for acts of violence committed by handguns. So far the courts have ruled in general that the Second Amendment protection of the right to bear arms trumps any claim to damage caused by firearms. Presumably, the same could be true in the case of films, except as protected by the First Amendment. In the case of motion pictures or guns, we have to make a choice: Do we want to restrict the constitutional protections provided to all or act to prevent the actions of deranged individuals?

So far the answer is no. A good test case in this regard is the Kentucky school-shooting case discussed briefly at the beginning of this section. In dismissing the liability lawsuit against the producers of video games and the film *The Basketball Diaries*, the court ruled that the producers of media could not be held liable for the criminal acts in question (the Columbine shootings), for three reasons. First, it was not foreseeable that someone would watch *The Basketball Diaries* or play a video game and walk into a school and start shooting; this is based on the principle of "duty care," or the obligation of manufacturers to take reasonable care that a product is not harmful. Second, manufacturers can reasonably assume with a few exceptions that people will not put their products to criminal use. Third, and probably most important, tort liability cannot be applied speech protected under the First Amendment, which clearly includes the movies but, interestingly, perhaps not the video games. The bottom line is that the defendants did not intend to create harm, nor were they negligent in the marketing of their products.[33] This ruling was so unequivocal that it seems unlikely that the tort law will be used successfully to sue filmmakers in the foreseeable future. But as we have seen, times do change.

In one area, government censorship of film will remain a possibility. Because children are impressionable and are limited in their activities (such as not having the right to vote until age eighteen), it *might* not be improper or unconstitutional to restrict the films they see. Therefore, a voluntary but strictly enforced rating system and the legislatively mandated V-chip seem completely appropriate (and prudent).

Another issue to consider is that of local standards. This issue is thorny because the courts still do not provide a completely clear guide in this regard. On the one hand, there is in the federal system a general guarantee of local autonomy. On the other hand, the protections provided by the Bill of Rights are supposed to be accorded to all Americans, regardless of where they live. Consequently, there are at least two constitutional principles in conflict here. While states' rights are protected under the US Constitution and there seems to be at least some leeway in the law for the judgments of local voters and juries, as long as films are a protected expression under the First Amendment, communities that want to restrict the screening of some films seem to have no legal recourse. This is particularly the case given the advent of on-demand, streaming video. Nevertheless, given that the first-run screening of films in theaters is the most lucrative source of revenue for the studios, restrictions on first-run screenings are still a problem, if not for the consumers, then at least for the producers.

But that is not the end of the issue. Market incentives can still be brought to bear, and they are. As a practical matter, film distributors constrain what films communities are likely to see. Certain theaters are at least informally designated "art houses" and are assigned a special category of film—foreign films, small-budget independent films, and the like. Most other theaters are slated for more mainstream fare. It is no accident that both small theaters all over rural American and suburban Cineplexes show the same films at the same time while more controversial films are slated for limited release (in large cities and on college campuses). The market incentive is at work. Fortunately for film buffs outside metropolitan areas, on-demand video allows them much the same access to film that one would enjoy in Greenwich Village.

Feature Film: *Spotlight*

One of my favorite films growing up was *Boys Town* (1938) with Spencer Tracy and Mickey Rooney. It is the story of the founding by Father Edward J. Flanagan of a school for orphaned boys outside Lincoln, Nebraska. I am not Catholic, but that film had a special meaning for me because my mother had been orphaned during the Depression, and, unlike the stereotypical depiction of orphanage life depicted in books (and films) like *Oliver Twist*, Mom had nothing but good things to say about her experience at the orphanage.

Spotlight, **Open Road Films (II)/Photofest, 2015**

So it occurred to me while I was watching *Spotlight*, a film about the *Boston Globe*'s investigation of child abuse and subsequent coverup by the Catholic Church, that I might want to look up Boys Town's record in that regard. As it turned out, Boys Town had also been rocked by scandal. None of the allegations have been proven in court, but after watching *Spotlight*, it seemed to me that all the indications of a scandal and coverup appear to be there, including a priest accused of child molestation having been transferred to Boys Town (!) after being accused of child molestation in another parish in upstate New York. I want to make it clear that Father Flanagan, who as of this writing is likely to be canonized, had nothing to do with any of this.

At the outset, let me say that *Spotlight* is an excellent film. It highlights the kind of investigative newspaper journalism that has probably gone the way of, well, the newspaper. Just briefly, the story is that the *Globe* is bought out by the *New York Times* and an outside editor is brought in from Miami to run the newsroom. The new editor sees a story in what has apparently been an open secret in Boston for many years—that there are a number of priests in the Boston diocese who are child molesters. No one in the newsroom sees a story in these rumors, mind you, because there is a kind of *omerta* in Boston surrounding the church and because, more to the point, they don't want to believe it's true. Furthermore, as a practical matter, who wants to take on the Catholic Church in Boston?

But the new editor persists, and the reporters, who are good journalists, begin to see the story as well. In the end they uncover a massive and systematic coverup that goes all the way up to the top. In one of the most dramatic scenes in the movie, Michael Keaton, playing the head of the investigative team, realizes that, as the metro editor on the *Globe* twenty years before, he had passed on investigating strong evidence of the scandal they were just uncovering now. How many children, he wonders, must have been abused in the interim?

That is when it occurred to me that *Spotlight* is a story about the damage wrought by censorship. In all the years that this scandal, appearing in plain sight, went on, hundreds and maybe thousands of lives were ruined. Thank goodness the First Amendment allows for the freedom of the press and even the entertainment media. But then another thing occurred to me: in the golden era of Hollywood cinema, under the production code, this film could have never been made.

EXERCISE

Review the modern ratings system for television and the movies as outlined by the Classification and Ratings Administration (www.filmratings .com). Within the bounds of the Constitution as interpreted by the Supreme Court, how would you revise those ratings, if at all? Is there any way to take into account the advent of streaming video and pay on demand when trying to protect children from unsuitable media content? Finally, can a film go too far?

SUGGESTED READINGS

Asimow, Michael, and Shannon Mader. *Law and Popular Culture: A Course Book.* 2nd ed. New York: Peter Lang, 2013.

Black, Gregory. *Hollywood Censored: Morality Codes, Catholics, and the Movies.* New York: Cambridge University Press, 1996.

Greenfield, Steve, Guy Osborn, and Peter Robson. *Film and the Law: The Cinema of Justice.* Oxford: Bloomsbury, 2010.

Jacobs, Lea. *The Wages of Sin: Censorship and the Fallen Woman Film, 1928–1942.* Berkeley: University of California Press, 1991.

Lasalle, Mick. *Complicated Women: Sex and Power in Pre-Code Hollywood.* New York: St. Martin's Press, 2001.

Leff, Leonard J., and Jerold L. Simmons. *The Dame in the Kimono: Hollywood, Censorship, and the Production Code.* Lexington: University Press of Kentucky, 2013.

Shindler, Colin. *Hollywood Goes to War: Films and American Society, 1939–1952.* Abingdon: Routledge, 2014.

Strub, Whitney. *Perversion for Profit: The Politics of Pornography and the Rise of the New Right.* New York: Columbia University Press, 2011.

Wilcox, Clyde, and Carin Robinson. *Onward Christian Soldiers? The Religious Right in American Politics.* Boulder: Westview Press, 2010.

NOTES

1. Mike Grigsby, *Marketing Analytics: A Practical Guide to Real Marketing Science* (London: Kogan Page, 2015).

2. See Melanie Wright, *Religion and Film: An Introduction* (London: I. B. Tauris, 2006); John Lyden, ed., *The Routledge Companion to Religion and Film* (Abingdon: Routledge, 2009); and William L. Blizek, ed., *The Continuum Companion to Religion and Film* (London: A&C Black, 2009).

3. Brian Godawa, *Hollywood Worldviews: Watching Films with Wisdom and Discernment* (Downers Grove, IL: InterVarsity Press, 2011).

4. Existentialism is the belief that there is no God and thus no preordained characteristics of man, commonly called human nature. Accordingly, "Man simply is. Nor that he *is* simply what he conceives himself to be, but he is what he wills, and as he conceives himself after already existing—as he wills to be after that leap towards existence. Man is nothing else but that which he makes of himself." That realization precipitates what is known as the *existential crisis.* Jean-Paul Sartre, "Existentialism," in *Existentialism from Dostoevsky to Sartre,* ed. Walter Kaufmann (New York: Meridian, 1969), 291.

5. Rebecca Barrett-Fox, "Congress at the Kitchen Table," in *The Great Recession in Fiction, Film, and Television: Twenty-First-Century Bust Culture,* ed. Kirk Boyle (Lanham, MD: Lexington Books, 2013).

6. Niall McCarthy, "Bollywood: India's Film Industry by the Numbers [Infographic]," *Forbes,* September 3, 2014, http://www.forbes.com/sites/niallmccarthy/2014/09/03/bollywood-indias-film-industry-by-the-numbers-infographic/#2715e4857a0b5f83ae3d7bf0 (accessed January 18, 2016).

7. Article I, section 8, clause 3, of the US Constitution empowers Congress "to regulate Commerce with foreign Nations, and among the several States, and with the Indian Tribes." Since the Great Depression, the federal courts have often used the commerce clause as a justification for ruling as unconstitutional a variety of actions taken by the states.

8. *Mutual Film Co. v. Industrial Commission of Ohio,* 236 U.S. 230 (1915), http://caselaw.lp.findlaw.com/scripts/getcase.pl?court = US&vol = 236&invol = 230 (accessed January 19, 2016).

9. Margaret Thorpe, *America at the Movies* (New Haven, CT: Yale University Press, 1939).

10. Because there were several Jews prominent in the Bolshevik Revolution, Jews have often been painted as agents of international communism.

11. Populism is the political doctrine that supports the rights and powers of the common people in their struggle against a privileged elite. Populist movements can come from the Left (Huey Long) or the Right (Father Coughlin), but they share a common purpose of class warfare. See Adrian Kuzminski, *Fixing the System: A History of Populism, Ancient and Modern* (New York: Bloomsbury, 2008).

12. Tina Balio, *Grand Design: Hollywood as a Modern Business Enterprise, 1930–1939*, volume 5 (Los Angeles: University of California Press, 1995), particularly chapter 3 by Richard Maltby, "The Production Code and the Hays Office," 37–72.

13. Even today booking agents collude to ensure that competing theaters do not show the same films. The fact that this seems to be a clear antitrust violation provides one explanation for why Hollywood is such an active player in national electoral politics.

14. For an excellent history of the founding and enforcement of the Hollywood production code, see Steven Vaughn, "Morality and Entertainment: The Origins of the Motion Picture Production Code," *Journal of American History* 77, no. 1 (June 1990): 39–65.

15. See "MPAA–The Motion Picture Production Code–MPPDA–OCTOBER 1927–The 36 Don'ts and Be Carefuls–Don'ts/Be Carefuls," http://www.filmson super8.com/censorship/censorship.html (accessed January 19, 2016).

16. This explains why Hollywood so enthusiastically embraced the code *even after* the US Supreme Court declared the NIRA unconstitutional in 1935.

17. *United States v. Paramount Pictures, Inc.*, 334 U.S. 131 (1948).

18. Source: Classification and Ratings Administration, which is an independent agency (as they put it) established by the MPAA. CARA is not a government agency but an organization that urges filmmakers (and television producers) to voluntarily submit their materials for ratings. Films that are not submitted to CARA for ratings are designated NR. See a rather opaque explanation of all this at CARA's website, filmratings.com. For a complete rundown on the rules of ratings, go to http://film ratings.com/downloads/rating_rules.pdf.

19. US Government, Federal Trade Commission, "FTC Undercover Shopper Survey on Entertainment Ratings Enforcement Finds Compliance Highest among Video Game Sellers and Movie Theaters," https://www.ftc.gov/news-events/press -releases/2013/03/ftc-undercover-shopper-survey-entertainment-ratings-enforce ment (accessed January 20, 2016).

20. Excerpted from the appeal from *Joe James v. Meow Media, Inc.*, 2002 Fed App. 0270P (6th Cir.), http://www.dinsmore.com/files/upload/James_v_Meow_Media _Sixth_Circuit_Opinion.pdf (accessed January 20, 2016).

21. "*Tort* from French for 'wrong,' a civil wrong or wrongful act, whether intentional or accidental, from which injury occurs to another. Torts include all negligence cases as well as intentional wrongs which result in harm. Therefore tort law is one of the major areas of law (along with contract, real property and criminal law) and results in more civil litigation than any other category. Some intentional torts may also be crimes, such as assault, battery, wrongful death, fraud, conversion (a euphemism for theft) and trespass on property and form the basis for a lawsuit for damages by the injured party. Defamation, including intentionally telling harmful untruths about another—either by print or broadcast (libel) or orally (slander)—is a tort and used to be a crime as well." From Law.com, http://diction ary.law.com/Default.aspx?selected = 2137 (accessed January 20, 2016).

22. *Brown v. Entertainment Merchants Ass'n*, 131 S. Ct. 2729, 564 U.S., 180 L. Ed. 2d 708 (2011).

23. *Burstyn v. Wilson*, 72 S. Ct. 777, 343 U.S. 459, 96 L. Ed. 1098 (Supreme Court 1952).

24. *Chaplinsky v. New Hampshire*, 315 U.S. 568, 62 S. Ct. 766, 86 L. Ed. 1031 (1942).

25. *Kovacs v. Cooper*, 336 U.S. 77, 69 S. Ct. 448, 93 L. Ed. 513 (1949).

26. *New York Times Co. v. Sullivan*, 376 U.S. 254 (1964).

27. *Roth v. United States*, 354 U.S. 476 (1957).

28. *Miller v. California*, 413 U.S. 15 (1973).

29. *Sable Communications v. FCC*, 492 U.S. 115 (1989).

30. US Government, Federal Communications Commission: "The FCC has defined broadcast indecency as 'language or material that, in context, depicts or describes, in terms patently offensive as measured by contemporary community standards for the broadcast medium, sexual or excretory organs or activities.' Indecent programming contains patently offensive sexual or excretory material that does not rise to the level of obscenity. The courts hold that indecent material is protected by the First Amendment and cannot be banned entirely. FCC rules prohibit indecent speech on broadcast radio and television between 6 a.m. and 10 p.m., when there is reasonable risk that children may be in the audience." *Obscene, Indecent and Profane Broadcasts*, https://www.fcc.gov/consumers/guides/obscene-indecent-and-profane-broadcasts (accessed January 21, 2016).

31. *United States v. Playboy Entertainment Group, Inc.* (98–1682), 529 U.S. 803 (2000).

32. In 2014 a Florida jury awarded a widow of a former smoker a settlement of over $28 *billion* against RJ Reynolds Tobacco Company. The amount was eventually reduced to just under $17 million, but there are still a number of such cases in different stages of adjudication.

33. *Joe James v. Meow Media, Inc.*

Conclusion

The central question in this book is: What do commercial films have to do with politics? The answer, as it has been laid out in the preceding chapters, is multifaceted and complex and can really be summed up in two parts. First, we must consider the degree of the film industry's influence on American politics. At various times, the industry's influence has more or less depended on the market for films, the technology of the time, and the political economy of the film industry itself. But the main question here is one of cause and effect. Do films promote certain types of behaviors and spread certain beliefs that are foreign to the sensibilities of the audience? Or are they in the main a reflection of prevailing attitudes? The answer is probably a little of both, but more one than the other. It is unlikely that in an attempt to corrupt the morals of our youth executives in the film industry will risk the profitability of their products by pushing a particular cause.

Second, the film industry is an instructive lesson in the politics of government-industry relations in the United States. But beyond that, how we have regulated the film industry tells us much about American political culture. The fact that the film industry has such a high profile and that it was in large part founded by an immigrant group outside the mainstream of American cultural life is an instructive example of how we regard and treat the "outsider." The development of the movie industry is one of the great illustrations of the American melting pot. Thus, in the main, this study of film politics is the study of American political culture. Furthermore, tangentially, the study of politics and film tells us something about the regulatory process and our evolving interpretation of the First Amendment. The story of politics and film is the story, through metaphor, of American political development in the twentieth century going into the twenty-first.

THE FILM INDUSTRY IN AMERICAN HISTORY

The role of commercial film in American society is a relatively recent one, really only since the turn of the twentieth century. But soon after its introduction, the film medium became the first entertainment medium for the masses. Up until then, theater, music, and the arts had been the relative province of the elite. But by the early 1920s, movies were regularly viewed by a large and growing segment of the American public. The problem for the elite then was how to react to this entirely new phenomenon. The answer, it seems, was to censor the content of films by establishing, with the blessing of the courts, film censorship boards at the local community level. Ultimately, the Hays Office and the production code were established as a form of censorship at the source. By gently intimidating studio owners, most of whom were first-generation immigrant Jews, and by intimating that their position in society was tenuous at best and subject to revocation, Main Street America was able to manipulate the content of film. The moguls, having experienced religious persecution firsthand in Europe, and for reasons related to their business, were more than willing to go along.[1]

This regime of elite control, better known as the golden era of Hollywood cinema, was reinforced by the vertical integration of the movie industry. Theater owners could show their product only with the permission of the studios because Hollywood had an effective monopoly over the production and distribution of films. Thus, the content of commercial films for the period from 1933 to just after the end of World War II was relatively homogeneous and, while often brilliant in execution, bland in character.

But as economists tell us, monopolies are bound to erode. The recovery of the European film industry, the advent of television, and the hunger among audiences for something new began to chip away at the edifice of the golden era. The film noir genre ushered in a new and more daring style of Hollywood cinema. While the Hays Office still exerted substantial control over film content, censorship at the local level was limited by the antitrust breakup of the vertical monopoly (in the *Paramount* decision of 1948) and, more important, the Court's reversal of its view that commercial films were not constitutionally protected speech (in the *Burstyn* decision of 1952). In some sense, the last gasp of the golden era was the imposition of the Hollywood blacklist when a number of filmmakers, writers, and actors (many of whom happened to be Jewish) were accused of being communists and were forbidden from working in the industry. The result was to intimidate the rest of the industry, including the moguls, who were beginning to pass the torch to a new generation.

Subject to the limitations of the blacklist code, uninspired filmmaking in the 1950s contributed to a decline in film attendance. By the early 1960s, the studio system had collapsed and was largely bought out by large industrial conglomerates. Eventually the parts of the movie industry were reconfigured, and the industry became what it is today, a modern commercial enterprise. The studios are a shadow of what they once were. They are subsidiaries of larger corporations that outsource the production of movies.

The result is a more commercial film, one that is more sensitive to the audience it hopes to attract. Critics and moralists from both the Right and the Left can object to this arrangement. After all, strictly speaking, business is not moral; it is not immoral; it is amoral. Conservatives argue that the appeal of commercial films to the lowest common denominator degrades the morals of our society. Leftists argue that the corporate monopoly in American film reinforces the corporate control of our economy and of our politics by reinforcing the belief in the status quo and excluding from the screen certain messages considered subversive by the bourgeoisie.

But both of these critiques seem just a bit disingenuous. If industrial filmmaking is simply the act of satisfying a demand, then the fact that films may seem immoral says more about our society and the audience for film than it does about the businesses that produce them. Furthermore, if there is a market for, say, religious films, the film industry has every incentive to tap that market. In fact, as noted in previous chapters, there is a small but vibrant market for Christian films. But it is not small because of some kind of Hollywood conspiracy; it is small because of the size of the market.

The same kind of argument can be made to counter the criticisms of the Left. If there were a market for movies extolling workers' rights, the film industry would have an incentive to produce those films. Furthermore, the vibrant market for so-called independent films (even though most indies are ultimately distributed by member companies—the major studios—of the MPAA) demonstrates that films with alternate messages can get screened and make money, they just have to be produced on a small enough budget. *Trumbo* and *Spotlight* are two such recent films. But maybe the market for these films is just limited. Neither film is on track to do much more than cover their costs.

If the content of film is more a reflection than a driver of the public mood, the movie industry tells us more about who we were than who we will be, which brings to mind the next major question addressed in this book: What behaviors would the screening of biblical epics or calls to a workers' revolution be likely to produce anyway? What are the causes and effects of commercial film?

CAUSE AND EFFECT

While there is certainly evidence to suggest that film is both a cause and an effect, the direction of causality is more one way than the other. Because the film industry is a business and, particularly in the modern era, produces films to meet a market demand, it seems fairly clear that the demand is driving the supply. There is a market for certain types of films, and the selection of those films tells us something about the audience that consumes those products. Therefore, we need to know something about the audience for film, and that appears to be changing.

With the advent of streaming pay-per-view video, the audience for film, particularly made-for-television serials, has expanded the market for original content. That audience is older and more mature than the audience for traditional movies screened in the theater. That means that serialized television is likely to be more sophisticated and nuanced in its plots and a better reflection of the voting public than traditional movies that derive a large part of their revenues from abroad. That being the case, what is the causal relationship between film and politics?

First of all, the relationship is not all that simple. Research indicates that the messages in media mainly "activate" and reinforce existing biases, preferences, and behaviors. So, in that sense, films can drive behavior.[2] But there are a couple of caveats that should be added to this conclusion. First of all, movies are one of the least obtrusive and affecting of the media. While watching the same film over and over may result in a cumulative effect on behavior (as occurred to John Hinckley in watching *Taxi Driver*), most moviegoers will see a film once or twice. And even if viewers are avid moviegoers, and even if different films reinforce similar messages, there is an absolute limit on how often one can go to the movies. Consequently, it is more likely that television, video games, and even recorded music will play a more prominent role in reinforcing the existing beliefs of those who watch, play, and listen to them. Furthermore, it's not only negative or objectionable messages that are reinforced in the media. Little has been done to measure the countervailing influence of positive messages in the media and whether, on balance, the positive outweighs the negative.[3] Finally, the commercial film attracts a surprisingly narrow audience.

In the days before the advent of television, film entertainment was practically the only game in town, with the exception of radio. As suggested, the movies may have been the first truly mass entertainment. A phenomenally large percentage of the American public went to the movies regularly in the 1920s, 1930s, and 1940s. But with the advent of television and other media outlets competing for the public's free time, moviegoing populations became narrower and more demographically distinct. Besides the fact that television, video games, and radio compete for the attention of the film audience, viewers have other ways of screening a movie than by doing so in a theater. Broadcast television, DVDs, pay-per-view streaming videos, and television channels that air commercially uninterrupted films all compete for the public's entertainment dollars. The consequence is that what used to be the most lucrative moviegoing audience could once fairly be described as being relatively young and affluent and without children and religious or civic obligations to occupy their time. It was for this target audience that most medium- and big-budget Hollywood films were made, and because of that, the content of film, while reflecting American society, reflected a relatively narrow segment of that society.

Now that the digitalization of film has allowed for much easier access to films (and television serials), the audience for film has become more reflective of the broader population. And that is reflected in the programming, particularly in the plots of the serials produced for television. In *Boardwalk Empire*, the story of the boss of the Atlantic City political machine in the 1920s, a substantial part of the narrative is reserved for a nuanced depiction of a parallel African American community. The same dynamic is at work in *The Knick* and in *Orange Is the New Black* (with the addition of a Hispanic riff). This addition would not be present in the films of the past or even in the big-budget films that are produced for theatrical release. The home viewing audience is more domestic, it's more cosmopolitan, and it's more diverse—thus, in serialized television, plots are different.

So when we talk of the film industry now, we talk of three different tracks. There are films prepared for theatrical release and tracked for triple-digit returns in the millions, films that are shot with a sixteen-year-old boy and a Chinese audience in mind. Then there are television serials shot for the domestic home audience. These can be prepared for a broadcast audience, a cable audience (basically the same as the broadcast audience but with a slightly different set of rules), and a subscriber audience, such as the one that purchases Netflix or HBO. Finally, there is a small segment of commercial film that is produced on a low enough budget that it can be profitable if prepared mostly for a niche audience.

Now it may be the case that rather than try to attract an audience they already have, Hollywood filmmakers can go out and seek audiences that don't go to the movies. But that is really not how marketing generally works. It is not an accident that the audience for films exhibits the kind of profile they do. Nothing that Hollywood can do will make it easier for the parents with children to get out for an evening's entertainment or for churchgoers to subsume their religious obligations or for the poor to come up with discretionary income to pay to see a film in a first-run theater. These are the realities of the market that drive not only the audience for movies but also the content of film. Calls for film censorship therefore represent not just, as the proponents of censorship suggest, a desire to protect the community but also an attempt by one part of the community— those who often don't go to the movies—to impose its control over those who do.

SUBJECTIVE EVALUATIONS

Several years ago the American Film Institute released its list of the top American comedy films. By and large the list makes lots of sense (see www.afionline.org). With interest, I did notice that the film *Shampoo* made the list. *Shampoo* (starring Warren Beatty, Julie Christie, and Goldie Hawn) is a morality tale about the loneliness of a serial womanizer. In the end, the main character, played by Beatty, is left standing alone on a hill pondering his fate. He has just lost the only woman he ever really loved; in fact, we get a sense that she may be the only woman he ever will love. To me, this movie is hardly a comedy. In fact, calling *Shampoo* a comedy is like calling Mozart's opera *Don Giovanni* a comedy. To go one step further, *Shampoo* is *Don Giovanni*. Now, *The Producers* (1968), with Zero Mostel and Gene Wilder, *that's* a comedy!

I bring this up to illustrate a central point of this book. Our evaluation of films, the parts that are really important to most of us, is highly personal; it doesn't include the technical quality of the film or the obscure references to film history that are the historical nods to the inside Hollywood crowd. In that sense, my reaction to *Shampoo* is hardly to think of it as a comedy. (A kind of subplot in the film concerns the presidential election of 1972, but that part made no impression on me at the time, and I may have to look at the film again from a different, older perspective.)

By the same token, one of the funniest films ever made, in my opinion, is *Showgirls* (1995), starring (all of) Elizabeth Berkley and Gina Gershon. I don't know whether the producers of the film meant this to be a comedy.[4] But when I saw this film a couple of years ago with a good friend of mine, we couldn't stop laughing. Some of the funniest scenes in film history are in this film. But let me issue a warning: If you don't tolerate nudity, foul language, and simulated sex, don't rent this film. This film is not about any of those elements, but there is plenty of each. And maybe, too, you won't get the joke. That's okay. That doesn't mean you don't have a sense of humor. It just means that you don't have my sense of humor. And thank goodness, too. What a boring world that would be if everyone thought like me.

All of this discussion of "different strokes for different folks" is pretty harmless until we get to the politics of film. The ideas that I consider harmless or even right on the mark other people consider objectionable. There is certainly some consensus as to what constitutes harmful films, particularly as they affect children. Thus, the film rating system is heavily weighted toward parental involvement. There is also a certain amount of consensus concerning the harm of screening hardcore pornography. So, as the rating system is enforced, it tends to be much more stringently imposed on films that are sexually explicit than on films that are violent or have some other kind of social or political message.

In looking over the critics' choices for the best films of 2015, we can see reflected in content the evolution of political themes in American society. With the exception of *Mad Max: Fury Road* (2015), which inexplicably has received critical praise, and *Bridge of Spies* and *The Martian*, and a couple of others the film cognoscenti really like, they are third-track films, films that are made on a reasonably low budget for a niche audience or the art theater crowd. Those films, among others, include *Carol*, the story of a lesbian love affair; *The Danish Girl*, a man in transition (to becoming a woman); and *Tangerine*, a story of transgender prostitutes in LA. This is not to mention the widely acclaimed television serials *Transparent* and *Orange Is the New Black* that feature prominent transgender characters. That makes 2015 the LGBT year in film, to coincide with the Supreme Court's ruling in June 2015 legalizing gay marriage in all fifty states. The big, blockbuster films don't explore these themes, mind you; foreign audiences may not be so receptive, but clearly LGBT politics are on the minds of American filmgoers.

What this suggests is that the reaction to film at the societal and even at the individual level tells us as much about the audience as it does about the film itself. The reaction to *American Sniper* is instructive in this regard. Beyond evaluations of the technical merits of the film, the range of reactions to the film is a veritable metaphor for the spectrum of American political debate. While *Sniper* is just one of the most obvious examples of this dynamic, film criticism in general can be regarded as metaphor even when the connection between the film being evaluated and public life is much more subtle.

During the Vietnam War, contemporary films often spoke of the current war in metaphor. It is hard not to associate the fictional recreation of the Korean War in *MASH* (1970) or the slaughter of the American Indian in *Little Big Man* (1970) or the senseless World War II bombing of an Italian village in *Catch-22* (1970) with the Vietnam War, especially after the Tet offensive in 1968 when the war in Vietnam wasn't going that well.

Even in times of peace, war films can attract quite a bit of controversy. Steven Spielberg's *Saving Private Ryan* (1998) was attacked from the political Right, ostensibly for its depiction of cowardice among American troops during World War II. I say "ostensibly" because one gets the sense that there is also a political agenda behind the attacks that reflect more of the Left-Right debate in the United States than the actual content of the film.[5]

But besides being an instructive indicator of where the film audience stands, subjective evaluations are not really that important until they are translated into action. That being the case, much of the politics of films involves the attempt of one group or another to censor the content of films.

CENSORSHIP AND CONTROL

Beyond the concerns for the morality of our youth, much of what passes for concern for morality is really an attempt at another purpose. What I am suggesting is that the politics of censorship are not as much about morality as they are about control. As discussed above, many of the early attempts to censor films were engaged as a kind of class warfare. The nickelodeon version of film was considered too crass and vulgar for the common man or woman, filled with too much sex and violence. From the elite perspective, film was a danger to the masses. The films of the carny sideshow had none of the refinement of, say, the bloodbath at the end of a typical Shakespearean tragedy.

Furthermore, when the movie industry fell into the hands of people with funny accents and apostolic religious beliefs, the problem was no longer the corruption of the masses by the medium but the corruption of the medium by the masses. The next phase of movie censorship came as an attempt to weed out "foreign influences" that had pervaded American films. The only thing that was particularly remarkable about this second era of censorship was that it was orchestrated by the Catholic Church in what is basically a Protestant country.

Maybe in the case of adults controlling what children see is there a justification for this kind of control. Children are assumed to be in their minority and thus unable to make responsible decisions for themselves. But adults are assumed to be able to draw their own conclusions. That is the definition of an adult. Thus, censorship of what adults see is nothing more than control. Viewed from that perspective, the golden era of Hollywood film was not so golden after all. Yes, some great films were made during that era, as they are today. But what viewers were allowed to see was controlled. So, before we start waxing poetic about that great era of Hollywood cinema, let us consider the implications of what was going on at the time. Who was being un-American and who wasn't: the censors, or those who wanted to defy them?

The golden era of censorship ended when the government intervened, as it should when there is gross distortion of the free market, and broke up the (vertical) Hollywood monopoly. Nevertheless, one gets the sense that the days of vertical-integration monopoly were numbered in any event with the advent of television and the recovery of the postwar European film industry. However, without the intervention of the government, the breakup would have taken many years, and that fact alone makes the government's actions in this case commendable.

So without the tool of monopoly to control the content of film, those who wished to control had to resort to other measures to assert their authority. In American politics, one of the primary tactics of achieving policy goals is through personal attacks. If one could demonstrate that filmmakers or newscasters were sick or crazy or disloyal, then one could intimidate them and thus discredit their wrongheaded politics. Taking advantage of the Red Scare at the end of World War II, Senator Joseph

McCarthy and his minions sought to discredit their political rivals by labeling them *communist*. It is no accident that the two main targets of the McCarthy era were opposition politicians and entertainers. The attack on the first group is completely understandable, and the second diabolically brilliant. It is not enough to defeat your opponents in politics—that is only temporary—but to control the interpretation of that defeat and reinforce the message that emerges, that is *real* victory.[6]

But eventually McCarthy fell victim to his own devices, and no one was more deserving. So discredited was McCarthy that *McCarthyism* has become a pejorative term in the English language. After McCarthy, the question for politicians became how to discredit political opponents without looking like McCarthy. The answer was science. After all, if scientific evidence could be brought to bear to prove that those who work in the entertainment industry are either sick or crazy, then their product would be discredited and the producers thereof intimidated. Thus, the junk science of media psychology was born. Literally hundreds of studies were conducted looking for a connection between media depictions of violence and actual behavior, with the same (surprise!) results. The weight of the evidence suggested that the media caused violence, with the inescapable conclusion that those who produce the entertainment media are either demented or evil.

I argue in chapter 4 that much of what passes for evidence that the media cause violence is simply wrong or can be completely misinterpreted. (To be fair to the researchers, their results are often misinterpreted or exaggerated by people with a political agenda.) But let's just assume, for the sake of argument, that research is right—that media depictions of violence *do* cause violence. Or, more to the point, that depictions of a liberal-friendly political agenda cause people to become liberals (or for that matter, conservative films cause them to become conservatives). Okay—now what?

I suppose we could return to the good old days of the production code and the Hays Commission. But, no, that wouldn't work. What made the production code work was the fact that the censorship board's decisions could be enforced. Films that did not meet code standards were simply not screened in the theaters that the studios owned or controlled. Nowadays films would be screened whether they were approved or not, as the vertical integration of the film industry no long exists.

Who would form a film censorship board? Our politics are now more diverse than they have ever been. With the advent of the Voting Rights Act, the eighteen-year-old vote, and other legislation that eased restraints on women, minority, and youth participation, it is highly unlikely that any consensus would form about the composition of a censorship board or its message. Certainly, it would no longer be the case that the Catholic Church would be ceded the right to speak for moviegoers. Additionally, what kind of censorship would be permitted and, more important, how much? This is a slippery-slope argument. Once we begin to censor film for story line content, there is no telling what direction that will go. Presumably, if violent films make people more violent, or sexually explicit movies make people more prone to having sex, then liberal films will make people more liberal and conservative films will make people more conservative. The battle over film content will ultimately become a battle for our hearts and minds, and the outcome will in no way reflect the market demand for entertainment: it will simply be the outcome of a battle for control. Fortunately, after 1952, when the Court reversed the *Mutual Film Company* decision, the courts would not allow it.[7]

There are, of course, exceptions to the rule. You are going to have a heck of a time finding a copy (or a viewing) of *Truth* (2015) with Robert Redford and Cate Blanchett. How could a film with two of the most bankable stars in history be basically unobtainable, you might ask? It might have something to do with the story. *Truth* is based on the backstory of a CBS *60 Minutes* segment anchored by Dan Rather and shown during the 2004 presidential campaign. The gist of the segment was that George W. Bush avoided the draft during the Vietnam War by enlisting in the Texas Air National Guard. He then, according to the story, had the bad form to quit showing up for service for the last year or so of his enlistment.

Some of the documentary evidence highlighted to support the conclusions of the report then proved to be unsourced and, perhaps, actual forgeries. CBS then fired the producer of the segment and forced Dan Rather to retire. Rather filed a breach of contract suit against CBS and its parent corporation Viacom. His argument was that he and his producer were being punished for annoying Sumner Redstone (the CEO of CBS's parent company Viacom) and his Republican allies. CBS convened a panel to investigate the segment and eventually recanted the story.

In any event, *Truth* is very critical of CBS and sympathetic to Rather's side of the story. He believes that the *60 Minutes* segment is completely true and that he and his producer were being punished for afflicting the comfortable. The film has gotten on balance mediocre reviews because those who are on the Left love it and those who are on the Right hate it. By the way, that highlights a problem with making a controversial film that has nothing to do with censorship. A film that produces a strong but split reaction is likely to receive a mediocre rating on a website like *Rotten Tomatoes*. But that's a topic for a different book.

More to the point, *Truth* insults the media, and a very powerful part of the media at that. Thus, to the extent that the film has been buried, that represents a form of censorship not because the film impugns the integrity of George W. Bush but because the film insults Sumner Redstone. The problem with that kind of censorship, as I pointed out in my review of *Spotlight* (in chapter 7), is that some stories might not get told, stories that could be actionable in the public policy realm.

But by and large, the censorship of film by the government at least is virtually nonexistent. The Supreme Court has taken a 180-degree turn from the original notion that film is product, not art. One gets the sense that the Court could at some point turn away from *Miller* (regarding the three-point obscenity test) and lift the First Amendment protections currently enjoyed by commercial films. One landmark lawsuit could allow the censorship of film, either directly or indirectly, through the artifice of liability law or some other legal principle that we haven't even thought of yet.

We have to consider what we will have lost if we subvert the First Amendment to censor movies. On balance, would it be worth it to keep *Taxi Driver* off the market if it meant that President Reagan wouldn't have been shot by John Hinckley? This is a classic security versus freedom argument. Reagan also might not have been shot had the private ownership of handguns been forbidden. But the right to bear arms is protected by the US Constitution. The same could be said for the untrammeled right to screen *Taxi Driver* in the theater. My guess is that Hinckley would have done something anyway (but probably not shoot Reagan to impress Jodie Foster). Even so, freedom of expression is the cornerstone of a free society. Movies don't kill people; people kill people, and so on.

Of course, it is true that film censorship was never mandatory. It existed mainly because studio owners of the golden era were intimidated by the circumstance of their own immigrant ancestry, by the context of world fascism, and by unclear court decisions on the First Amendment status of film. But nowadays, owners of the studios *are* the elite. The conservative Right cannot intimidate them because they are sometimes themselves the conservative Right. In fact, they are probably more frightened of their shareholders. Furthermore, it is not clear that the religious Right goes *to* the movies. And if they do, there is now an industry that caters to the niche market for their limited dollars. Therefore, from the market perspective, the religious Right has little or no leverage (although for a moment the success of *The Passion of the Christ* seemed to, but in fact did not, change all that). Thus, the likelihood of voluntary compliance with something like the code in the modern era is quite unlikely.

Now, it is possible that if it were patently clear that movie violence caused actual violence, appeals could be made to the collective conscience of studio executives. And indeed, theater owners have made a good-faith effort to enforce the ratings system. But more than that is unlikely. This, I have argued, is a function of the fact that the film industry is increasingly publicly held and the distribution end of the business is more often than not part of a large conglomerate. Studio executives couldn't restrain themselves if they wanted to. Corporate headquarters wouldn't allow it. If it is clear to the studios that films with a certain type of content are more salable, then market forces will prevail.

The reason why a focus on feature films is particularly interesting in this regard is that voluntary compliance with some kind of code is unlikely, and, thus, the market for films is about the least encumbered of any in the entertainment media. Political activists have some leverage in the market for television because the Federal Communications Commission issues broadcasting licenses. Through the licensing procedure, political pressure can be brought to bear to influence television programming content. However, as broadcast television goes the way of the dinosaur (along with cable TV), even that is coming to an end. The same can be said for radio. But in the market for movies, there is no FCC. Short of an unanticipated court ruling that attaches to film some sort of product liability or dictates that film exists as product and not expression, there exists for film a market that is about as free as one can be.

Even so, marketization has its own bias, which is mainly associated with the availability of money to finance production. Money for production and distribution is readily available for *Rocky* or *Star Wars* sequels—and other such tedious nonsense (actually *Creed* [2015], the Rocky sequel, and *Star Wars: The Force Awakens* [2015], are pretty good films). And I suppose corporate America will be reluctant to finance and screen films that are critical of corporate America or are controversial in general. In the early 2000s, Miramax Films (owned by Disney) refused to distribute *Fahrenheit 9/11*, a film directed by Michael Moore critical of President George W. Bush. Disney probably regrets that decision, as the film was eventually purchased by the film's producers, Harvey and Bob Weinstein, and distributed at their expense. Even after paying Disney back for the financing ($6 million) and, as part of the deal, donating 60 percent of the net to charity, the Weinsteins made a good amount of money, pocketing a cool $85 million (at a gross of $222 million).

After that experience, the Weinsteins left Disney to form their own production company. The Weinstein Company has produced two films that have been awarded the Academy Award for Best Motion Picture, *The King's Speech* and *The Artist*, in consecutive years, 2010 and 2011. The Weinsteins by and large make a living on producing small-budget, quality films. Their top grossing film was *Django Unchained*, which grossed $425 million on a $100 million production budget. That is a lot of money, to be sure, but it isn't in the same class as *Avatar*, *Jurassic World*, or *Star Wars: The Force Awakens*. And the Weinsteins have to pay for art (or what some people would call "vanity") projects on the budgets of their successful films. There was some grousing from investors about the lack of (enough) profitability of the Weinstein Company.[8] Furthermore, the Weinsteins have recently announced, befitting the times, that they will deemphasize movie production in favor of television.[9] But in the main, the Weinstein brothers have proved that quality films can be made profitably in a competitive market.

But commercialism is a bias in content that is present in all American media. This would certainly alarm a Marxist—the capitalist conspiracy to control the thoughts and minds of the proletariat and all that—but it is more likely that because of our preference for free market liberalism, Americans get the films that they want to watch. We are limited in what we see not because of some kind of plot orchestrated by the ruling class.

Nevertheless, because *The Blair Witch Project* (1999; one step above a bunch of kids in their backyard with a video camera) can get made and screened, one gets the sense that anything can get made and screened. And with the fragmentation of the market that allows for an economic return on films made for almost the smallest niche, I would have to say that now, not 1939, is the golden age of American cinema. There is more product now of a wider variety and better quality than ever before. American movies are so popular that many countries, including Korea and France, have been "forced" to set quotas on the number of American films that can be screened in domestic theaters in order to protect their own domestic film industries.

In terms of content, what exists now is a pretty benign environment. I have pointed out that we should mostly ignore the junk science that supports the politics of control. Most of us who go to the movies see what we want to see and aren't much the worse for wear. People who don't go to the movies, mostly cultural conservatives, are horrified by what we watch, but it shouldn't really be their call. Let us not forget for a minute that the culture wars are not about culture; they are about control.

That last point is why it is so important to discuss film and politics in the same context. Films are meant to be entertainment, but they also tell us something about who we are as a people. The debate over film content as part of the culture wars tells us something about the politics of our society. We are engaged in a constant struggle over the untrammeled rights of expression guaranteed to us under the US Constitution. There will always be those in society who are not satisfied with their own status unless they can control others as well.

The intersection of film and politics is just a piece in the complex mosaic of American political culture. While at a superficial level, many people would not see a connection between politics and film, and in this book I have outlined some of the ways that the film industry both reflects and drives the policies of the country. Ideally, in reading this book, students of politics will begin to consider how this and other seemingly innocuous aspects of our national life affect the politics of our larger society. By the same token, students who read this book and are getting into the making of movies will have a better idea of what they are really about. Ultimately, if all I have done in this book is to introduce to the students of politics and of film a different perspective on politics through the study of the media, then I have more than succeeded at my task.

Feature Film: *The Hateful Eight*

If you are looking for a soul-deadening experience, one that makes you wonder whether humans as a species are any better than amoebas, then Quentin Tarantino's *The Hateful Eight* is for you. At the end of the day, life may be meaningless and the solar system an atom in a table leg, but even if that is true, we don't have to act like it. Watching *The Hateful Eight* makes me sorry to be human (and even sorrier to have paid for the experience).

One of the things that make the arts and literature so important is that they transmit in no other, comparable way the complexities of human life. No textbook on philosophy can do as good a job as Tolstoy did in *War and Peace* in transmitting the idea that we are merely "sticks in a stream" and that life is a series of events largely beyond our control that eventually lead to death. That's a pretty depressing conclusion, but in the novel, Tolstoy makes the case in a way that enhances the human experience. In fact, he does it so well that his book is essentially an argument against its own central message. It makes life worth living.

So even when we face the existential crisis or the realization that we are insignificant and will soon be forgotten after we are dead, the arts allow us to at least act as though life has some meaning. *The Hateful Eight* doesn't allow any of that.

There is nothing about *The Hateful Eight* that is elevating, uplifting, or even truthful. It simply is. The movie is one cruelty after another—artfully done, I'll give Tarantino that, but for no purpose. Now I can understand that Tarantino is still dealing with his own existential crisis, but we don't have to go along for the ride. I got over that when I was in my early twenties, so I find his struggle not only tiresome but also unpleasant. Thus, here is my recommendation.

Live with it! Embrace it. If, in fact, life has no meaning, then at least act like it does. You will have lost nothing, and life will be more fun and will, at least, seem more fulfilling. And if at the end of the day life has no meaning, then you won't know it anyway because you will be dead. But in the meantime, by embracing joyful and compassionate behavior and even sometimes sobering intellectual pursuits, you can at least enhance the experience of life (and the lives of others).

There is none of that in this film. Perhaps when he grows up Tarantino will find a soul. In the meantime, when Jennifer Jason Leigh got punched in the face for the first time I was ready to get up and leave (but I was with friends; now I'm sorry I didn't). I don't mind violence in film; *The Wild Bunch* is one of my favorite films, and there is a lot of violence in that. But what I can't stand is violence without a purpose.

Take the difference between erotica and porno. Erotica, no matter how graphic, explores the intricacies of lovemaking while pornography simply photographs the act. Erotica is always more compelling, but it's a lot harder to do. *The Hateful Eight* is in that sense pornographic. Making a film with meaning is a lot harder to do. So in this film Tarantino got lazy. Or maybe he expended all his energies on the technical side of the production. But for whatever reason, it's important that you don't see this film (or wait until it gets to the dollar theater).

Don't agree? What do you think?

EXERCISE

Did you ever have one of those "the emperor has no clothes" experiences? Did you ever walk out of movie that had been critically praised feeling as if you lived on another planet? Here is an opportunity for you to get it off your chest. Write about a film that is generally well regarded but that you think is, to put it gently, excrement. Why are you right and why are they wrong?

NOTES

1. In general, American Jews responded to the anti-Semitism sparked by the Great Depression "by increasing their efforts to assimilate or *by* keeping a low profile. This attitude is reflected in the screen portrayal of the Jew during the 1930s and 1940s." Patricia Erens, *The Jew in American Cinema* (Bloomington: Indiana University Press, 1984), 4. For a more positive take on this idea, see Ted Baehr, "How Church Advocacy Groups Fostered the Golden Age of Hollywood," in *Advocacy Groups and the Entertainment Industry*, ed. Michael Suman and Gabriel Rossman (Westport, CT: Praeger, 2000), chapter 7.

2. For example, see Nicholas A. Valentino, "Crime News and the Priming of Racial Attitudes during Evaluations of the President," *Public Opinion Quarterly* 63, no. 3 (Autumn 1999): 293–320. In the summary of his findings, the author states, "These results suggest that implicitly racial issues are connected in memory and can be simultaneously activated by common news coverage." See also Roberto Franzosi, "Narrative Analysis, or Why (and How) Sociologists Should Be Interested in Narrative," *Annual Review of Sociology* 24 (1998): 517–54; Nicholas A. Valentino, Vincent L. Hutchings, and Ismail K. White, "Cues That Matter: How Political Ads Prime Racial Attitudes During Campaigns," *American Political Science Review* 96, no. 1

(2002): 75–90; or Jennings Bryant, Susan Thompson, and Bruce W. Finklea, *Fundamentals of Media Effects* (Long Grove, IL: Waveland Press, 2012).

3. Richard E. Petty, "Two Routes to Persuasion: State of the Art," *International Perspectives on Psychological Science* 2 (2013): 229–47.

4. I think they meant it. In 1995, at the annual Razzie awards (for the worst in filmmaking), director Paul Verhoeven turned up in person to accept the awards for Worst Director and Worst Picture. He was the first director to ever collect the awards in person. The picture actually turned out to be enormously profitable in the home rental market.

5. For example, see the column written by Ken Masugi, who, at the time, was a senior fellow at the conservative Claremont Institute, titled "Saving 'Private Ryan' from the Conservatives," http://www.leaderu.com/humanities/masugi.html (accessed August 5, 2005). At the end of the column, he writes, "How can a conventional liberal such as Spielberg make such an impressive movie? One might recall that the morally obtuse Woody Allen has made deeply spiritual films about morality and the family such as *Bullets over Broadway* and *Mighty Aphrodite*. It is good that bad men are hypocrites. That is the only way they can be tolerated. The answer to this paradox may lie in a fact this low: Spielberg is simply a whore of the marketplace, and what sells is patriotism. What does not sell are political depictions of America such as the Clinton clone movie *Primary Colors* or the even more repulsive *Bulworth*. In at least that regard, we Americans are good, or at least better than our filmmakers and a lot of our critics."

6. See Larry Ceplair and Stephen Englund, *The Inquisition in Hollywood: Politics in the Film Community, 1930–1960* (Garden City, NY: Doubleday, 1980); Robert Griffith, *The Politics of Fear: Joseph R. McCarthy and the Senate*, 2nd ed. (Amherst: University of Massachusetts Press, 1987); or Reynold Humphries, *Hollywood's Blacklists: A Political and Cultural History* (Edinburgh: Edinburgh University Press, 2008).

7. The court ruled that films were largely artistic expression protected by the First Amendment in *Joseph Burstyn, Inc. v. Wilson*, 343 U.S. 495 (1952).

8. Michael Cieply, "The Weinstein Brothers Have Oscar Gold. Now They Need Cash," *New York Times*, December 19, 2015, http://www.nytimes.com/2015/12/20/business/media/the-weinstein-brothers-have-oscar-gold-now-they-need-some-cash.html (accessed January 25, 2016).

9. Brent Lang and Ramin Setoodeh, "Harvey Weinstein to Release Fewer Indie Films (EXCLUSIVE)," *Variety.com*, http://variety.com/2015/film/news/weinstein-company-movie-distribution-cut-tv-1201647083/ (accessed January 25, 2016).

Index